CUPID STUNTS

THE LIFE AND
RADIO TIMES OF

KENNY
EVERETT

To Georgia, Connie and Clementine

CUPID STUNTS

THE LIFE AND RADIO TIMES OF

KENNY EVERETT

DAVID & CAROLINE STAFFORD

OMNIBUS PRESS
London / New York / Paris / Sydney / Copenhagen / Berlin / Madrid / Tokyo

Cover designed by Fresh Lemon
Picture research by Jacqui Black

ISBN: 978.1.78038.708.6
Order No: OP54945

Exclusive Distributors
Music Sales Limited,
14/15 Berners Street,
London, W1T 3LJ.

Music Sales Corporation
180 Madison Avenue, 24th Floor,
New York,
NY 10016,
USA.

Macmillan Distribution Services,
56 Parkwest Drive
Derrimut, Vic 3030,
Australia.

Every effort has been made to trace the copyright holders of the photographs in this book but one or
two were unreachable. We would be grateful if the photographers concerned would contact us.

Typeset by Phoenix Photosetting, Chatham, Kent
Printed in the EU

A catalogue record for this book is available from the British Library.

Visit Omnibus Press on the web at www.omnibuspress.com

FOREWORD

by Andrew Marshall

I imagine that for most people who recall Kenny Everett their predominant memory is likely to be of a funny little bearded man in a dress, ostentatiously crossing and re-crossing his legs in a somewhat silly manner. Delightfully warming and chuckle-inducing as this image may be, however, it's very far from an illustration of the full range and essence of the remarkable palette of qualities that made the former Maurice Cole of Seaforth, Merseyside, to some of us, a very unusual and beloved figure in British broadcasting.

Imagine BBC Radio in the early sixties: the 'Light Programme' starts each day with a portentous orchestral rendering of 'Oranges And Lemons' by the BBC Northern Heavy Orchestra conducted by the Home Secretary; kitsch children's dreck is played all Saturday morning by a one-legged man, with the faintly sinister alias of 'Uncle Mac'; Sunday afternoons consist of *Semprini Serenade* – nineteen hours of piano playing by an Italian from Bath – building up to *Sing Something Simple,* a funereal-paced programme of singalong tunes for the gently suicidal.

Into this miasma of Postwar Doldrums stepped the Pirate Radio DJs, and in particular, Kenny.

There had never been anyone on the radio quite like him. He had absolute control of the medium. He was funny. He was cool. He knew The Beatles! And he said just whatever popped into his head at any moment, a quality that was simultaneously stimulating and delightfully dangerous: dangerous for Kenny definitely, as we were to discover; and sometimes dangerous even for us – when, for instance, he turned up a Conservative Party Rally and blithely defied what many would have liked him to have said in his continuing devotion to the supremacy of the stream of consciousness.

Oddly, no one ever seems to reflect that one of his later sackings from Radio 1 was for relating a joke that referred to Margaret Thatcher as a part of the female anatomy, illustrating his delightfully complete lack of any kind of political consistency. The first time he was fired, in contrast – for following an ingratiating news report that the Minister of Transport's wife had just passed her driving test with his quip "Bet she pressed a fiver into the examiner's hand" – resulted in the arrival, a week later, of his replacement, Noel Edmonds, handily providing as a bonus a completely legitimate reason for cool listeners to loathe Noel for the rest of his life. Thus nature balances itself.

That unexpected initial sacking was the first major clue as to what made Kenny particularly endearing. He provided a kind of energizing, benevolent, skewed commentary on the world in which he functioned as a Pop-era Puck – naughty, friendly, sometimes incisive, sometimes invigoratingly silly, eccentrically distant but always somehow still approachable: an uncontrollable force of disorder that you might nevertheless safely invite to tea with Godfrey Winn, but, on the other hand, the sort of personality that was always going to have what one might call an "eventful" career.

Like Edward Lear, Lewis Carroll, Will Heath-Robinson, Spike Milligan and others, Kenny had the means and talent to create within his chosen medium an entire absurdist world of his own to reside in; but also, like them, he found the actual world a somewhat less amiable land in which to dwell. We have a knack of creating these Lords of Misrule in Britain, perhaps a deep need for them, and the price they pay for being our Beloveds is often a less than satisfactory daily existence than we ourselves would be comfortable with.

It was perhaps inevitable that it was difficult for Kenny to discover a completely suitable long-term partner (although arguably no more difficult than it would be for the average famous person) or set down one completely definitive piece of work (he was far too unfixed a point in the universe for that) or leave behind a tiny Everett or two to continue the mayhem (can you imagine?).

But despite this, and an earlier death than a just Fate might have provided, it isn't at all accurate to think of Kenny's life as especially tragic. He was consistently happy in his work, was a kindly and thoughtful man to have as a friend, and when all else failed would always be cheered up by the thought of his apartment being thoroughly steam-cleaned tomorrow. And although he is gone now, there is much to be remembered about him that made us all happy. He interviewed John and Paul on their tour of the USA in the name of Bassett's Jelly Babies. He coined the phrase 'Naughty Bits'. I often reflect that his beautiful singing voice was never commented upon (he was a former choirboy) or his astonishing ability to perform complex fugues in multi-track. And I have to confess, seeing him crossing and re-crossing those legs does still make me laugh. But as you will now discover, with the aid of the astonishing literary varifocals of Caroline and David Stafford, there was a lot more to him than just that ...

Andrew Marshall *wrote* 2.4 Children, Whoops Apocalypse *and many other hit TV shows. He was also one of the writers on* The Kenny Everett Television Show *and a close friends of Kenny's.*

ACKNOWLEDGEMENTS

We are grateful for the many absorbing hours we spent at the British Library, the British Newspaper Library and the BBC Written Archives Centre, and to the many people gave us far more of their time than we had any right to expect and/or generous permission to quote for their work. They include (in alphabetical order): Keith Ames, Eddie Baines, 'Bull's Head' Bob, Francis Butler, Sue Calf, Annie Challis, Grace Clarke, Michael Coveney, Andrew (*The Crosby Herald*), Barry Cryer, Yvonne Cureton, Wilfred De'Ath, Tessa Ditner, Brian Dooley, Charlie Dore, John Edward, Neil Fleming, Ray Gearing, Roberta Green, Brian Gregg, Jo Gurnett, John Haines, 'Whispering' Bob Harris, Tom Heavey, Christine Kavanagh, Cheryl Kennedy, Tony Kennedy, Richard Kerr, Vicki Lambeth, Bernard 'Clem' Lawson, Peter Leyden, Maisie (*The Oldie* magazine), Andrew Marshall, Margie Davies Macdonald, David Mallet, Dennis Maughan, Paula McGinley, Nick Micouris, Jon Myer, Trudie Myerscough-Harris, Hilary Oliver, Mike Orme, Harry Parker, Nigel Planer, Richard Porter, Elsie Prescott-Hadwin, David Prest, Ian Rawes, Rowland Rivron, Alexei Sayle, Linda Sayle, Warren Sherman, Keith Skues, Sheila Staefal, Sheila Stanley, Ed 'Stewpot' Stewart, John Sugar, Jeff Walden, Clive Warner, Alison Webb, Mike Webster, Tim Whitnall, Natalie Wright and of course David Barraclough, Jacqui Black, Chris Charlesworth and Charlie Harris of Omnibus Press.

Apologies in advance to anyone we've missed out.

Wherever possible we have sought permission for lengthy quotations, but in cases where we have failed to do this and have exceeded the limits of 'Fair Usage' we would be grateful if the copyright holders could contact us.

CHAPTER ONE

It seemed unlikely that you could actually be hanged at Execution Dock for taking to the high seas and hijacking radio frequencies, but could you be sent to prison? Admiralty Law and the Law of The Sea, so reassuringly inflexible when it came to cabotage, flotsam and lien, were vague on the matter. To be on the safe side, Ben Toney, Programme Controller of Wonderful Radio London decided, when the station first went on the air in 1964, that it would be wise for the disc jockeys broadcasting from the *MV Galaxy* to assume false identities. Thus Paul Kazarine became Paul Kaye, Dave Wish became Dave Cash, Neil Spence became Dave Dennis and Tony Withers became Tony Windsor.

There are conflicting accounts of how Maurice Cole came upon his new name, none of which can ever be definitive. Here's one to be going on with. Maurice Cole from Crosby, Liverpool had recently seen *It's A Mad Mad Mad Mad World,* 1963's top-grossing movie which featured a cameo from Edward Everett Horton, the fine character actor who'd appeared in nearly as many Fred Astaire films as Ginger Rogers. 'Everett' had a ring to it. It was cod-posh – the name at least of a snooty butler if not a senior partner. There was something about its dactylic rhythm – DIDdle-ee – that gave it a sing-song, away-with-the fairies quality. Its similarity to 'Ever Ready' suggested unflagging energy. Its similarity to 'Everard' suggested postcard filth.

'Kenny' arrived out of the blue. It undercut the poshness of 'Everett' (no butler or senior partner was ever called Kenny) while enhancing the rhythm. Kenny Everett. Happy Holiday. Sunny Saturday. Floppy Antelope. Lacy Calico.

Maurice Cole had thrown up in the little boat that took him from Harwich out to the *MV Galaxy* and by his own testimony continued to throw up for the next two months. He'd never been to sea before. It was just before his 20th birthday, which, like Jesus', fell on Christmas Day. It would be the first birthday he'd spent away from home; the first Christmas he'd spent away from home; the first time he'd been a disc jockey anywhere except in his bedroom in Crosby; the first time he'd ever introduced himself, "Hi, I'm Kenny Everett."

Seasickness, homesickness, shyness and abject terror would have put him on the next boat back to land were it not for the fact that there was no next boat back to land. A dispute between the tender company and the owners of the *Galaxy* kept the ship without transport or fresh supplies for six weeks. Unless he felt like braving the icy waters and swimming to Frinton, he was stuck. There was no going back to Maurice Cole. From now on he was Kenny Everett.

* * *

In his unreliable autobiography, Kenny Everett depicts little Maurice Cole, his childhood self, as a ragged-arsed urchin from a back-to-back slum, trying to survive on the mean streets of Liverpool. You can't blame him. Rags to riches always made a more entertaining story than nicely-turned-out to quite-well-off, and Kenny's compulsion to entertain was his heartbeat.

Hereford Road, Crosby, where Maurice was born and brought up, is a street of neat bay-windowed houses, these days selling with two receps, kitchen, three beds, bathroom and a bit of front and back garden for not much below the national average. They're not quite as posh as 'Mendips' where John Lennon, another 'working class hero', grew up over the other side of Liverpool, but still several streets and three or four pay scales away from anything you could call a slum.

Crosby provided all the ingredients of an idyllic childhood. Potter's Barn Park, with swings and roundabouts, was just the other side of the Crosby Road from Maurice's house; beyond that came miles of dunes where dens could be built, wars fought, hiding places found, used condoms collected, troubling sexual episodes encountered; and beyond that the beach, the Mersey estuary and the Irish Sea. The beach at Crosby was always a favourite day out for the people of Liverpool. From the train station, you'd walk down the main street, past Woolworths, past ice cream parlours and chippies and shops that sold buckets and spades. You'd take sandwiches and a thermos. There'd be vans near the beach that used to fill your flask for sixpence.

The sixpenny tea vans have gone, but it's still proper seaside, with the added value that it's also home to Antony Gormley's art installation *Another Place*, an eerie collection of 100 life-size cast-iron human figures, facing out to sea and anchored in the sand so as to remain unbothered by partial or total submersion when the tide comes in.

Crosby wasn't a bad place and 1944 wasn't a bad year in which to be born. The end of the war was only a few months away and although great tracts of the major cities were smoking ruins and rationing had turned jam, smokes and decent bacon into prized luxuries and bananas into an improbable dream, there was a general sense that good times were just around the corner. "When the lights go on again all over the world," sang Vera Lynn, "... then we'll have time for things like wedding rings and free hearts will sing."

The theme of the King's Christmas Speech that year was 'The Journey Home' and was possibly the first bit of wireless that Maurice Cole, born at 3 a.m. that Christmas morning, ever heard.

Little Maurice's world, everybody knew, would be a blessed one; and so it came to pass. Hitler, bombs, scratchy serge and utility furniture would gradually be superseded by hi-fi, front-loading washing machines, witty T-shirts, tremolo arms, coloured telephones and cradle-to-grave health care. Atomic-age research scientists in Hank Marvin spectacles would bring about advances in the field of psychopharmacology that would make the drugs Spitfire pilots had used to stay awake, go to sleep and ease the pain look like Junior Aspirin. Sex, according to Philip Larkin, would be invented.

Maurice's dad, Tom, worked on the tugboats, guiding the great ocean liners and merchant ships up the Mersey into Liverpool docks. Eventually he'd become a tugboat captain, a working class aristocrat, not hugely well paid but as respected as a train driver. Best of all, during the war, working the tugboats was a reserved occupation, exempt from the call-up. This never put him out of harm's way — he was still out there, doing his job while the bombs rained on the docks — but at least he could come home at nights, and he could see his newborn son.

Mum, Elizabeth, known as Lily, had had a tragic childhood. Her big sister died of meningitis at the age of three. The grief, it seems, took her dad six months later. When Elizabeth was 14, a heart attack took her mum. She was brought up by an aunt and remained, understandably, a little overprotective of her own children.

In the fine distinctions of class that bedevil the world, living in Crosby, at least in the forties and fifties, put you a cut above those who lived in most of Liverpool proper; having a dad who was a tugboat captain put you a cut above those whose dads were casuals at the docks, or on the lines making washing machines at English Electric; living in a house with two or three feet of front garden put you a cut above those with only a stone step between front door and pavement. In other words, in comparative terms, the Coles were posh; even posher when Lily ran a sweet shop thereby propelling them, in strict Marxist terms, out of the ranks of the proletariat and into the ranks of the petty bourgeoisie.

Finding yourself a cut above your neighbours can send you in various directions. Some recognise that their elevated status is still only a hair's-breadth from starvation and devote their lives to helping those less fortunate. Others feel alienated, a pearl among swine, disgusted by scabby knees and the absence of dry-cleaning. "I hated Liverpool," Kenny told *Cosmopolitan* in 1979. "It was just mean streets and buildings. I had no friends."

Biographers and autobiographers have a tendency to seek in the childhoods of their subjects presentiments of greatness to come. They put great stress, for instance, on the enthusiasm with which the five-year-old entertainer-of-the-future put on shows for mummy and daddy, conveniently ignoring the abundant evidence that most burger flippers and nearly all chemistry professors, when they were five, also provided their parents with quality entertainment.

"I always knew, deep down, I was going to be famous some day," says the diva, neglecting to enquire whether her make-up stylist, her puppy handler and her sous-chef also knew, deep down – and as it turned out mistakenly – that they, too, were going to be famous some day.

Even worse is the biographer's tendency to play Dr Freud.

"I once had an enema," Kenny told the *Daily Mail* in 1970. "I was a little boy and we used to have an outside loo in the back yard in Liverpool where I lived, and I hated it because it was full of spiders. So when they'd say, 'Maurice go and poo,' I'd go out and walk back in. Eventually they found out and had to take me to hospital."

Don't start.

Give or take the odd enema, infancy was unruffled by great trauma or overexcitement. A Lucozade bottle, filled with wee that – according again to his unreliable autobiography – his sister gave him as a joke, was drunk without apparent ill-effect. Twice or three times a week he went to his grandma's house. She gave him money for liquorice and flying saucers. Nobody choked. Then he went to school.

St Edmund's was a Roman Catholic primary school a mile or so away up the Oxford Road. It had some distinguished alumni. Thirteen years before Maurice was signed up, Tony Booth, the actor who played Mike Rawlins, the 'scouse git' in the Sixties TV sitcom *Til Death Us Do Part*, had been there and it was where Tony sent his daughter, Cherie, who later became Cherie Blair, top barrister and Prime Ministerial wife.

At St Edmund's, Kenny first encountered a need, never fully met, to develop survival skills. Full-grown he was five-foot-five and could be lifted with one hand. In an age when boys were called John, Brian and Keith, he was a Maurice. Sometimes this was shortened to 'Mo', which was, in the playgrounds of most secondary schools and some of the more sophisticated primaries, also a shortening of 'homo'. He was a bit posher than his schoolmates. He had a mop of blond curls. He had allergies. Wool next to the skin brought him out in an itchy rash. Sometimes, according to David Lister's 1995 biography, *In The Best Possible Taste*[1], his mum dressed him in "little dickey bows and gleaming white trousers and white shirt". He didn't stand a chance.

"I wasn't really built to be born in Liverpool," he told the *Daily Mirror* in 1979[2]. "I was even thinner as a kid than I am now, and I tended to get hit a lot. Beating up people is a big thing in Liverpool."

Childhood acquaintances agree that he almost certainly exaggerated the beatings. Schools in the fifties were violent places, but then as now, bullies soon learned that the threat of violence was always more effective than an actual kicking. To the true megalomaniac, far more satisfying than giving the victim a bloody nose is to watch the victim wet himself with fear. And anyway, towering above even the vilest bullies in the school was the scariest bully of them all.

"We were all terrified of God," Kenny wrote. "They'd tell us frightening stories to keep us in line at school. 'God is always watching you,' they'd say, making him out to be some kind of beady-eyed spiritual Big Brother. 'He's everywhere,' they'd say, 'inside you, outside you, watching your every move.' I was frightened to fart in case I upset him."[3]

Tom and Lily were devout Roman Catholics. Little Maurice knew the gut-wrenching disappointment of coming home for tea to find a priest at the table, telling his beads. Mass was a Sunday ritual but it had its upside. Maurice was an altar boy and sang in the church choir, which, apart from a few abortive violin lessons, was the only formal musical training he ever had. The experience nonetheless left him with the uncanny grasp of harmony that later allowed him to construct jingles dripping with overdubbed, self-performed – and presumably improvised – layers of Bach-style counterpoint, sometimes approaching fugue.

In Catholic schools of the time, the basis of all religious education was the Penny Catechism, a document that defines the principle tenets of the Roman Catholic faith, in a form that supposedly even the most unspiritual of children can understand. It consists of 370 questions and answers.

"*1. Who made you?*
God made me.
2. Why did God make you?
God made me to know him, love him and serve him in this world, and to be happy with him for ever in the next."

Until everything began to get liberal in the sixties, most Catholic schools and Sunday Schools insisted that at least some of it be learnt by heart. Kids were made to recite random passages. The consequences of faltering, stumbling or mumbling were unthinkable.

"*72. When will Christ come again?*
Christ will come again from heaven at the last day, to judge all mankind.
73. What are the things Christ will judge?
Christ will judge our thoughts, words, works, and omissions."

The Penny Catechism, once installed, cannot be uninstalled. Like nursery rhymes, playground chants and the lyrics of every pop song you heard before the age of 20, it remains as part of the hard-wiring of the brain. Odd phrases surface at cruelly appropriate moments.

212. Are immodest plays and dances forbidden by the sixth Commandment?
Immodest plays and dances are forbidden by the sixth Commandment, and it is sinful to look at them.
213. Does the sixth Commandment forbid immodest songs, books, and pictures?
The sixth Commandment forbids immodest songs, books, and pictures, because they are most dangerous to the soul, and lead to mortal sin.

In later life, little Maurice Cole became a champion of immodest songs and in his television shows made a notable feature of immodest dances.

327. Which are the four sins crying to heaven for vengeance?
The four sins crying to heaven for vengeance are:
1.   Wilful murder (Gen. 4)
2.   The sin of Sodom (Gen. 18)
3.   Oppression of the poor (Exod. 2)
4.   Defrauding labourers of their wages (James 5)

As far as we know, Kenny was innocent of wilful murder and was never known to oppress the poor or to defraud labourers of their wages. The second of those four 'sins', however, must have given him pause for thought.

To say that Roman Catholicism gave him a great guilt complex about his homosexuality is as self-evident as it is a gross oversimplification. There are as many gay Roman Catholics who've never felt a twinge of discomfort about their sexuality as there are gay Protestants, Jews, Muslims and atheists traumatised by self-hatred and remorse. Besides, it's unfair to lay all the blame on religion. Before 1967, when homosexuality was decriminalised – and for a long time afterwards – religion was only one element in an endless parade of headlines, glances, jokes, movies and laws designed to make gay people feel shitty about themselves.

"When did he discover he was gay?" asked *You*[4] magazine in 1991. "'The first stirrings were when I was five years old,'" he said, "'and one of my male relatives dangled me on his knee.'"

Sex education came in the form of a book his dad chucked on his bed one day and advised him to read. The book, called *What A Young Boy Ought To Know* and published in 1897 was 'transcribed from the cylinders' – Edison recording cylinders – of sermons given by Sylvanus Stall, a Lutheran pastor from Elizaville, New York. It was the first of several similarly pious works – including *What A Young Man Ought To Know* (1904), *What A Young Husband Ought To Know* (1899) and *What A Man Of Forty-five Ought To Know* (1901). The essential message of the *Young Boy* edition can be summarised in two words, "Don't wank."

"You will see," says Sylvanus, "from what I have said, that this secret vice is attended with most serious consequences. But I have not yet told you the worst. If persisted in, masturbation will not only undermine, but completely overthrow the health." He warns that 'imbecility' and 'insanity' are the best you can hope for. In order to effect a 'cure', boys "often have to be put in a 'strait-jacket', sometimes have their hands fastened behind their backs, sometimes their hands are tied to the posts of the bed, or fastened by ropes or chains to rings in the wall."

As Kenny put it, "Can you imagine anything more designed to turn people into sado-masochistic freaks than reading that sort of advice while they're still in short trousers?"[5]

Maurice was never much of a mixer. "He was very quiet and shy, although a very nice lad," says John Haines, whose siblings were classmates. "There was no sign at all then of what he would become later."

"I always thought he was a little shit," says another classmate who prefers to remain anonymous and was unable to provide further enlightenment.

"To be honest, I always thought he was a bit strange as a child," says Elsie Prescott-Hadwin another childhood acquaintance.

Cleo Rocos, who later became a sidekick in life and on his TV show, gives a fine example of the strange way his brain worked – a story that Kenny's mum told her.[6]

When Maurice was about seven, he and a friend, playing on a disused railway line, lit a little fire in a derelict carriage. The fire got out of control and soon the carriage was a blazing inferno. Their efforts to put it out were useless and anyway soon they saw adults approaching, so they legged it. Eventually they shook off their pursuers, but were still terrified they'd been recognised and would be reported to their dads, or their schools, or the police. Then Kenny had a brainwave. Disguise. "Let's swap jackets," he said. "Then they'll never recognise us."

He was given a toy record player called a Kiddiegram. It had a horn and a needle, like all pre-electric gramophones, but just one fixed record, 'Mary Had A Little Lamb'. There was a junk shop next door to St. Edmund's called Rosie's where brand new 78 rpm records of the Great Classics could be purchased for 3d (1½p). Kenny would buy these. At home he butchered his Kiddiegram, ripping the horn off so that he could amputate 'Mary Had A Little Lamb' ("It's boring, innit") and, holding the needle and horn in place with one hand while spinning the record at approximately 78 rpm with the index finger of his other hand, play his Great Classics.

Once a week, Saturday morning pictures provided a few hours' blessed relief from the endless round of bullies, God and arson.

"I went to the cinema a lot when I was small – at the Odeon, Crosby," he told the *Sunday Telegraph*[7] in 1990. "It cost sixpence and you got your pea shooter confiscated at the door and hoped you'd get the same one back when you left. The rest of the time we'd be busy flicking used chewing gum into girls' hair. I loved the Flash Gordon serials on Saturday mornings, when we used to sing a rousing song that ended with, '… we all intend to be good citizens and champions of the free,' at which point I'd dissolve into tears of laughter."

The Odeon, later renamed the Plaza, was a ten minute walk up Crosby Road North. The usual fare on Saturday mornings was a triple bill: a comedy – *Three Stooges, Abbot & Costello* or maybe an old *Laurel & Hardy* – followed by a jungle film or a western – Roy Rogers, or Hopalong Cassidy – followed by the serial – *Rocket Man, The Curse Of The Crimson Ghost* or – everybody's favourite not just Kenny's – *Flash Gordon* starring Buster Crabbe with Jean Rogers as Dale Arden and Charles B Middleton as Ming the Merciless, ruler of the planet Mongo. In the pre-TV world, Saturday morning pictures had the kind of profound and lasting effect on the impressionable young that Goebbels could only have dreamt of. Peek into the psyche of any spirited lad who sat through those jungle films, for instance, and you will find an enduring sexual fetish for jodhpurs and pith helmets, a snake-phobia and a good spattering of residual racism. Flash Gordon became Kenny's alter-ego, an imaginative retreat that kept him safe in the playground and, later, as Captain Kremmen, a bold ally in his adventures on radio and TV.

Audience participation was an essential part of the Saturday Morning Pictures experience: not just singalongs, but talent shows and yo-yo competitions. This was the arena in which Kenny won his first great showbusiness victory, albeit a Pyrrhic victory that came close to providing a Contributory Negligence plea – "he was asking for it" – to all subsequent bullies.

He won a skipping contest.

Maurice, with his blond curls and possibly his dickey-bow, won a skipping contest.

"I desperately wanted the first prize – a gorgeous jigsaw of a train coming out of the Canadian Rockies," he told the *Mail On Sunday* in 1987.[8]

"But of course how stupid of me – skipping! Back at school I got beaten to death for it. And my dad, he used to drive a Liverpool tugboat – very heave-ho me hearties. He didn't go much on skipping either."

Worse still, Kenny didn't even win the jigsaw fair and square. An older, bigger girl skipped more skips than he did, but the novelty of awarding a skipping prize to a *boy* – and such a weedy looking boy at that – swung the judges' decision. He was, in other words, beaten by *a girl,* and given the prize out of *pity.* Any passing bully who didn't give him a kick after that would have felt bad about it for the rest of his life. (And if any of the bullies were Freudians, what japes they could have had with Kenny's passion for "a train coming out of the Canadian Rockies".)

In 1956, Maurice took his 11-plus, the exam to decide whether he'd be elevated to the grammar school or dumped in the secondary modern. He failed.

St Bede's Catholic Secondary Modern had all the muscular Christianity, bullying and brutality that Kenny had grown used to at St Edmund's, but much, much worse. "It was a strict school," says Yvonne Cureton, an old St Bedeian herself. "The headmaster used to use the strap on girls and boys. Also the boys used to get hit on the backside with a pump, as in gym shoe."

"They'd bring out the cane, and that was horrendous," said Kenny. "All that weight and viciousness concentrated into a stick. It hurt like hell. I used to prefer the strap. Because there was the same weight and force but spread over a wider area.⁹"

The teachers at St Bede's were not cut from the same cloth as say, Miss Jean Brodie or Mr Chips. "The worst one," says Yvonne Cureton, "was Mr Parkinson. Maths teacher. Read the racing pages in the lessons. Hopeless."

When an alternative presented itself, Maurice leapt at it. Peter Terry, a pal from around the corner whom Kenny had known since they were toddlers, had been going away to boarding school: the St Peter Claver College at Stillington Hall, founded in 1949 by the Verona Fathers, an Italian missionary order, as a training school for boys eager to minister to the godless and underprivileged in Africa.

Tom and Lily filled in the forms. A priest arrived to interview Maurice. He was deemed acceptable. A uniform – grey trousers, grey blazer, grey cap – was bought and sewn with Cash's Woven Name Tapes. A suitcase was packed.

For lads from Liverpool, Manchester and Leeds, Stillington Hall was a gobsmacking gaff with the sort of staircase Margaret Lockwood might descend in order to say something haughty to poor James Mason cowering in the vaulted entrance hall below. A movie-star staircase. Walking up it – hearing the thud of your own boots on the oak, smelling the polish – was as exciting as climbing the mountains of the moon. One brave kid tried to slide down that formidable banister, fell off, hit the floor and was taken unconscious to hospital. He was considered lucky to have survived.

The hall was ten miles outside York, in the placid bit of North Yorkshire, next to the then tiny Stillington village. Not quite the middle of nowhere, but near.

"The feel of the whole village was calming after the experience of inner-city living," says Mike Webster, who started at Stillington the same day as Maurice. "With only 58 or so pupils it was less hectic than secondary modern schools and had a gentler academic pace. Also the nature of the students entering the school added to the overall calmer atmosphere."

As well as the students, "there were two resident lay teachers, the Father Rector and six teachers who were Verona Fathers. In addition to the local Yorkshire accent, there were strong accents from various parts of Scotland, Ireland as well as a couple of students from overseas."

The brazen, the belligerent and the bullies had been weeded out by the selection process. "The discipline was there, but not strict in the normal sense of the word."

A level one offence would mean a missed meal. A level two meant chores – usually working in the orchard or the vegetable patch. A level three mean a black mark and could mean missing a film show or a day out.

There were no beatings. Instead "The staff set an academic example for all to follow." The intention was for everyone to develop into 'rounded' people.

There is a photograph of Kenny, perched on a stone bollard taken outside against a side wall of Stillington Hall. His shorts come down to his knees. He's taken off his tie. He has his hands folded on one raised knee and he's looking, calm and self-assured into the camera, well on his way to becoming a 'rounded' person.

The school photo shows Maurice at the end of the line, standing to attention with his feet at ten-to-two, in shorts and buttoned blazer. His socks are pulled up. He has a camera hanging on a strap around his neck.

The camera was a short-lived obsession. In *The Custard Stops At Hatfield*, he talks about impressing his classmates – if only for a fleeting moment – with his ability to take a snap, vanish into the darkroom and emerge with a damp print no more than an hour later; a miracle in those almost pre–Polaroid and certainly pre–digital times. Mike Webster has no memory of this, but does remember photographs of "trees in front of the house… individual students and bits of the buildings in the grounds. The quality was what you would expect of someone of that age and limited skill."

Kenny's version of the truth, particularly about his childhood, was always woven with a latex thread, enabling it to be stretched for personal and celebrity purposes. In *Custard* he represents himself as faking a 'vocation' in order to get into the place – although, again according to Mike Webster, the priests, as one might expect, weren't so unrealistic as to expect the boys to be St Bernadette or Sister Lúcia of Fátima and were more concerned that they had roughly the right attitude and sense of service rather than anything so grand as a 'vocation'.

Anyway, in the ethos of the college, and apparently in the eyes of many of the priests, belief in the might, majesty and wonder of God only marginally outranked belief in the might, majesty and wonder of football. They played a lot of football. One of the priests, Fr Antonio Colombo, had a relative who played for Internazionale Milan and through him had acquired full strip for all the boys in Inter's black and blue home colours.

Most Stillington Old Boys recall their time at the college as a period of *Cider With Rosie* bucolic innocence. Sometimes Geoff 'Bullethead' Cullen would show off by ramming a stone column on the front lawn with his skull. Sometimes the Major from the Old Rectory would attend church services and cause a stir by bringing his daughter with him. And sometimes trips to the village would be blessed with a glimpse of the cobbler's daughter. "Nothing wrong with admiring God's handiwork," the accompanying priest would murmur as he caught sight of the boys' widening eyes and blushing cheeks. Once one of the boy's mothers caused untold excitement by breast-feeding on the front lawn.

Otherwise it was a time of country walks, birds nesting, scrumping, the odd scrap with a village boy, pillow fights and wild garlic to hide the stink of sneaky cigarettes. Bernard 'Clem' Lawson, another pupil at Stillington in the late fifties, praises young Maurice's impersonations of "an English teacher called Mr. Durrant known as Da Di; an older gentleman with glasses and a moustache who had a sort of scooter. Not quite a Mr. Pastry or Mr. Bean but ideal for Maurice Cole – Kenny Everett – to impersonate."

At times Kenny and his friends would run around the grounds singing a pointless song Kenny had made up in praise of the school: "A place (pronounced pla-y-ce) for infants to go. A playce for infants to go." It was almost certainly his first ever jingle: or perhaps more of a station ident for the school.

He put on little shows for the amusement of his friends, fragments of comedy he'd heard on the radio, doing all the voices himself.

It couldn't last.

One Christmas holiday, Tom and Lily received a letter from the Father Rector, suggesting that Maurice's talents might be better served at some other seat of learning.

Kenny later liked to suggest that he was expelled as a troublemaker. There may be some truth in this. Tom Heavey, another classmate, remembers him "as a skinny, sickly-looking boy, very giddy, and always up to mischief. If I remember rightly he was involved in that April Fool stunt when ink was poured into the holy water fount at the entrance to the chapel. The most amusing (and, for some, embarrassing) aspect of that trick, was the evidence of how badly some of us – including the priests – made the sign of the cross."

Another story widely disseminated, not least by Kenny himself, suggests that he was part of an expedition to the cellars where his skinny frame allowed him to slip through the bars and hand out bottles of communion wine to his partners-in-crime. A misplaced faith in the absolute confidentiality of the confessional led to his subsequent discovery. It's a story that 'Clem' Lawson dismisses as "a good old myth". Mike Webster says a far more likely explanation for Maurice's 'being advised not to return' is straightforward homesickness.

"Quite a number of students returned home as a result of homesickness," says Mike. Though the tranquillity of Stillington had much to offer, the regime of "early mornings and study and the religious aspect to the life" were hard for some: as was the complete absence of female reassurance. Even the equivalent of a school matron – the great comforter in so many boys' boarding – was a priest.

The Housemasters and the college's Spiritual Director were both charged with keeping an eye on the boys' general welfare. If a boy was unhappy, they'd know. If a boy was unsuited to the life, they'd know. "If they believed a student had the wrong attitude or intellectually would find the life difficult then they were counselled to give serious thought to returning to their home area and picking up their education there."

For Maurice, returning home meant the chill feeling that he'd let his parents down, after they'd bought the uniform and the Cash's Woven Name Tapes, and made the local priest feel he was having some sort of impact on his flock. Even worse, "picking up his education there" meant St. Bede's Catholic Secondary Modern.

"I was hopeless at school," Kenny told the *Daily Mirror*[10] in 1979. "I wasn't really good at anything, except geography – and that was only because I liked the teacher. She was cute, Miss Geography, or whatever her name was. It was a terrible place anyway. All the kids there were budding criminals who spent their time carving daggers out of bits of their desks. Anyone who was caught actually listening to lessons was considered a cissy and was beaten up in the playground afterwards."

By now Maurice was acquiring a few rudimentary survival skills,

"I remember there was this bloke called Fletcher, or Fletch as he was tremblingly known at school," he told the *Sunday Express*[11] in 1982. "A great big hulking kid who terrified small fry like myself. Fortunately Fletch had a sense of humour and he laughed at everything I said. I became his best pal and we went round everywhere together. Like salt and pepper. Talk about an odd couple! But at least I never got my brains bashed about by him like most of the other kids. And I've been making people laugh ever since."

There were other attempts to fit in. Maurice became an unenthusiastic member of a gang and tagged along while they nicked tins of baked beans from grocer's shops. Sometimes he helped out at his mum's sweet shop, where he nicked one sweet from every jar and amassed a huge stash. But increasingly, he just retreated.

"When I got home from school I used to turn on the telly straight away and escape into it," he told the London *Evening Standard*[12] in 1978. "Television always seemed much better than life to me. You either watched telly all day or allowed your brain to turn a somersault on itself and go off into fantasy. The programmes were terrible, things like Katie Boyle. But telly was still a great escape for me because Liverpool was such a drag. I'd get home at night and plant myself in front of the screen and stay there. I never saw Liverpool again. Just that tube.[13]"

The Cole family bucked the trend for buying a TV in 1953 to watch the Coronation (they watched it on the new telly installed at the Labour Club instead) but gave in a year later and had the apparatus installed. Before 1956, when ITV came to Liverpool, 'changing channel' was something they did in America. Here we were stuck with the BBC whose schedules were usually so grim that "allowing your brain to turn a somersault on itself" must have seemed infinitely more attractive. At primetime on, to pick a random date, Monday February 11, 1957, BBC was showing *Panorama,* followed by *Television Dancing Club* (joyless ballroom), followed by *The Prime Minister At The English Speaking Union Dinner In Honour Of General Lauris Norstad.* Thankfully ITV was running an episode of *Alfred Hitchcock Presents,* so brain somersaults could be postponed for an hour or so.

Wireless was always better. It was the soundscape of Maurice's childhood and he never stopped loving that sound: a box filled with funny voices, most of them alien to Liverpool ears.

"That, for me, was civilization," he told the *Mail on Sunday*[14] in 1987. "The voice of Alvar Lidell [BBC radio announcer and newsreader, 1936–1969, full name Tord Alvar Quan Lidell], 'Good evening, and welcome to the wireless.' Sitting there by myself, just listening to those voices made me feel all warm and cosy. They never said anything horrible or hurtful."

On the same night as the Prime Minister was honouring General Lauris Norstad on TV, the Light Programme – BBC Radio's entertainment station – was playing the highlight of Kenny's week: *The Goon Show,* a comedy series, mostly written by Spike Milligan and starring Milligan, Peter Sellers, Harry Secombe and Michael Bentine (1951–53). Some 238 episodes were made between 1951 and 1960. It brought Peter Sellers movie stardom, Harry Secombe a knighthood and a nation's affection, and Spike Milligan several long bouts of mental illness. In other parts of Europe, *musique concrète* – the assembly of musical and other noises with voices (sung and spoken) into compositions unconstrained by the conventional rules of melody, harmony or structure – was a serious art form, funded by governments and pursued by earnest intellectuals. Here it was something comedians and BBC technicians did (much better) for gags: for this was a radio cartoon, mixing a schizophrenic's cast of voices, which mauled language and often didn't bother with words at all, catchphrases, with the cool jazz stylings of the Ray Ellington Quartet and, for some reason, a solo from Max Geldray, who played the mouth organ.

The sound effects were cutting edge. On one occasion, for instance, to achieve a particular quality of squelch, Spike Milligan filled his own socks with custard from the studio canteen.

"Back in the studio," said Harry Secombe, "Spike had already placed a sheet of three-ply near a microphone." He swung the socks around his head and then bought them crashing down to make the squelch. "There were (in the studio), I think, four turntables on the go simultaneously, with different sounds being played on each – chickens clucking, Big Ben striking, donkeys braying, massive explosions, ships sirens – all happening at once."[15]

The Goon Show's influence on most British comedy – and indirectly American comedy, too – and some British music, including the Beatles, is well documented. Like *Monty Python*, *The Fast Show*, and *Little Britain,* it also spawned a million schoolboy imitators and office wags who would 'do the voices' and repeat the catchphrases endlessly in the mistaken belief that people would laugh and this might make them popular. Maurice was among their number, but with knobs on: for whereas others would make a half-hearted stab at 'doing the voices' he owned them. And not just the voices off *The Goon Show*. He could do Alvar Lidell, he could do the sound of the spaceship doors opening in *Journey Into Space,* he could do the time signal and the sig tunes and *The Shipping Forecast*. And just as he owned the voices, the music and the sounds, they came to own him. They came to invade his speech patterns such that a single sentence could encompass four or five different voices, an explosion, a raspberry and a couple of bars of *The Archers* theme. All the noises that came out of the big valve wireless at home. Years before he got near a microphone, Maurice *was* that wireless.

A whole different repertoire of voices came from Radio Luxembourg, the forerunner of pirate radio, which, helped by what was at one time the world's most powerful radio transmitter, broadcast commercial radio in English to Britain. In an age when pop on the BBC was as rare as bananas had been a decade earlier, Luxembourg was luxury: Keith Fordyce's *Rockin' To Dreamland,* Benny Lee's *Record Hop,* Alan

Freed's *Rock'n'Roll*, played chart records, interrupted only by chat and ads. What has now become the bog standard radio format, available all across the dial, was then limited to a faraway, static-shrouded signal on 208 metres, medium wave. The non-pop programmes were worth listening to as well, if only for curiosity value: the quiz shows, *Double Your Money* and *Take Your Pick,* both subsequently snapped up by ITV; the serials, *Dan Dare Pilot Of The Future* (like *Flash Gordon* but cosier, as befits a programme "brought to you by the makers of Horlicks, the food drink of the night"); and the US-made and paid-for evangelist shows like *Frank And Ernest* "revealing the Gospel's relevance to everyday life" and sponsored by the Dawn Bible Student's Association of Rutherford, New Jersey. Luxembourg not only gave Maurice his first notions of what radio could be, it also gave him access to a whole range of non-BBC, American voices to filch: the unctuous adman, the stern announcer, the Bible-belt bigot.

The voices, BBC and Luxembourg, were, of course, an indispensable form of camouflage. Now you see him, now you don't. Will the real Maurice Cole please step forward. They presented a moving target of register, a dissolution of identity, a deconstruction of the power/discourse narrative and an implosion of meaning that must have made many post-modernists kick 'emselves for not having thought of it first.

Then love came into Maurice's life.

Some men love women. Some men love men. But for some men the greatest love of all – the love to which they remain true all their lives while lesser, human loves, come and go – is for a team, a crankshaft, a two-stroke, a maple-topped mahogany-bodied six-string, a pair of 12-bore over-and-unders.

Maurice Cole found such a love and its name was Grundig.

CHAPTER TWO

The tape recorder was a German invention. Its ancestor, the wire recorder, had been around since the 1890s but its horribly lo-fi quality confined its use to indistinct dictation. Then, in the twenties, Fritz Pfleumer, an extraordinarily versatile engineer who had already made major contributions to the development of plastics, MDF and cigarette holders, came up with a technique for sticking iron oxide to paper tape. The electrical company AEG acquired the patent and, at the Berlin Radio Exhibition of 1935, unveiled its new Magnetophon, the world's first fully working tape recorder, to an audience of wide-eyed visitors including some of the nation's most influential Nazis. A year later, the London Philharmonic Orchestra, conducted by Sir Thomas Beecham, was recorded on tape playing Mozart's 39th Symphony on the Berlin leg of their European tour. Beecham, unimpressed, saw no future in the medium.

During the war, few outside Germany bothered much with the miracle of iron oxide. British and American radio engineers could only envy the Reich Broadcasting Corporation's ability to transmit repeats of Goebbels' best routines in such click and hiss-free quality. But at the end of the war, the US military got hold of the technology and took it back home. Bing Crosby invested $50,000 and within a year was making all his records and radio shows on tape. By the early fifties, smaller, cheaper versions of the big broadcast machines were being developed for the domestic market.

From the start the tape recorder could have been designed specifically with the nerd market in mind. Its combination of mechanical clunkiness and atom-age electronics gave it an irresistible Heath Robinson/Dan Dare appeal. The cheap ones had something called a magic eye to measure the input level. It throbbed greenly. The posh ones had actual dials that swung, sometimes dangerously into the red sector. Ownership gave one the right to talk about "frequency response" and "dynamic range" and "red leader' – or even better "wow" and "flutter" – with an air of self-righteous authority. And that combination of hot Rexene, warm cellulose acetate, fizzing electricity and curious mustiness meant they smelt good, too.

Perhaps more importantly, if you put the microphone in the bathroom and spoke sonorously, you could be the Pope addressing the assembled faithful in somewhere like Westminster Cathedral. If you recorded the same thing at 7.5 inches per second and then played it back at 3.75 inches per second, you were the voice of God. If you recorded the Lord's Prayer and then turned the tape so that it played backwards you could, according to ancient myth, raise the devil. With a little editing block, a razor blade and some custom-made tape – or failing that a pair of nail scissors and some Sellotape – you could have some serious fun. Some boys (and, yes, they were always boys) removed everything except the intros and middles from Cliff Richard records so as to be left with a medley that was all Hank and no Cliff. Some boys took a recording of a County Class (4-6-0) steam loco entering the Box Tunnel just outside Swindon, and spliced it with a completely separate recording of a Modified Hall Class (4-6-0) loco exiting the self-same tunnel thereby giving the impression that the train had *magically changed identity* while within the confines of the tunnel. Some boys – with a taste for political satire – took all the 'not's from one of Mr Macmillan's speeches so as to make him say the exact opposite of what he meant: with precision editing – a painstaking but worthwhile skill to acquire – they could even isolate individual syllables and make him say, "Look at my bum".

In other words, a tape recorder gave the weedy, the disenfranchised, the overlooked and the bullied a chance to control the world, to remake it in their own image and put it on a seven-inch reel, duly labelled and stored with its alphabetised fellows on a bedroom shelf.

Maurice had always been a tinkerer. The Cole family was accustomed to having radios, clocks, watches and pianos ritually disassembled and modified. Not long after the Stillington adventure, he found himself cutting out pictures of tape recorders and pasting them into a scrapbook.[16] They cost a fortune, though. In 1956, an entry level Grundig, the TK5, cost 52 guineas (£54.60). The national average wage was about £15 a week.

Maurice would often claim in later life to have bought his first tape recorder with money he saved from a paper round. Given that it wasn't unusual for paper boys to be paid as little as 5s (25p) a week in the fifties, it seems unlikely that this was the only source of funding, but one way or another the money was found and Maurice got his Grundig.

The next difficulty, one that faced all keen tape recordists, was, once you've got your hands on a machine of your own, once you've checked it over for wow and flutter, once you've tested the frequency response and dynamic range to make sure they matched the manufacturer's promises, once you've made a train *magically change identity,* what do you do with it then? Boys quickly realised that going out and about with your machine in order to build a library of interesting sounds was ultimately dismaying when the realisation dawned that the only people content to keep still long enough to listen to collections of interesting sounds were coma victims.

Unlike those other boys, though, Maurice knew exactly what he wanted to do with his Grundig.

Jack Jackson was a trumpeter whose big band wowed the smart set at the Dorchester Hotel in London from 1933 to the outbreak of war. He did his bit to defeat the Nazi peril by drawing propaganda cartoons for the Ministry of Information and when peace was declared, re-formed the band and got himself a gig at Churchill's club. Then the BBC invited him to compere a big band show for the Light Programme (the precursor of Radio 2). A year later he was spinning discs on the Light Programme's *Record Round Up* – later renamed *Record Roundabout* – a show that ran for 20 years. He eventually relocated to the Canary Islands where he built himself a little studio to put his programmes together, sending the tapes in neat parcels to the BBC.

"Jack Jackson was finding new creative and interesting ways of linking music," says DJ legend 'Whispering' Bob Harris. "The links weren't just links. They were events within themselves. There would be characters or there would be different voices or he would talk up to the vocal of the record he was playing so that, for instance, the first line would answer a question he asked."

(viz: JACKSON: What do you fancy for dinner? AL HIBBLER [US RECORDING ARTISTE]: [SINGS] Oh, my love, my darling, I hunger for your touch …)

"He used to cut in little snippets of other shows and have conversations with Tony Hancock. It's difficult to describe. There wasn't anything else like that around."

Jackson delighted in mayhem. He conducted an ongoing argument with his "boss", the Senior Programme Suppressor. He invited contributions from his cat, Tiddles. The result made the speakers fizz, scream and bubble. If he'd delivered his aural collages at concert halls and galleries instead of the BBC, Jackson would have been hailed as a Dada genius – a direct descendent of Duchamp, Tzara and Schwitters. As it was, he had to make do with being the BBC's top disc jockey (a term that was gradually being introduced by suede-footed hipsters) with an audience peaking at 12 million.

Throughout his life, Kenny cited Jack Jackson as a primary influence.

"Oh, yes, he was terrific," said Kenny[17]. "Loved him to death. I used to record all his shows. He used to get hold of an hour and do a lot of work in it. It just sounded really good, and fun, and jolly. And all the rest of the guys on the Light Programme were just going, 'That was Robert Ditch singing 'Melodies Are Made Of Thing' by the Northern Dance Orchestra. It's ten past eight.' That was it. But Jack Jackson had a studio in the Canary Islands so he was free from all this collar and tie stuff. So he just used to throw a few records together with comedy sketches and bits of daft LPs and things and he knitted together quite a jolly show. That's the secret of wireless. Sound like you're having fun."

The similarity between Jackson and Kenny's styles is unmistakable, but Kenny took Jackson's mayhem several stages further. For a start, he did voices. Jack Jackson always played the role of the dignified, if put-upon, moderator – a bit like Kenneth Horne in *Round The Horne*.

Kenny engaged with the mayhem, fully immersed, matching the mood and the music with his own inflections, accents, rhythms and scream.

The trouble is you can't create Jack Jackson-style mayhem with just one Grundig. A razor blade edit is a harsh and sudden jolt. If you cut the tape at a 45-degree angle it becomes slightly less sudden, but the 'mix' only lasts a tiny fraction of a second. If you want to carry on a conversation with clips from *Hancock's Half Hour* or *The Goon Show*, you want your sound and the clip to flow together. Hancock delivers his line. The studio audience laughs. You deliver your line over the laugh. You can't do that with an edit. You need to play in one lot of sound from one machine while at the same time re-recording that sound, together with your own voice, into another machine. In other words, you need two Grundigs.

Maurice left school at 15. Like most secondary modern students, he was never even given a shot at paper qualifications. Nevertheless, a career, or at least a job, had to be found. The lack of O levels put most white-collar jobs out of reach. The weedy physique made the idea of following his dad on the tugs or down the docks a non-starter. With vague notions of wearing a tall hat, throwing tantrums about soup and pronouncing his name with the accent on the second syllable, Maurice expressed an interest in becoming a chef. A job was found at Coopers, which seemed a promising start. It was a posh shop – Liverpool's equivalent of Fortnum's – that sold delicacies, still comparatively rare in the fifties, like French wine and fresh coffee. Kenny was sent to the bakery where he was given the job of scraping gunge from used sausage-roll trays.

On the following day he was given the same job. And the day after. The pay was £7 10s a week. His surly colleagues did not need to mention that a French accent would not impress.

The job did, however, provide him with the means at least partly to subsidise his escalating Grundig habit. He acquired his second tape recorder and, by fiddling with wires, hooking in the family gramophone and soundproofing the odd spot of wall with egg-boxes, figured out how to be Jack Jackson.

There is, in fact, no end of stuff you can do with two tape recorders.

Among the regulars on Bing Crosby's radio show was a trio led by guitarist Les Paul. Les was intrigued by the new machines Bing was sponsoring. He began to experiment and soon discovered the joys of playing with himself.

If you tape a guitar part and then re-record that first guitar part into a second machine while at the same time playing a second part, you end up with a recording of two guitars, both of which, miraculously, you have played yourself, thereby making massive savings on the fees involved in hiring another musician. It's called double-tracking. If you slow down the tape while recording, but play it back at normal speed, you can play finger-busting, if tinkly, solos. Similarly, if you speed up the tape while recording, your guitar turns into a bass. Les Paul would layer anything up to a dozen guitar parts, recorded at various speeds, then add his wife, Mary Ford, again overdubbed a dozen times, singing with herself in dense harmony. Their 'Vaya Con Dios' spent 11 weeks at number one in the *Billboard* Top 10. 'How High The Moon' did nine weeks. Then Les invented the guitar that still bears his name.

Kenny had been in the church choir. He sang pure and in tune. He had an entirely intuitive but remarkably sophisticated sense of harmony. By doing a Les Paul with his two Grundigs, he could be a one-man choir.

Maurice – just like Les Paul, Paul McCartney, Jeff Lynne, Dave Edmunds, Brian Wilson, Steve Winwood, Prince, Mike Oldfield, Dave Grohl and thousands of others – discovered that playing with yourself, overdubbing, provides a level of control, comfort, security and pleasure offered by no other human activity. Through all his days it remained his great and enduring love.

One day, Elsie Fleming, a part-time market researcher, was dispatched to No. 14 Hereford Road to interview a prospect about a recent purchase – a Grundig tape-recorder. The lad who invited her in answered all her questions about the purchase in intricate technical detail, and suggested areas where improvements to the product could be made. "He also proceeded," says Elsie's son Neil, Elsie being sadly no longer with us, "to demonstrate some of the recordings he had made himself, with the latest music interspersed with talk, jokes, double tracking of items and so on." Elsie left some time later, so impressed that she told her son when she got home. When Maurice eventually emerged as Kenny, she rightfully prided herself on her talent-spotting abilities.

Kenny lasted three months at Coopers before walking out. For the rest of his life, 'scraping gunge off sausage-roll trays' remained a benchmark for degradation. Three months on the dole were a worrying time, but the next job was a definite step up.

Douglass & Co was an advertising agency on Chapel Street. Kenny started there as a copy boy (these days more likely called a runner), rose to the rank of Assistant Production Manager and left, with glowing references, to take up an even better post in the advertising department of *The Journal Of Commerce*. His time there was somewhat curtailed, though, by The Great Moment In The Life Of Maurice Cole.

Maurice was a keen and regular reader of *Tape Recording Magazine*, 'First And Foremost In This Field, Monthly, 1s 6d'. This was top-class magno-porn where, in a single issue you could read about the Grundig TK40's "better than 50db signal-to-noise radio, its pressure sling and its cine socket", full details of the Lustraphone mic, and a fascinating article about local tape recording clubs which included news that the president of a Lancashire club lived just round the corner from Maurice. The next month's issue advertised the launch of the Sony Professional 777 at a bankbusting £570 but with specs to make a grown man drool.

In the September 1962 issue, regular contributor Alan Edward Beeby began a "brand new series" cataloguing the humorous scrapes that he and his tape-recording friend Harris got into on their sound effects collecting expeditions. On one, for instance, they had, for their own security, to pretend that their mic (he doesn't mention whether it's a Lustraphone) was an electric razor. With predictably hilarious consequences.

Then, in the April 1963 issue, Beeby's 'Tape Talk' column mentions, in its usual breezy style, "if you've got a worrying little query, opinion or problem you'd like to get off your chest, just drop me a line and I'll be only too pleased to help if I can. ... or you can send me a tape if you like – I'm not fussy! SO that's that. Are we in business?"

Four issues go by before Beeby's offer is mentioned again. Then, in the August issue, under the sub-heading "Tape Talent", he writes, "I have some advice to offer to any talent-scout who may be reading this column. It is this: 'When you've finished signing up guitar-bashing, hollering teenagers with about as much talent as a mentally retarded orang-utan, take time out to pay a visit to young Maurice Cole who lives in Seaforth, Liverpool 21. Take him back to the recording-studio, provide him with a tape-recorder, a record transcription deck, a pile of records of his own choice and an editing block. Then leave him to it. Don't try to direct, produce or stage-manage him – just leave him alone to get on with it. You'll have quite a pleasant surprise.'

"How do I know about Mr Cole? He was among the readers who responded to my recent invitation to 'send me a tape.' What makes me think he has talent? My 16-years as a semi-professional variety producer – and it takes one hell of a lot to make me sit up and beg for more.

"Mr Cole just talks and plays records. Doesn't sound very original, does it? It isn't – until Maurice takes over the DJ chair. It's difficult to describe his style, but if you've ever watched and listened to Timothy Birdsall (*TWTWTW*'s madcap cartoonist) [a reference to the innovative late night satire show *That Was The Week That Was*] you may get some idea.

"In my humble opinion, he's well worth a spot on 'Sound.' ARE YOU TAKING THIS DOWN, BBC?"

Maurice had sent Beeby a Jack Jackson style mash up of records, links, sound effects and funny voices called *The Maurice Cole Quarter-Of-An-Hour-Show*. Either he, or more likely Beeby, sent it to the BBC.

1964, like 1944, was a watershed year. In the UK, Harold Wilson's 'White Heat' Labour Government took over from the crusty aristocrats of the Conservative Party who'd been running the country for 13 years. The British cultural invasion of America, spearheaded by the Beatles, Lionel Bart's *Oliver* and Anthony Newley's *Stop The World I Want To Get Off*, had planted the possibility in people's minds that England might swing like a pendulum do. TV acquired a third channel with the birth of BBC2. The Rolling Stones and the Kinks released their first LPs. Philips launched the cassette recorder, Roald Dahl wrote *Charlie And The Chocolate Factory*, Dr Martin Luther King was awarded the Nobel Prize for Peace, and, on May 4, Maurice Cole, of Hereford Road, Crosby, got a letter.

"Dear Maurice Cole
You will have heard from Mr Beeby that we are very interested in your tape 'The Maurice Cole Quarter-of-an-Hour Show.' It seems

to me and my colleagues to show tremendous promise and I would be very interested to meet you at some time in the near future. I do not know whether you are prepared to come to London to see me, but if so the date I have in mind is 13th May. It is just possible (although I cannot promise this at the moment) that we may be able to transmit a part or all of your tape in the Home Service magazine programme 'Midweek' on that day. Provided you were agreeable, of course. If you were to come down then, you would probably have to travel on Tuesday, stay overnight, and return on the Wednesday. In this case, I think the BBC would be prepared to cover your travel and overnight expenses.

"I shall look forward to hearing from you about this in the next day or two. If you prefer not to write, you can always telephone my office and reverse the charges if you ask for me personally. In the meantime I would be very interested to see and receive any other material you may have produced

Yours sincerely
Wilfred De'Ath
Producer, Talks Department"

Maurice replied that he would be agreeable to a trip to London. A telegram arrived to say that he and his tape were scheduled to appear in the *Midweek* programme. He stuck the telegram to the handlebars of his NSU Quickly (49cc of throbbing power, top speed 25 mph) so that he could read and re-read it on his way to work.

A long time after Maurice had gone from Hereford Road, Grace Clarke's daughter bought the house. While stripping paper from a bedroom wall, she came across some writing. It was blurred and hard to make out. "BBC" was clear enough, though. And a huge, excited exclamation mark.

★   ★   ★

Wilfred De'Ath was a young Talks and Current Affairs producer, not long down from Oxford. He had a brand new show on the drawing board with a killingly with-it title: *The Teen Scene*. It was slated to start in

June of 1964 late night on the Light Programme. Because of this, most 'youth related' stuff got redirected to his desk, which is why *The Maurice Cole Quarter-Of-An-Hour Show* had landed there.

He loved it. "I remember I played and played it in my office and drove my colleagues mad," he says. "It was his links that impressed me, the commentary. It was obviously influenced by *The Goon Show* but it had something new. It had, what I believe I called at the time, 'comic genius.'"

De'Ath's initial idea was to invite Maurice down to London and audition him for *The Teen Scene*. Then he was asked to fill in for a couple of weeks as a holiday relief producer on another show, *Midweek,* a 20-minute lunchtime magazine programme that had then been running for about two years and, in a different time-slot and with a slightly different format, is still running today. He decided to kill two birds with one stone. He'd throw Maurice into the deep end and audition him live on air as part of the *Midweek* programme, "… which was a bit of a risk because I was only a very junior producer and I had management sitting on top of me watching my every move".

Maurice arrived on May 12, the day before the *Midweek* broadcast. London, he said, "… was everything I'd ever seen in the movies. I arrived at Euston station, walked along the road and saw a building called Castrol House. I remember staring up at it and thinking 'Wow a real skyscraper!'"[18]

Broadcasting House itself, of course, was designed with awe in mind. It was, and is, an Art Deco monolith, a 'battleship of modernism', dwarfing Nash's All Souls church next door in such a way as to leave no one in any doubt at all about the BBC's status relative to God. In the foyer is a sign, its letters carved in stone, declaring the place to be a "temple of the arts and muses" and exhorting those within to banish "all things foul or hostile to peace", to "tread the path of virtue and wisdom" and to incline their ears to "whatsoever things are lovely and honest". The BBC meant it, too. Then. But there were still a few years to go before John Peel invited listeners to incline their ears to the lovely honesty of Napalm Death's 'Retreat To Nowhere, Scum'.

De'Ath met Maurice in reception. "He was very overawed and impressed by being at the BBC." And the BBC, on that first encounter, was as impressed by Maurice as Maurice was by the BBC. "He was a very nice chap," says De'Ath. "Very vulnerable, but everybody liked Kenny. Everybody was nice to him."

De'Ath gave him a guided tour. Beyond the foyer were studios, in green baize and walnut, and offices, some of them with wall-to-wall carpets. "Back in Liverpool carpet was a little bit of a thing in the middle of the lino," said Kenny. "And at Christmas and Bank Holidays you would all step off the lino and on to the carpet as a special treat."[19]

Some of the studios were still using the Marconi Type A ribbon microphones, the big ones with the silhouette so recognisable that it's become one of the little computer icons for 'audio'. In the offices, clubbable men, swathed in pipe smoke, rubbed tweed shoulders with earnest intellectuals (Senior Service) and louche theatrical types (Embassy tipped), while full-skirted secretaries (Consulate – cool as a mountain stream) typed words of import and wisdom on huge clanking Imperials. Some of the women, far more than in most other industries, weren't secretaries or tea-ladies at all but seemed to be in charge. Some of the men, Maurice was pleased to notice, called each other 'darling'. People at *The Journal Of Commerce,* back in Liverpool, didn't do that, and they certainly didn't do it in the playground at St. Bede's. The chances that any of these people might start a fist-fight seemed negligible.

Best of all, for Maurice, was the gear. To a keen tape-recordist, the EMI BTR2 'Large Green' tape machine was the stuff of rumour and travellers' tales. Here, there were ranks of them. Indeed, so accustomed to their presence had the BBC people grown that the temptation to kneel before them and worship had all but subsided. There were endless rows, vanishing into the distance, of TD/7 record decks too, each set in a huge metal box bristling with the sort of knobs a Bond hero might turn to increase the pain. Carpets, darling, large green machines: when the sausage-roll tin scraper had dreamed of a better life, this was exactly the better life he'd dreamed of.

After the guided tour, Wilfred took Maurice back to his flat in Swiss Cottage where his wife was preparing a spot of dinner.

"I offered him a 'snifter'. He teased me about that. A 'snifter'. For years he used to introduce this 'snifter' thing into conversation. I gave him a large gin and tonic and he just drank it down like water and asked for another one. He'd never drunk a gin and tonic before and he'd had a couple of large ones before he realised you didn't have to drink it all down in one go. He got a bit pissed over dinner."

Maurice's hick-from-the-sticks ignorance of dinner-party conventions showed itself in other ways, too. "I remember my wife had cooked veal escalope and she put a piece of bread on to his side plate and he took it on to his main plate and cut it up with his veal into little squares." It didn't matter. "We just got on very, very well. Although he did bring out a protective side in everybody he met. Needy. That's the word. He was a very needy person right from the word go. But a very nice guy."

After dinner, Wilfred walked Maurice to the taxi rank outside the John Barnes department store and poured him into a cab. He'd been booked into the Mascot Hotel, on York Street, near Baker Street station, a place regularly used by pop and wireless people. Six guineas a night with breakfast. He was ticking off the firsts. First time at the BBC. First sighting of an EMI BTR2. First G&T. First middle-class dinner party with escalopes and side plates. First time on his own in a hotel.

He showed up at Broadcasting House, good and early, suit brushed, hair slicked. "He wasn't nervous at all," De'Ath says. "It was as though he was a professional already. It was quite astonishing."

The programme's presenter was Ronald Fletcher, a staff announcer who, like Alvar Lidell, John Snagge and Wallace Greenslade, was one of the voices that back then defined the BBC's identity: impeccable breeding, good school, absolute authority, but, in Fletcher's case, just enough raffishness to make a distinction between the BBC and the Institute of Chartered Accountants. It was the sort of voice that had lived inside Maurice's wireless and in his head for years and which he could impersonate to a perfectly enunciated T.

Maurice's radio debut in nearly all respects established the boilerplate that defined the rest of his career.

"He started taking the piss out of the BBC," says De'Ath. "He just took it over as far as I can remember. He was the only item. We played most of *The Maurice Cole Quarter-Of-An-Hour Show* and then Ronald interviewed him. Ronald was a very kind, avuncular person and Maurice was very cheeky. He was taking the micky out of Liverpool and out of the BBC. I knew he was going to be a handful but also rather a pleasant person to deal with. He was only 19 but he was witty and not at all frightened."

Wilfred was delighted with the programme. It was different. It was young. It was cheeky. He was a young gun out to prove himself. He'd stirred things up a bit.

"Of course, I got into terrible trouble. I had a terrible woman who was Head of Talks or Magazines or something – and the Head of the Department – and they were outraged that I'd put this young man on. I defended myself. I said, 'I think we've discovered someone very talented'. They gave me a bad time. I remember getting one of those nasty memos, you know, those internal memos, 'You are never to do this again. This type of item belongs in showbusiness,' and all that kind of thing."

At some point after the show, Maurice asked the question that had been bubbling on his lips, "Can I have a job here, please?"

Wilfred De'Ath tried his best to oblige. He sent the tapes of Maurice's *Midweek* interview and *The Maurice Cole Quarter-Of-An-Hour Show* off to colleagues in the Light Entertainment and Popular Music Departments along with a note declaring that, "Maurice is 19, lives in Liverpool with his parents, and spends all his time playing with tape recorders. I feel that he has quite exceptional ability and may prove of use to you."

A grudging audition was arranged with Derek Chinnery, later to become the controller of Radio 1, then a producer in Light Entertainment. This time De'Ath was not available to guide and encourage. Maurice went in cold and alone. There are indications that he may have had a couple of snifters to brace himself. He was presented with a pile of random gramophone records and invited to link them. It was intimidating, clumsy, inappropriate, " … having Derek Chinnery glaring icily at me as I played records was enough to put anyone off. So I failed the audition. I remember thinking, 'Oh God I'm stuck in Liverpool for ever now.' I went home in tears."

"I'm sorry that there appears to have been some kind of mix up at your audition," wrote Wilfred De'Ath. "I must say I had a feeling that this might happen if I was not there to supervise the situation. Anyway I am investigating the problem and will be in touch with you again soon."

For the *Midweek* appearance, Maurice got five guineas (£5.25) plus £4 17s (£4.65) for his train fare. The powers that be refused to shell out for his hotel. In the end, De'Ath had to put his hand in his own pocket.

Maurice, it seemed, had had his 15 minutes of fame and the only professional fee for broadcasting he'd ever know.

But De'Ath stayed true to his protégé. In the first broadcast of *The Teen Scene,* transmitted at the end of June, he featured a short clip from *The Maurice Cole Quarter-Of-An-Hour Show.*

Chris Peers was a record producer and agent, then working in Artist Promotions for EMI. Everybody knew Chris Peers. He got around. "He was a friend of mine," says De'Ath, "who used to come into *The Teen Scene* – we had a hospitality suite – looking for talent." De'Ath sang Maurice's praises and made sure Peers heard the tape. Chris wasn't looking for DJs or presenters but, as it happened, knew somebody who was: an advertising executive by the name of Philip Birch who had recently started work for a new kind of radio station.

From such chance encounters, mighty careers are made.

CHAPTER THREE

A radio disc jockey can become a valued friend, an irritating but cherished brother or sister, a bloke in the pub who knows a lot of stuff, a woman you often chat to on the bus. A DJ is somebody you get used to, whom you look forward to hearing again, who shapes your day. When DJs get fired, people – and not just stupid people – cry.

To get that sort of reaction the DJs don't necessarily have to be amusing or even interesting – although God knows it helps if they are. Many popular DJs are unashamedly banal, and seem to understand, like a Buddhist master, the great power of banality to soothe the vexed and anxious spirit.

"This week we're talking about rain and we've got Bernie on the line from Lowestoft. What have you got to share with us, Bernie?"

"I just wanted to make the point that if it wasn't for rain, things wouldn't be green would they?"

"That's a very good point, Bernie. And you like green, do you?"

"Well, it's not my favourite colour. That'd have to be blue. But you can't deny green looks nice on a shrub."

And suddenly the ironing's all done and you've hardly noticed the time passing at all.

The real key to a radio DJ's success isn't in what they do or what they say. It lies in their power to engage – a nebulous but nonetheless vital quality in the world of ephemeral entertainment. The power to engage is what sends one pop song double platinum while another similar song is dropped from the set list after two gigs. It is what causes one video of a cat playing the piano to go viral while another video featuring a slightly different cat playing the piano – even though this cat plays like Oscar Peterson – never breaks double digits. It's what makes *Angry Birds* infinitely more popular than *Street Viking IV – Shovels Of Rage*.

What the Manhattan Project was to nuclear physics, what the Bauhaus was to design, the pirate radio ships were to this art of engagement: a hothouse where young men, living and working cheek-by-jowl, were given the freedom to experiment, the freedom to fail, the freedom to take a passing notion into the studio almost as soon as it had occurred and test its potential for becoming a workable wireless notion – the kind that has the power to engage.

It was an evanescent sort of research. No concrete findings emerged, no research papers or equations, just a vast body of experience that still defines and informs most of the radio you find on the dial.

Those pirate ships were Kenny Everett's university, where he learned his job – where he helped to invent the job.

"Everything seemed, in an amazing way, to collide through those few years," says Bob Harris, "and pirate radio seemed to be the realization of all this energy – oh, the Beatles have just started and here's pirate radio to play them. And all these British bands – and the Byrds and the Beach Boys from America – and, oh yes, we've now got 15 pirate radio stations playing all this new music where 18 months ago there had been nothing except *Housewives' Choice* and *Two-Way Family Favourites*."

"The moment I got out there, I knew we were going to alter the whole of broadcasting in this country," said Tony Blackburn.[20]

"Exciting just isn't the word for it," said Kenny in his autobiography[21]. "It was like having been in prison for 18 years and someone saying: 'Here's a hole in the wall.' What would you think? You wouldn't sit and think about it, would you? You'd do what I did. Vroooooooom!!"

There was nothing new about pirate radio. Almost as soon as the BBC was granted a monopoly of British airwaves, chancers were trying to break it. European stations, most notably Radio Luxembourg, had been transmitting English language programmes, paid for with English language adverts, aimed at a British audience, since the thirties. But even Luxembourg's huge transmitter provided an iffy signal. Weather and ionosphere permitting, you might get passable reception on the big wireless in the living room with the outside aerial, but on your little Decca Debonaire under the bedclothes you didn't stand a chance. "Your baby doesn't love you any more," Roy Orbison would sing. And dissolve into static.

A radio station on a boat, anchored far enough out at sea to be beyond the law, but still close enough to send a signal that could penetrate bedclothes, was a much better idea.

Radio Mercur, the first, began broadcasting from a ship anchored in the Øresund to a pop-starved Denmark in 1958. It lasted four years before the Danes found a way to ban it.

Mercur's ships (by this time there were two of them) promptly turned around and began transmitting to Sweden as Radio Syd. The Swedes banned that almost as soon as it went on the air, but it carried on defiantly for another good few years.

Ronan O'Rahilly, the pioneer of British marine radio, was the grandson of *The* O'Rahilly – the great rebel, *Mícheál Seosamh Ó Rathaille*, eulogised by W.B. Yeats for his heroic role in the Easter Rising of 1916 – and therefore genetically coded to cock a snook at English law.

He was a mover and shaker in the pop business. One day, driven mad by his inability to get airplay for one of his acts, Georgie Fame & the Blue Flames, he made, if legend is to be believed, a great vow. "If none of the radio stations will play the record," he swore, "then I shall start one that will."

True to his word, he founded Radio Caroline, which went on air in March 1964 broadcasting from a former Danish ferry, the *Fredericia*, now re-christened *MV Caroline* and anchored a few miles out from Harwich on the Essex coast. In July, it merged with a rival station, Radio Atlanta, based on the *MV Mi Amigo* anchored nearby. Atlanta was rechristened Radio Caroline South and stayed where it was while the *MV Caroline* upped its anchor and sailed to a point just off the Isle of Man where it broadcast as Radio Caroline North. In Crosby, Liverpool, you couldn't pick up Radio Caroline South, but the Isle of Man signal came through strong and exciting.

"Looking out to sea, just beyond the horizon," said Kenny, talking about a walk he once enjoyed on Crosby beach not long after he flunked that first BBC audition and hope seemed vain, "was Radio Caroline North. It had just sailed up the Mersey Estuary and I was walking along with this really heavy transistor radio. I think it was one of the first. It was an old Philips, with bits of elastic and old springs sticking out of it. And I was listening to all these guys and they were having a terrific time. 'Hey! There's a seagull on the transmitter.' And they were playing all these records and having a really good time... and I thought, 'That's for me.'"[22]

Meanwhile, in far away Florida, the *USS Density*, a 100 ton World War II minesweeper, was receiving yet another humiliating makeover and name change. The vessel had once known glory, serving with great distinction in the face of repeated attacks from *kamikaze* during the invasion of Okinawa, but, decommissioned after the war, she had fallen into the hands of new owners, been renamed the *MV Manoula* and pressed into service as a humble freighter until, early in 1964 she was impounded by the port of Miami, Florida for non-payment of harbour fees.

Soon afterwards, a group of Texans arrived in Miami, shopping for a boat. They represented a consortium of car dealers and radio entrepreneurs, initially led by Don Pierson, Mayor of Eastland near Dallas, TX, who, astonished to discover that the UK was a commercial radio virgin and inspired by Ronan O'Rahilly's marine adventures, were eager to join in the deflowering. The *Manoula* seemed to meet their needs. A deal was done. The Texans changed the ship's name once again, this time to the *MV Galaxy*, installed a 50kw transmitter and a 120 ft mast (212 ft was usually claimed in publicity) and on October 22, 1964, set sail for England.

The ship was a rust bucket. The engines had to be shut down from time to time to prevent their overheating. The huge mast made the craft unstable in the heavy seas and, perhaps the supreme irony for a ship carrying such a 120 ft liability, the ship-to-shore radio was permanently on the blink. Nevertheless, her Atlantic crossing was – give or take some screaming panic and the odd touch of mutiny – uneventful. A month or so after leaving Miami, she reached her anchorage, about four miles off the Essex coast, and went into business as a pirate radio station.

One of the Texans, Gordon McLendon, had a long track record in radio and even some experience with the European pirates. He'd been in on some of the Scandinavian adventures and had an interest in Radio Atlanta, but more significantly he was the co-founder of KLIF (the Mighty 1190), which had earned its place as Dallas' top rated station by playing non-stop pop – no jazz, no standards, no polkas, no old-time country, just pure Top 40 radio.

The original idea for the British venture was simply to repackage KLIF programmes complete with the American DJs and the US charts, and transmit them in the UK as Radio KLIF London. Wiser heads advised that, whatever the Texans might believe, England was not, yet, the 51st state of America, and neither did it want to be. A product more specifically tailored to the British market would be better received. Accordingly, the name was shortened to Radio London, and though the principles of Top 40 radio would be rigidly applied, that Top 40 would be British and so – give or take the odd Canadian and the even odder phony accent – would the DJs.

The call went out to find or invent a crack team of British DJs. Philip Birch, a three-passport British/American/Canadian ad man who'd been taken on board to flog advertising spots on the new station, began scouting for talent. He put out feelers. Some of the recruits had actual DJ experience on foreign stations. Others were actors with nice personalities and lovely voices who hadn't quite had the breaks they deserved. Yet others had had no experience at all but showed promise and, more importantly, were prepared to endure big waves, small wages and tainted food.

Philip Birch knew a chap called Chris Peers who knew a chap called Wilfred De'Ath who was terribly enthusiastic about a 19 year old called Maurice Cole. An offer of £15 a week was made. Out there on the high seas, the lad was told, there were tape recorders and microphones. With nary a thought for the big waves and tainted food, young Maurice eagerly signed up as ship's company.

On December 23, 1964, the recent storms had abated. The wind in the English Channel was moderate to fresh, with good visibility and a slight to moderate sea. Maximum temperature for East Anglia was a bracing 3°C. Long before dawn, the transmitters had been switched on, warmed up and tested. At 6 o'clock, the mic was opened. "Good Morning, Ladies and Gentlemen," said Paul Kaye, the station's Head Of News. "This is Radio London transmitting in the medium wave band on 266 metres, 1133 kilocycles." Paul Brady stuck Cliff Richard's 'I Could Easily Fall In Love With You' on the turntable. Radio London, Wonderful Radio London, the Big L, the 'new concept sound', was on the air.

The newly christened Kenny Everett had been on board for a few weeks but was still having trouble keeping solids down. Nevertheless, the following afternoon, at six o'clock on Christmas Eve, he was shoved in front of a microphone. And he started as he meant to go on for the next 35 years. Stirring it. Putting the wind up his bosses.

The running order said he had to make a Public Service Announcement about the Perils Of Drunk Driving.

"Tonight," he told his listeners, "I want you to get very, very, very drunk." Anxious looks were exchanged. "Forget all this don't-drink-and-drive stuff. I want you to get really plastered." A finger reached for the 'off' button. They had clearly hired a lunatic. "So drunk that you'll be completely incapable of even finding your car!"

Ah, the twist at the end. Do you see what he did there? Clever. Smiles broke out. Paul Kaye realised they had "a natural on our hands".

On the *Galaxy* the walls were steel and mostly painted battleship grey. Everything smelled of seaweed and diesel. The washbasins were rusty. The showers dribbled and spurted hot then cold. There were no baths. The DJs slept two to a cabin.

"It was fairly primitive," says Ed 'Stewpot' Stewart. "There were double bunks in each cabin, very narrow, and if you were on the early shift, you'd take the lower one so you didn't disturb anyone when you came back."

When the snoring got too bad, it was not unknown for a room-mate to hoik his mattress up to the bridge which, the ship being anchored, was usually deserted. That's if they had a mattress to hoik. In the early days, before the studio was properly finished, bedding was often pressed into service as an improvised baffle to counteract the lively acoustic of the steel walls.

Kenny's first room-mate was Dave Dennis, 'The Double D', one of the 'actor DJs' who'd put in some time on the *Mi Amigo* during the brief life of Radio Atlanta. Kenny complained (on air) that his feet smelled and he had a terrible temper. On the other hand since Kenny was still chucking up every couple of minutes, the antipathy was almost certainly mutual. Later, Kenny made a jingle for Dave with the lyrics, "Dave Dennis swings!" Few of the jocks could resist appending, "Yeah, but from which tree?" Even later still, after he'd left Radio London, Dave Dennis had a shot at pop stardom with a record called 'Yes, Virginia, There Is A Santa Claus', a sentimental song that reassured an eight-year-old girl called Virginia that... you can guess the rest. Remarkably it went Top 40, but then so did a lot of Ken Dodd records.

Food was basic and eating communal. "There was one long table in the middle of what was probably originally the captain's quarters," says Ed Stewart. "Part of the kitchen was next door and there was a cage in there – I don't know what it had been used for in the war when the ship had been a minesweeper, but the first Christmas I was aboard one of the crew got badly drunk and started threatening everyone with a meat cleaver, so the captain eventually talked him into this cage and we locked him in and kept him there until the police came out from Harwich and took him ashore."

The DJs, unless they brought their own supplies of alcohol on board, were rationed to two small bottles of Heineken a day. In sharp contrast to the BBC where some of the most respected presenters were never known to enter a studio without a few stiffeners under the weskit, at the Big L, on-air drunkenness was all but unknown. "Maybe some of the older ones would have a drink," says Ed, "the spirits drinkers. But on the whole we were sober. We had to be. We valued our jobs."

Entertainment was a problem. In the early days there was no telly on board. Rummy was played around the clock. Sometimes Paul Kaye would get his guitar out and they'd all have a bit of a sing-song. Small wonder they all sounded so cheerful on air. Anything must have been better than bloody rummy and sing-songs.

In the summertime when the weather was fine the braver ones would dive over the side for a swim and from time to time there were accidental duckings, too. A ritual developed whereby birthday boys would be taken by the ankles and hung over the side of the boat. Those, like Kenny, whose birthdays fell in mid-winter, risked death by hypothermia every year.

"The worst thing about the boats was no freedom," says Ed, "not being able to go anywhere. We used to look at the lights of Frinton which was three and a half miles away on shore and we used to say, 'Oh, I could do with a motorboat to go into Frinton and have a pint,' not realising that Frinton was in fact a dry town – it didn't even have a pub."

"While you were broadcasting it was this really vibrant exciting place," said Johnnie Walker, who was on the *Mi Amigo* just a couple of miles away, a smaller boat with even more rudimentary living conditions, "but if ever it went off air you realised you were just on this rusting hulk in the middle of the sea and you wanted to get off."[23]

Wistfully, Johnnie, during the course of his Caroline programme, would sometimes make 'is anybody out there' contact with the outside world by encouraging the 'Lay-By' lovers of Frinton and District to point their cars out to sea and flash their lights. "Go on," he'd say, "flash your lights now. Let's see you in Frinton." The coast would light up like a Christmas tree and the distant DJs would know they were loved.

Inevitably, a WW1-battle-of-the-Somme-style camaraderie developed between the DJs. Nicknames came almost immediately. Tony Windsor, an Australian DJ who'd come aboard around the same time as Kenny, had a habit of endowing people with lovelier names. His own 'Windsor' had been chosen to celebrate his 'queeniness' and he assumed the identity of 'The Queen Mother' as a matter of course. Tony Blackburn became 'Bessie', Keith Skues was 'Samantha', Ed 'Stewpot' Stewart was 'Sally' and Kenny became 'Edith'. Later they all were christened with even lovelier chocolate names: 'Nut Log' for Tony, 'Hazel Cluster' for Ed, 'Strawberry Whirl' for Kenny.

The close confinement, the camp presence of Tony Windsor and the unsavoury presence of Chris Denning (who, at the time of writing, is serving a five year sentence in Slovakia for producing child pornography) might have encouraged Kenny to experiment a little.

"He didn't know himself whether he was into women or into men," says shipmate Ed 'Stewpot' Stewart, "but one or two of the older generation on board did start making passes at him, suggesting that he might like men rather than women."

By all accounts, the passes were shyly rebuffed and Kenny retreated behind a comforting shield of innocence.

When the North Easterlies blew, the sea was fierce.

"The whole thing was moving around, in gales especially," said Kenny[24]. "Cups would go crashing across the tables and people would be falling over and being ill all over the place. It was quite dramatic."

A tale is told that one day the waves drove a hole through the rusty hull. Water gushed in. With great presence of mind but scant regard for standard naval procedure, Tony 'Bessie' 'Nut Log' Blackburn grabbed the nearest frozen chicken and plugged the hole. It is a sobering thought that if the hole had been a few inches bigger or no frozen fowl immediately available, the entire history of British broadcasting would have been altered.

For the seasick and the potentially seasick the studio was the worst location on the boat. The anchor chains ran from the bow. The studio was in the stern. As well as rising and falling, it skittered and swung.

"We were down a couple of flights of stairs, almost where the bilge used to be, very cramped," says Ed Stewart. "We used turntables. It was rough at times, but that never used to upset the turntables. The only time they were upset and jumped was when the tender was coming close by to drop packages or people or whatever and it jolted the side of the ship. That was the only time the needle jumped."

This, of course, only made a difference if the record decks had the power to turn round.

"We had this generator that powered the turntables, cartridge machines, all the things you need on a show except the microphone, that was powered independently and the transmitter was, too," said Kenny.[25] "And one day, the nuts fell out of the generator and it went crashing across the deck and over the side. Very dramatic, blue flames everywhere. And, of course, everything came to a grinding halt except the microphone and the transmitter. I knew this. I was down in the studio all by myself and I went, 'Oh, dear, well we seem to have lost our power for the tunes, so I'll just keep chatting away here.' And I started to tell the story of my life and – it just shows how young I was – I ran out after 30 seconds. And there was about 10 minutes before the DJs upstairs who were casually listening while they were eating heard the sound of terror in my voice and came running down to tell sort of jokes and things."

"The studio moved at least 20 feet up and down in the sea swell," says

41

Dave Cash in his biography[26]. "The thought of any creative thinking, let alone production, seemed impossible. Staying upright was the only priority. Kenny had found a way by holding tightly onto the desk-frame with one hand and operating the equipment with the other."

The music was terrific, though. That first Christmas, when Kenny took to the air, the Beatles' 'I Feel Fine' was number one in a chart that also featured Petula Clark's 'Downtown', the Rolling Stones' 'Little Red Rooster', P.J.Proby's 'Somewhere', Twinkle's 'Terry', Elvis Presley's 'Blue Christmas', the Supremes' 'Baby Love', Georgie Fame's 'Yeh Yeh', the Kinks' 'All Day And All Of The Night', Dusty Springfield's 'Losing You', the Moody Blues' 'Go Now', the Shangri-Las' 'Remember (Walkin' In The Sand)', Gerry and the Pacemakers' 'Ferry Cross The Mersey' and Roy Orbison's 'Pretty Woman' – all quality product that made the lame dance and the deaf hear and even now has the power to sell comparison websites and compensation lawyers on ITV3.

The music was good, but from the point of view of the American owners, the DJs were a shambles. The American model of Top 40 radio was slick, up, positive and authoritative. Worryingly, the Brits often sounded as if they were taking the piss. They made light of their technical fumbles and turned them into gags. They were resolutely odd, eccentric. Most baffling of all for the Texans, sometimes they were self-effacing. It was a few months before a compromise was reached whereby the DJs – some of them anyway – figured out how to be more positive without sounding stupid and the American owners got used to the fact that the British do things differently. It would be pretentious to say that in those tin studios on those bucking boats a new art form – the art of the British DJ – was forged, so, since pretentiousness in a British DJ is a career-killer, we won't.

Kenny rarely opened his mouth without taking the piss out of something. It was the tone of voice that did it. He took the piss out of the camp little weed he felt he was. He took the piss out of the macho heterosexual muscle-man he wanted to be. He took the piss out of wanting to be something that he wasn't. He took the piss out of authority. He took the piss out of those in rebellion against authority. He took the piss because it's the only healthy response to a world in which all is vanity and nothing is knowable, least of all yourself.

Perhaps in deference to his American bosses, or more likely still to take the piss some more, in his early broadcasts he does adopt his American accent more frequently than he was prone to in his later career. It's not, though, the kind of American accent of which the Texans would have approved. It fluctuates, but defaults to something more *The Pink Parrot* than *Ed's Rib Shack*; more Cupid Stunt than Wolfman Jack; more of a shriek than a rumble.

Best of all, Kenny took the piss out of the form. No sooner had he learned how to do this US-style Top 40 radio thingy than he figured out how to subvert it with his ace in the hole, the pièce de résistance that would remain his pièce de résistance until his very last broadcast, his showpiece of the tape recordist's art − his jingles.

The British jingle was a novelty: a form that appeared to have been fresh-minted for the fresh-minty taste of the adverts on ITV. The power and persuasiveness of those early TV jingles was frightening. Overnight, they wormed their way into the consciousness and entered the culture.

On *The Goon Show*, Eccles − one of Spike Milligan's characters − asked, "I wonder where the yellow went?" and got a big laugh because the lyric that had wormed its way, insistently and permanently, into every skull in the country at the time went, "You'll wonder where the yellow went, when you brush your teeth with Pepsodent."

Women left the house to a chorus of kids chanting, "Rowntrees Fruit Gums, yum yum yum, five fruity flavours in your tum tum tum, one thing's certain beyond dispute, in Rowntrees Fruit Gums you taste the fruit."

Those crippled by indecision in the tobacconist's would remember that, "today's cigarette is a Bristol, a real cool flavour you'll never forget, Bristol is today's cigarette." And then go off to "drink Red Barrel near or far in pub or club or any bar, it's always good wherever you are, Watney's draught Red Barrel."

The ad jingle in fact went back much further than the birth of ITV. It had been a feature of American radio − usually performed live by the station's house band − since the twenties. In the forties, Gordon McLendon at KLIF in Dallas, the Big L's role model and mentor, was among the first to extend the use of jungles from ads to station idents and self-promotion. Why limit their use to advertising mere products when they can be used just as effectively to advertise yourself?

The KLIF house band, Bill Meek's Early Bird Orchestra, would put the station idents together in their down time. "Doodle oodle di doo dah dey," the trumpets would bray and the singers in Four Freshmen close harmony would sing, "Wonderful KLIF."

When Bill Meeks eventually left KLIF to set up an ad agency called Production Advertising Merchandising Services (PAMS) he carried on making jingles, for ads and for stations. He figured out a way of amortising the cost of jingles, thereby increasing profits *and* reducing the price to the consumer, by making a standardised product, a package of jingles that could be sold to station after station with only a slight adjustment to the lyrics. His vocal group would stand around the mic and sing, "Start going steady with WGDY." Then, to the same backing tape, they'd sing "Start going steady with WABC." Then "Start going steady with WMGM." And because, unless they travelled, WMGM listeners could not pick up the WGDY signal, or the KLIF signal, the impression of exclusivity remained. Who'd have known that your station's jingles were every station's jingles?

In later years, the same PAMS chorus having done, "The happy sound of WYNR" would go on to "The happy sound of Radio 1"; for PAMS became Jingle Manufacturers by Appointment to BBC Radio 1 and Radio 2.

It went without saying that Radio London would be equipped with a full package of nearly 50 hand-crafted PAMS jingles. Mostly these consisted of the words "Wonderful Radio London", sung in a variety of styles ranging from classical to cha-cha-cha, but defaulting at big band swing. Sometimes the words, "Biggest Sound Around, Big L" or "Miles Of Music" were appended. "You're hearing things (you're hearing things) on Wonderful Radio London" made a nice change, while a shameless rip-off of the Beatles' 'It Won't Be Long' – "We're gonna groove, yeh, yeh, yeh, yeh, yeh, yeh, we're gonna groove, yeh, yeh, yeh, yeh, yeh, yeh" – made it clear that this was a station with its finger on the pulse. And if you were wondering what the sea conditions were like and just what level of success this new, wonderful sound was enjoying, your questions were answered with the words, "It's smooth sailing, with the highly successful sound of Wonderful Radio London."

As soon as the jingle tapes came on board, Kenny started messing with them. He cut up every instance of the word 'wonderful' into a montage of 'wonderfuls'. He nicked bits of Radio Caroline's jingles and butchered them. He (or at least most people assume it was him) stuck together bits of jingle from at least four different sources to make the still hotly debated and very bizarre 'Pussycat' jingle (best guess at the words – "You're a pussycat; and you're where it's at, the one that's in on every play, the in sound, Big L") used by the Who on their 1967 album *The Who Sell Out*.

"Kenny didn't like meeting people particularly," said Keith Skues[27]. "He was very shy. But we would get together at meal times. He would come in for the meal, although he wouldn't eat a great deal, and then he'd vanish. And where would he be? He'd be below the water level, downstairs in the studio where nobody could see him, putting together these brilliant programmes. And he was, I suppose, a bit of a loner."

"Like everybody on the boats," says Bob Harris, "Kenny had time on his hands between shows. And he had this creative drive in him, so he was in the studio messing around all the whole time – you know – trial and error, finding out what works and what doesn't work. He took certain things on air that didn't work, but he'd take other things on air that were absolutely genius moments."

It took a while for the results of his fiddling to find a place in his programmes. In February 1965, six weeks or so into his tour of duty on the *Galaxy*, he sounds for the most part like a ho-hum DJ, speaking in the approved mid-Atlantic accent, faithfully relating chart positions and enthusiastically endorsing the records – "Manfred Mann and 'The One In The Middle'. That's number 28 in the Fab 40 and it's probably their best record yet." But then it goes:

OLD MAN VOICE FROM NOWHERE: Ladies and Gentlemen ...

KENNY: Whaaa-aaat?

OLD MAN VOICE FROM NOWHERE: ... you are TUNED ...

KENNY: Yes?

OLD MAN VOICE FROM NOWHERE: ... to the Kenny Everett programme.

MUSIC: FINAL TRIUMPHANT BARS OF A SYMPHONY

KENNY: (MR ANGRY VOICE) What happened to the big hand

I was supposed to get? This is terrible! (WHINY, NEEDY CAMP AMERICAN VOICE) Where's my publicity manager?
 RHYTHMIC HANDCLAPPING LEADS US INTO 'LET'S GO' BY THE ROUTERS

It's not Dylan Thomas' *Under Milk Wood*, but it was a start.
 A year or so later, though, it went:

JINGLE: Wonderful Radio London, Where You're Hearing Things, Where You're Hearing Things
 KENNY: (OMINOUSLY) And now ...
 MUSIC: SPOOKY EXPECTANT STRINGS.
 KENNY: (OVER THE STRINGS) It's that moment, folks, that you've all been waiting for.
 SOUND EFFECT: VERY FAST BEEP BEEP MORSE CODE
 MUSIC: UPTEMPO VERSION OF 'JA-DA'
 KENNY: Yes, ladies and gentlemen once again this is Everett of England introducing Top Deck Time brought to you by the makers of ...
 VOICE FROM NOWHERE SHOUTS: Rumbaaaaa.
 KENNY: (ON TAPE)... which is flavoured with real Jamaican rum.
 KENNY: (LIVE) And now a word from our producer Bob Brooksby.
 DROOLING INCOHERENT OLD MAN: Eeeh huh houugh uh huh.
 KENNY: Somebody put a record on quick.
 MUSIC: NEIL CHRISTIAN, 'THAT'S NICE'
 KENNY: (AMERICAN VOICE) There we are folks, 'That's Nice' from Neil Christian. (ORDINARY CHATTY VOICE) I met him the other day and he said "Hi," and I said "Hi", so now we know each other (CAMP VOICE) intimately.

And so it went on. And it didn't half give a lift to radio fans brought up on a diet of *Housewives' Choice* and *Workers' Playtime*. Kenny littered his programmes with sound effects, cut ups, home-made bits, blasts of the classics, voices: out-Jack-Jacksoning Jack Jackson at every turn for speed, dazzle, slickness and rhythm; running effect into funny voice into record into ad and, best of all, making the whole thing sound utterly effortless – as if no preparation had gone into it at all and it was all no more than the off-the-cuff throwaways of a guy who happened to have the Superpower to conjure boings and bips and DAAAHS and da-doo-ron-rons out of thin air.

"He spent hours and hours and hours putting all this stuff together," said Tony Blackburn[28]. "The radio show reflected his brain which was all mixed up. It was all crazy. And he was a crazy person, really."

The show is also the sound of a man doing something he excels at and is passionate about. He loves this. "That's the secret of wireless. Sound like you're having fun."

And he loves the toys – bigger and better tape recorders than he could have ever have afforded at home, mixing desks, banks of eight-track cartridge machines, and the state-of-the-art electronic effects. He hung out a lot with the Big L's sound engineers, Russ Tallowfield and Dave Hawkins, learning, taking the machines apart, suggesting innovations and modifications, experimenting. A lot of what he did would now be called 'sampling'. In pre digital days, this meant, if the 'sample' was long enough, making loops of tape to go round and round the machine endlessly, or, if it was a short 'sample', copying it repeatedly onto other bits of tape and then laboriously editing them together. There were other tricks, too.

"He played Herman's Hermits' 'No Milk Today'," says Bob Harris. "It started just regularly and then it started phasing and whirling round. They'd had phasing of a sort on records back to Toni Fisher's 'The Big Hurt' in 1959, but that was way, way in the background. Kenny's show was the first time I really heard it working. You could hear specifically what it was. And Kenny had created it, way before 'Itchycoo Park' or 'Rainbow Chaser' or any of the Phasing Favourites."

Dave Cash came aboard the *Galaxy* just four days after Kenny. He was older by a couple of years. Born and educated in Britain, he'd spent much of his childhood in Canada so appeared impossibly cosmopolitan and sported an impressively authentic-sounding North American accent. He could even boast of broadcasting experience, having done a few voice-overs and bits and bobs for a Vancouver station – enough at least to tell the difference between a microphone and a hairdryer and to know it's a bad idea to blow your nose on air.

Kenny and Dave hit it off. They became friends, conspirators and collaborators. Both nerdy fans of radio as well as practitioners, while the other boys played rummy and enjoyed their sing-songs, they actually listened to the off-air recordings from KLIF that the Texans sent over now and then to educate and inspire the pirates. They were particularly excited by something called *The Charlie And Harrigan Breakfast Show*.

Harrigan was Ron Chapman, a DJ who had served behind a mic since High School, eventually winding up at KLIF in Dallas. He has a calming radio presence, extending and deepening key vowel sounds in a way that brings a honey buzz to even the baby speakers of a tiny transistor.

Charlie, at least the Charlie that Kenny and Dave Cash would have listened to, though there were others, was Dan McCurdy, a skew-minded pal of Ron's who'd been working the KLIF graveyard shift.

Charlie and Harrigan's combination of gags, sketches, characters, quizzes, news, comment and jingles with the Top 40 playlist sounded, to Kenny and Dave's ears, like the *ne plus ultra* of groovy. It's a menu that's since become a staple of British, American and probably Mongolian broadcasting, the basis of the 'zoo' format loved by the likes of Steve Wright, Jonathan Ross, Danny Baker and Adam and Joe.

On Groundhog Day, Charlie and Harrigan followed the groundhog down to his burrow, with snuffles and echoes. Here they found a Hugh Hefner-style bachelor pad where a rodent party was in full swing. They instituted the 'KLIF Lucky Matchbook', "Just walk into any 7–11 store and say, 'I would like a KLIF Lucky Matchbook.' The proprietor will give you a blank look. Friends, fill out this blank look and mail it to the Milkman's Matinee… " And so on.

Kenny and Dave got to work, wrote scripts and in the dark hours of the night, when Big L was off air and the wind screamed through the rigging, worked on their inserts and jingles.

On April 6, 1965, *The Kenny And Cash Show* went on air.

The Goon Show permeates Kenny and Cash to the core, just as it did everyday conversation in offices, pub and playgrounds around the country. Eccles, Bluebottle and Moriarty voices pepper their conversation: the nasal Seagoon, "It's a lie, I tell you!"; the posh Peter Sellers, "I wouldn't do that if I were you, Neddy."

Their pursuit of the perfect sound effect was as painstaking as Milligan's experiments with the custard-filled sock. DJs would be queued outside the bathroom, waiting while Kenny, mic in hand, portable Ampex at the ready, dropped apples into a sink filled with water in an endless quest to find the perfect 'plop'.

Eventually they invented characters of their own, Myra Crelge, Auntie Maud, J. Walter Beethoven. They obsessed about knees. They even went so far as to release a single called 'Knees'.

To give a flavour – in July 1965, they got hold of an advance copy of the Beatles' new LP, *Help*, weeks before the BBC. Abandoning the Top 40 format, they played the album in its entirety, but still found time to run Kenny over with a train, put Dave on a couch while Kenny, in a German accent, psychoanalysed him, to overenthuse about the new fluorescent lights they'd had installed in their cabins, and to rant about weather forecasters who, "stand on the Air Ministry roof playing draughts all day" and still get paid £29 a week. "Let's be weathermen," they decided.

A technical glitch, a whoop of feedback could lead to a couple of minutes' improvisation. Ordering food through a speaking tube to the galley upstairs, "two boiled eggs four minutes apiece and some shredded toast" could give rise to a three-act farce and recruit an unwitting chef as a co-star.

Half a century later, the show's still remembered with affection by those who heard it. But it was never the gags, or the voices, the sound effects or indeed anything you could exactly put your finger on that made it so engaging. It was in the mood it generated. The relaxed, couldn't-care-less anarchy that had to be so carefully scripted into *The Goon Show* here was unavoidable. Somewhere, if you thought about it long enough, you'd realise that the Big L was a money-spinning enterprise. Somewhere, miles away, people were selling ads, doing deals, but there were only occasional shreds of skimpy evidence that the moneymen were actually listening. As far as the DJs were concerned, they could do what they liked. They could order boiled eggs on air. The only people involved in this enterprise were them and the fans, the only people in the world, locked in an intimate conspiracy, cooler and groovier and hipper and more switched-on than the prosaic world of buses, school and weather could ever know. And in between the chat they served up the Beatles, Dusty and Roy Orbison. How could the fans repay such unstinting generosity?

Miss Judy Sparks of Croydon sent the pair a Gonk 'so big we couldn't fit it through the door'. Mary, Mozz, Jenny and Lyn from High Wycombe sent in a 15-foot scarf. Miss Cherry Calder of Tunbridge Wells wrote in wanting personal details about Kenny's ears. Fans bonded together in 'The Knees Club'.

From time to time, the Marys and Mozzes and Judys and Cherrys, together with a few Barrys, Larrys and Garys would hire a boat and sail out so they could meet their heroes. The DJs called these fans, after the weather-protective clothing they invariably wore, 'Anoraks' – a name synonymous with obsessives ever since. For complicated legal reasons the Anoraks were not allowed to board the *Galaxy,* but would float slowly past craning their necks for a glimpse of the stars. Kenny erected a big sign: "Please don't feed the DJs".

The *Music Echo* commissioned the two of them to write a weekly 'Kenny and Cash Kolumn' in which the great controversies of the day were debated: Dylan or Donovan – who's groovier? Are there enough female artistes in the charts? On a more serious note, they also engaged in a searing discussion about the British Government's right to attempt to pass legislation imposing restraints on the activities of the pirate stations – with Chubby 'Let's Twist Again' Checker. There were competitions to find the 'The Most Hated Group' and nominations for 'The Out Crowd'.

Kenny's shifts gave him two weeks on the boat and one week on shore. Rather than go back to Liverpool when he was on land, he shared a flat on London's Lower Sloane Street in the very fashionable borough of Chelsea with Dave Cash and Pete Brady. Time on shore was never time off. Radio London DJs would be signed up for a full round of personal appearances at discotheques and clubs.

Attempts to stage something called the 'Big L Club' in the fusty surroundings of Lyons Corner Houses – a flagging restaurant chain that had been around since before the First World War – did not set the world on fire, but other gigs proved scarily successful. At the Marquee Club in Wardour Street, Kenny was mobbed by a crowd of girls who wanted a piece of him.

This was something new. BBC DJs, inasmuch as they could be called

DJs – Pete Murray, Brian Matthew, David Jacobs and the like – urbane and matey though they might be, did not get mobbed. They might be approached in the street by smiling hand-shakers who admired their work, but nobody tried to tear their clothes off.

The pirate DJs, on the other hand, were regarded as stars just as if they were Rolling Stones or Kinks. It was unsettling. And not only did girls mob Kenny, music press polls consistently placed him number one DJ in the country. What had begun as a harmless tape-recording hobby was galloping out of control.

Radio London's bosses, realising Kenny's value, upped his wages, eventually to £30 a week. His expenses, while he was on the boat, were zero – no rent, rates, gas, electricity or even food. Creatively energised, financially flush, mobbed by girls, feted in the music press, top bunk to sleep in, three meals a day on the table. His bum was in butter.

Some commentators have suggested that Kenny had a self-destruct button; that he had to sabotage any success he achieved because of deep-seated feelings of unworthiness. And so on.

Others reckon that, like all spirited individuals, he acknowledged that rules are there to be broken, boundaries there to be pushed, grass to be walked on, locks picked, clocks dismantled.

"We all like a bit of fun," as his geography teacher might have said, "but some people have to take it that little bit too far, don't they? I think *you* know who I'm talking about, don't you, *Maurice Cole?*"

One day, Ed 'Stewpot' Stewart was reading the news, announcing in suitably sombre tones the death of some prominent and much-loved statesman. For the spirited individual – especially the spirited individual confined to a ship with other spirited individuals – there is only one sane response to the sight of Ed 'Stewpot' Stewart announcing the death of a prominent and much-loved statesman: you suddenly appear in his line of sight, gurning with bits of chalk stuck up your nostrils. Ed 'Stewpot' Stewart looked up. He tried to suppress the laughter, failed, recovered, failed again, recovered, failed again, and cut to a jingle.

Ed had already been in trouble with the bosses.

"Keith Skues and I got fired for an April Fool's Day prank. We got one of the crew guys who was very 'ooh arr have you got a loight, boy,' very Norfolk, to come on. And we cut him in in the middle of a record and he said, in this accent, 'This is Radio Norfolk on 267 metres on the medium wave band.' Well, that was only one away from 266, which was us. And then we kept doing it. And this guy would talk into the microphone and pretend he'd crashed our station. He said he was broadcasting from a disused signal box on the Kings Lynn to Yarmouth railway. Keith and I pretended we knew nothing about it – didn't know the records were being interrupted and so on. We fooled everyone including the Sunday press, and including the Radio London bosses in Curzon Street who panicked. Thought we'd been taken over by a rival station.

"Another time, Keith Skues made this wonderful newscast – made up stories – about an escaped zebra crossing the road in Slough. 'Would anyone who's seen this zebra crossing please phone this number?' And we gave out the number of our programme director, Alan Keen. He didn't get off the phone all weekend. We made another one. Jayne Mansfield was touring the country and we announced that unbeknownst to most people she was a great collector of antiquities and antique vases and we announced that she had in fact the finest pair of jugs in the country."

Kenny's first sacking offence came about by accident rather than design. "I'd go off air at 9.00 when I first joined," says Ed, "and after the show this one summer's evening, Kenny and I went up on deck. We had a radio with us and we were twiddling the knobs and we found Radio Luxembourg. They were playing Paul McCartney's 'Yesterday' and I said to Kenny, 'That music is so beautiful. It's like having... like having a musical orgasm.' And the next day he goes on air in the afternoon and he says, 'Here's a piece of music I'm going to play for you now that gives Ed Stewart an orgasm every time he hears it.'"

In these loucher times the word 'orgasm' is acceptable in polite company and may even be something they discuss endlessly on CBeebies, but in 1965 it counted as unutterable filth. "He got fired but was reinstated when he swore blind he didn't know what an orgasm was. The management believed him. We all believed him. Because that's how innocent he was."

As a lad who'd trained to be a Catholic missionary, Kenny might have been able to claim innocence about the human reproductive system, but never about religion. And religion was his downfall.

One of Radio London's biggest sponsors was the Worldwide Church of God, based in Pasadena, California. The church paid a hefty sum for a nightly 30-minute spot during which their leader, Garner Ted Armstrong, preached a sermon under the generic title, *The World Tomorrow*.

Garner Ted Armstrong was not a tub-thumper in the hellfire tradition. At one point in his life he had wondered whether night-club singer would suit him better than preacher. He had an affable, twinkly radio manner. Nevertheless, he did talk, on the wireless, about God, and thus gave his British audience – unfamiliar with American-style evangelical radio and culturally unsympathetic towards most forms of God-bothering – no option but to take the piss. Even people listening alone felt obliged to blow a quiet raspberry.

Like the Radio Luxembourg football pools wizard Horace Bachelor, Garner Ted merited a mention in the Bonzo Dog Band's 1967 B-side 'The Intro And The Outro'. After Adolph Hitler on vibes ("Looking very relaxed", "Nice"), Princess Anne on sousaphone and Liberace on clarinet came Garner Ted Armstrong on vocals ("doop doop do-be do-be doo").

Could Kenny buck the piss-taking trend? Of course he couldn't. Apart from anything else, Garner Ted was embedded right in the middle of his show, interrupting the flow and encouraging dial fiddling.

"I used to think this was a huge interruption to my show," said Kenny[29], "because a) I didn't agree with what he said and b) I used to think, 'Why me? Why has it been plonked in the middle of my show? Everybody's going to turn off.' So at the end of the show, I used to say snide little comments about him. And one day he came to England on a little tour-ette. And I didn't know he was there, and I said one of my funny little things at the end of his show. And he rang Radio London and said, 'Get that shit off my show.'"

Kenny Everett was the most popular DJ in the country whose value to Radio London could never be measured in mere money. Nevertheless Garner Ted's value to the station could be measured in money, and there was nothing mere about it. It was keeping the ship afloat. Kenny got the chop.

Unfazed, he walked straight into a job at Radio Luxembourg, happy for the time being to be working in a studio that didn't rise and fall 20 feet when the wind blew from the wrong direction, and to be working in London, where the shows were pre-recorded. The pleasure was short-lived. His Luxembourg show was a meagre 15 minutes and, like many of the Luxembourg shows, was sponsored by a single record company, in his case CBS, which used the airtime to boost its product and nobody else's. This meant, for instance, that Kenny could never play anything by the Beatles (on Parlophone), the Rolling Stones (Decca), the Kinks (Pye), Dusty Springfield (Philips), or a score of other hitmakers. The recently electrified Dylan and the new breakthrough group Simon & Garfunkel were on CBS, but it's tough to craft even a short 15-minute programme when all you've got worth playing is 'Stuck Inside Of Mobile With The Memphis Blues Again' and 'Homeward' bloody 'Bound'.

By spring 1966, the Big L, presumably while Garner Ted was looking the other way, reinstated Kenny. He was back where he belonged, with his head over the sick bucket.

In July, he warned that if the Critters' song 'Younger Girl' didn't make the charts, he'd resign from Big L and go back to Little L (Luxembourg). When the song edged up to number 42, he decided it was close enough and hung around. This was fortunate because soon after came what Kenny later called "The Greatest Day Of My Life".

"I was sitting around twiddling my thumbs," he said, "and the phone rang, and it was Alan Keen, who was the Programme Director of Radio London, and he said to me 'How would you like to go to America? I'd never been before, and I nearly died of happiness. And he said 'We want you to go to over there and do loads of shows,' and I thought, 'Oh fabulous, America – New York, Chicago, L.A …'

"'What's the purpose of it?'

"He said, 'We'd like you to follow the Beatles around, 32 cities in 40 days.'"

Jelly babies made it happen. At a 1963 Beatles concert in Britain, a fan had thrown some jelly babies on stage. George picked one up and popped it in his mouth. After that the Beatles performed in a hail of jelly babies. Eventually the issue had to be addressed head on.

"We used to like them," said Paul, "in fact we loved them. But since then we've been getting them in boxes, packets and crates. Anyway, we've gone right off jelly babies, you see. But we still like peppermint creams and chocolate dots and all that sort of thing."

It didn't make any difference, the jelly babies kept coming.

In the US, jelly babies were unknown, so fans, having heard of the tradition, substituted jellybeans, a much harder sweet which rained on the stage like machine-gun bullets. The Beatles, fearing for their sight, put out a more desperate request for the custom to end and by 1966 it had withered away.

Bassett's, the maker of jelly babies, was not going to take this renouncement of its product lying down. Unwilling to let anybody forget that its confections had once had the Beatle endorsement they ran ads in the paper: "We name no names, but a certain pop group is believed to rate JELLY BABIES top of the sweet parade. YEAH, YEAH JELLY BABIES!" To further cement the association, the company stumped up money so that the nation's most popular pop radio station could send the nation's most popular DJ on a jolly in America with the world's most popular pop group, heavily lacing his reports with references to the YEAH YEAH quality of its product. Kenny would, in the missionary style he was trained for, promote the doctrine of the Holy Trinity, the Three In One: Big L, Beatles, Bassett's.

In fact, the Beatles were long past the jelly-baby stage. Though their records, as we've already heard, still had the power to bring Ed 'Stewpot' Stewart to orgasm, John, Paul, George and Ringo were not happy. None of them much wanted to be Beatles any more. Not poseable-figure Beatles, anyway.

They'd grown up a bit. Their lyrics had progressed from, "She loves you yeah yeah yeah" to "She said I know what it's like to be dead". You can't stand on stage and sing, "She said I know what it's like to be dead" while pre-pubescent girls wet their pants with excitement and pelt you with jelly babies. It doesn't make sense.

Substances had a lot to do with it. After Bob Dylan introduced them to marijuana in 1964, they couldn't get enough of it, finding it a nourishing and enjoyable confection, more so even than jelly babies. When George's dentist laced his and John's coffee with lysergic acid diethylamide (LSD) a year or so later, they all had a pretty shrewd idea what it's like to be dead.

Indeed, death became a pressing possibility as their 1966 world tour

– of which Kenny's bit, the US leg, was the highlight – developed into a catalogue of life-threatening ordeals.

In July, they had visited Tokyo where it had been deemed wise to confine them to their hotel rooms for fear of violence from right-wing activists who accused them of desecrating Bodokan, the venue, built on the site of a sacred shrine, in which they were booked to appear.

A few days later in the Philippines, a polite refusal to attend a reception at the Presidential Palace was interpreted as a deliberate snub to the revered tyrant Ferdinand Marcos and his First Lady, Imelda. Their police protection was withdrawn. Mal Evans, their roadie and pal, was beaten up. They were punched and abused at the airport and didn't breathe easy until the plane was at cruising height.

And now, along with Kenny, they were flying into the eye of a religious hurricane.

Earlier in the year, in an interview for the London *Evening Standard* with Maureen Cleave – a journalist the Beatles known for years (and with whom John, allegedly, had had an affair) – John went banging on, as was his way, about God. "Christianity will go," he said. "It will vanish and shrink," adding, "We're more popular than Jesus now."

In Britain nobody took any notice. But in the land of Garner Ted Armstrong things were different. *Datebook*, 'The Magazine Everybody's Talking About, Written For & By Teens Themselves, Now Monthly', was, by 1966, pretty much entirely given over to Fab Four pix and fax. It reprinted part of the *Evening Standard* interview with the cover line, "I don't know which will go first—rock 'n' roll or Christianity."

Outraged by the blasphemy, station KLUE in El Paso, Texas, declared that John's comment "made it impossible for them to carry on playing Beatle records" and invited local teenagers to toss their Beatle records onto a public bonfire they'd be lighting. The day after the bonfire, KLUE suffered severe damage when a lightning bolt hit its transmitter aerial. Go figure.

Undeterred, KEEE in Nacogdoches, KEAN in Brownwood, KNRO in Conroe and other stations in Alabama, Florida and all over the Southern Bible Belt jumped on the anti-Beatle bandwagon. There were other bonfires. The Ku Klux Klan nailed 'I Want To Hold Your Hand' to a burning cross.

...ay, but not as we know him. Big L publicity still, 1965.

Stillington Hall. Right to left: Father Tavano, Thomas Donnelly, Maurice Cole, Peter Terry (Maurice's best friend) and Mathew Dunn. TONY KENNEDY

Clean living Kenny in the sixties.
S&G BARRATTS/EMPICS ARCHIVE

Stillington again. Right to left: Tony Ritchie, David Watt, Maurice Cole, with Father Tavano behind.
TONY KENNEDY

y and Dave Cash on dry land, 1965.
HOFFMANN/REX FEATURES

Kenny and Cash doing the business. JOHN LAIT

ting morale on two small Heinekens a day—below decks on the *Galaxy*.
LAIT

Above and below: Kenny backstage with the Fabs and Joan Baez, at Candlestick Park, San Francisco on August 29, 1966—the last Beatles concert. JIM MARSHALL)

ny, Lee, horse and tablecloth leaving Kensington Register Office after their wedding in 1969.
RCHIVE/PRESS ASSOCIATION IMAGES

ded bliss, Wales 1973.
N MCCREETH/REX FEATURES

Kenny in the BBC doghouse, 1970.
ASSOCIATED NEWSPAPERS/REX FEATURES

Kenny and Dave Cash, together again.
JOHN CURTIS/REX FEATURES

Left to right, Smokey the Parrot, Bosie the Great Dane, Bowbells the Chihuahua, Kenny the DJ and some cats.
FREMANTLEMEDIA LTD/REX FEATURES

1 Class of 1967: back row, left-right: Tony Blackburn, Jimmy Young, Kenny Everett, Duncan Johnson, Station Manager Robin
, David Ryder, Dave Cash, Pete Brady, David Symonds; centre row, left-right: Bob Holness, Terry Wogan, Barry Alldiss, Mike
ox, Keith Skues, Chris Denning, Johnny Moran, Pete Myers; front row, left-right: Pete Murray, Ed Stewart, Pete Drummond,
Raven, Mike Ahern, John Peel. BENTLEY ARCHIVE/POPPERFOTO/GETTY IMAGES

al Gold class of 1988, left to right: Tony Blackburn, Liat Goodson, David Hamilton with Rachael Welsh, Kenny, Jackie Colley.
HIVE/PRESS ASSOCIATION IMAGES

Kenny with macaw, Michael Bukht's office, Capital Radio, 1973.
CLIVE WARNER

All it takes is an inch of trigger.

Cancellation of the US tour would have cost the Beatles something like a million dollars, a sum that Brian Epstein, their manager, didn't think was unreasonable for keeping them alive. Their American representatives, though, assured him that everything would be OK if John apologised. John grudgingly did so when the Beatle plane touched down in Chicago on August 11.

If Kenny was aware that he had a front row seat for a key stage in the socio-religious World Cup between Christian Fundamentalists and Normal People, the outcome of which still remains undecided, he seemed blissfully unaware of it even 26 years later. "That was the tour with all the problems with all the 'Beatles are bigger than Jesus Christ' stuff? Oh was it?" he asked Richard Porter, in a 1992 interview for the London Beatles Fanclub magazine[30]. "We didn't have any problems on the tour, apart from trying not to get eaten by a million fans in every town, and they kept rushing the bus and bashing on the side of the van, and running across the fields to the guitars. But apart from that it was very well behaved. Everyone just screamed and that was it."

Even given there may have been a touch of disingenuous irony going on here, there's no doubt that Kenny was woefully ill-equipped for the role of radio journalist. He was 21. He'd never been to the US before. The closest he'd ever come to meeting a Beatle was when he was working as a copy boy at Douglass & Company and had to pick up packages from Brian Epstein's Liverpool shop. Though sparky enough on mic on his own or with Dave Cash in the studio, face to face with strangers he was shy.

Bold extroverts who might find themselves no more than a little tongue-tied were they to meet, say, Jesus Christ, when confronted with an actual Beatle tended to mumble, stumble and lose control of their basic motor functions – in which respect at least, Lennon's assessment of the band's fame and influence was perfectly accurate.

"I was a bundle of quivering jelly nerves at the prospect of spending a lot of time with the Beatles because I was only too well aware of my shortcomings, especially when it came to interviewing: I was the pits, dear! I would dangle my microphone under the nose of whichever Beatle I was talking to… and wait for him to say something."

Kenny was one of an army of journalists embedded in the tour. He didn't even have an exclusive for pirate radio. Jerry 'Soopa' Leighton from Caroline and Ron O'Quinn from 'Swinging' Radio England had both boarded the Beatle plane, too.

He could never have been anything other than what he was – a gushing, hysterical fan, which, as luck would have it, was exactly what Radio London and, more importantly, Bassett's the sponsor, wanted him to be. His other gleaming qualification was his place of birth. The Beatles always gave preferential treatment to fellow Liverpudlians.

"I remember getting on the plane to go to America, and I heard Paul McCartney's voice saying, 'Which one's Kenny Everett?' and we introduced ourselves. And that was it."

The Beatles took pity on his neediness. Paul, ever the PR pro, would from time to time take him to one side and, regardless of Kenny's stuttering questions, put enough fab Beatlisms on his tape to last him a few days.

It didn't make a lot of difference anyway. These were primitive times, and there were legal restrictions on ship-to-shore communications with the pirate ships. Kenny got the Beatle banter to the *Galaxy* by putting through an international call (a feat in itself) to Paul Kaye, on hand at the Big L offices in London. He'd hold up his portable tape recorder near the mouthpiece of the phone and play back whatever Beatle interviews and bits of actuality he'd managed to record. Paul Kaye would record all this, from the earpiece of his phone and into another tape machine at the other end, bundle his tape over to the *Galaxy* where it would be edited with more chat, ads and music into a half hour programme. In other words the signal went through the speakers in Kenny's tape machine, into the phone, over an international line, out through the phone in London and into another tape machine. Then it was broadcast from Big L's transmitter. By the time it was picked up by the fan's defective Decca Debonaire, it went …

"… dressed in white… STATIC AND/OR SCREAMING FANS… Ringo … here they come… STATIC AND/OR SCREAMING FANS, MORE LIKELY, GIVEN THE CONTEXT, SCREAMING FANS… Ringo is twiddling… how are you?… Greyhound bus which takes us over to Cleveland… flashbulbs… SCREAMING FANS OVERLOAD MIC… KENNY IS, BY NOW, SCREAMING HIMSELF… and here it is. 'Rock And Roll Music' courtesy of Radio

London... SCREAMING AND POSSIBLY SOME NOTES OF WHAT MIGHT BE MUSIC."

The tour was, to say the least, eventful.

It was "Armageddon mixed with a bit of Götterdämmerung", said Kenny[31]. "There was one particular moment when I thought I was going to be killed. We were in somewhere like Minneapolis or somewhere anonymous like that in this gigantic stadium. It was, like, from here to Crystal Palace."

The Beatles' dressing room was, according to Kenny, in the middle of the stadium "on the green bit", protected by a "thin, blue line" of cops.

Kenny was "on stage saying 'how nice to be here' and all that stuff. And suddenly a guy ran out from four miles away, past a policeman. And all the policemen from that segment went forward to get this guy, so that left the floodgates open."

Fans surged through the breach. They swarmed around the Beatles' caravan. "And it was going thrrwwpp thrrwwpp boing. It was rocking like crazy as these millions of people tried to get Ringo's leg, Paul's arm, just a bit of one of them as a memento of the occasion. That was terrifying."

Kenny was there in Cincinnati, Ohio, when it pissed with rain and the band cancelled after Mal Evans touched a wet amp and was thrown halfway across the stage. He was there when the Ku Klux Klan picketed the Mid-South Auditorium in Memphis, Tennessee and somebody let off a firework which George thought was a gunshot and almost fainted. He was there for the last gig of the tour at Candlestick Park, San Francisco, California – the last live gig, apart from the 1969 rooftop foray, that the Beatles ever played.

Kenny was a witness to history. He recorded every moment on tape, and broadcast it to the nation. And it went... "Ringo is twiddling... how are you? ... Greyhound bus which takes us over to Cleveland... flashbulbs... SCREAMING FANS OVERLOAD MIC."

And when the tour was finished, Kenny went back to weekly showers, an undulating studio, inedible food and smelly feet.

Not for long, though.

CHAPTER FOUR

Sackloads of cards arrived at Radio London's Curzon Street office in the run-up to Christmas 1966, too many to send out to the *Galaxy* for fear of capsizing the tender. Joy was unconfined when, on Christmas Eve, the DJs let it be known that from now on the Big L would be on air 24 hours a day: round the clock Top 40 radio. At midnight, they all – Kenny, Ed Stewart, Tony Windsor, Keith Skues, engineers, cooks, deckhands and cabin boys – crammed into the tiny studio and gathered around the mic to sing carols, then, in honour of Kenny's 22nd, they sang 'Happy Birthday To You'. The year turned.

1967 was a year of wonders and miracles, a year of bells and beads, of peace and love and anger and violence. Elvis got married. Christian Barnard performed the first heart transplant. The Velvet Underground and Pink Floyd released their first albums. Pulsars were discovered. *The Graduate, Cool Hand Luke, In The Heat Of The Night* and *Bonnie And Clyde* all did well at the Oscars. Washoe the chimpanzee learned American Sign Language. Otis Redding and Che Guevara died. It was the year of the Six Day Arab-Israeli War, further escalation by the US in Vietnam, and the start of the Nigeria-Biafra war which left one million dead.

It was also the year of the first great global TV spectacular, *One World*, made possible by the miracle of the communications satellite, three of which were used to carry the programme's live signals all around the world to be watched by an estimated half a billion people. The show featured Maria Callas and Pablo Picasso, but its undoubted stars were the Beatles, performing the song they'd tailor-made for the gig, 'All You Need Is Love'.

In the previous year, the Beatles had proved that they could take the name of the Lord in vain and, far from being struck dead, go on in triumph and majesty while their accusers were scourged with thunderbolts and wrath. To seal their reputation as Lords Of Creation, on June 1, 1967, they released *Sgt. Pepper's Lonely Hearts Club Band*, the album still regarded by some as the greatest pop record ever made and by still more extravagant thinkers as the apotheosis of human culture and understanding. The influence and dominance of *Sgt Pepper* was so immediate and absolute that other bands, producers and graphic artists could not but eat crow, suck sour grapes and reflect on the knowledge that their lives were worthless. After hearing it, Brian Wilson of the Beach Boys suffered what his friend and lyricist Van Dyke Parks described as "a nervous collapse". The LP held the number one spot in the UK album chart for 23 weeks.

And thanks to Bassett's, the maker of jelly babies, Kenny Everett found himself a trusted acolyte of the Lords Of Creation – not perhaps in the inner circle itself, but certainly no more than six or seven circles out. The connection was strengthened by his romantic involvement with Peter Brown, Brian Epstein's personal assistant and close friend, described at the time as resembling a "30-year-old Ernest Hemingway". Peter, who went on to run the Beatle's company, Apple Corps, and got a namecheck in 'The Ballad Of John And Yoko' ("Peter Brown called to say, 'You can make it OK ...'") had a lot in common with Kenny. Both were from Liverpool and both had been brought up as Catholics. Kenny felt comfortable in Peter's company. Their sexual relationship lasted for less than a year but was, by Peter's account at least, affectionate and relaxed.[32]

The privileged position Kenny enjoyed enabled him, for instance, to scoop the world by playing 'Strawberry Fields Forever' on Radio London ages before its official UK release. He was even an occasional house guest in the Fabs' homes.

"I went to his [John Lennon's] house once," he told Richard Porter.[33]

"We were leaving a club in Margaret Street, the Speakeasy. Those were the days when Traffic would play, just get up out of the audience and do a set. John was there and we went outside after we'd finished clubbing, and he said, 'Do you want a lift?' and I said 'Yeah, I live in Lower Sloane Street.' And he said 'Oh great, we'll drop you off.' So I jumped into the back of this gigantic thing. And it was Terry Doran driving, with one arm out the window and one finger on the wheel. He was a maniac. When we got to Lower Sloane Street, he went straight past my house and I thought, 'Oh, well, I'd rather be in this car than in my house.' So I just kept quiet in the back and before we knew it we were in Weybridge at his house and I stayed for a couple of days. It was rather fun. It was a gigantic place. It's not the sort he'd want now if he were still alive. It was a stockbrokery sort of place, mock Tudor monster and yards of lawn."

Kenny stayed the night. The next day, John asked whether he fancied a spot of LSD. "Yes, John. Anything you say John. Tell me to turn into a pickled gherkin and I'll do it."[34]

Gently tripping and with a light rain falling, they took a hallucinogenic walk on the undulating fairways of St George's Hill Golf Course, next door to John's house. Kenny remembered they were both wearing 'wizard cloaks' and at one point, incongruously, a helicopter landed quite nearby, or it may have been a bird.

"There was an occasion in the house when there was a girl spotted at the door. She'd somehow climbed over the wall. And someone said, 'Oh John, there's a fan at the door.' And he walked all the way down the path and chatted to her for a while and then just gently led her out and said goodbye. And I thought that was very pleasant. He could have had her shot or unleashed the odd dog. But he went out to speak to her. That was rather sweet."

"I first heard *Sergeant Pepper* in George's house. He had a low-slung white goes-on-forever house in Esher. And a bunch of us including Tony Hall from Deram records were invited to George's place to hear this new album. He had an acetate of it. He put it on the gramophone, and we all sat around and this thing started and blew us away. We were completely gone and on another planet. It was a quantum leap and we thought, 'Music can stop right here, nobody is ever going to produce anything better than this, so all musicians can go back to bed now'. It was the best thing we'd ever heard. And George said, 'It's quite good isn't it?' The night before they'd all had a party and they'd decided to get spray cans of coloured paint and spray 'God is Love' and other things all over the walls of the house, this wonderful million-dollar house, and they sprayed flowers and words all over it in a stoned orgy the night before. He'd woken up the next morning to get the milk in and had horror written all over his face at what they'd done."

All across the nation there was a strange vibration which was felt even offshore in the bilges of the *Galaxy*.

The station had hired another Liverpudlian. John Peel had spent time in America. He had a taste for the outré and the arcane which could never be constrained by the Big L's Top 40/new release/revived 45 playlist. His chance to sneak a few in past the defenders came when he was offered the graveyard slot and invented a show cheekily named after a classic work of erotic literature, *The Perfumed Garden*.

"The way John explained it," says DJ Bob Harris, "was that the show was on between 12 and 2 a.m.; a time when, in theory at least, you're not getting a huge number of people listening, so it's much more difficult to sell advertising space. But in the playlist schedule allowances were made for three ad breaks an hour. Also in terms of staffing, I don't think they had a one o'clock news bulletin, so there's another three minutes an hour. What John did to start with was he just put in his own favourite tracks to fill those holes. Then people responded to the fact that they were hearing the Doors or Quicksilver Messenger Service or something like that for the first time and he started getting feedback. So he started gradually nicking a little more space. Then, of course, he starts getting all the correspondence and the poems and the stuff people sent. And by the time, as John told me, the station management woke up to the fact that this had all happened it had already become established."

The Perfumed Garden became a repository for all things hippy, Bush Telegraph Central for anything underground, alternative, freaky or out there. John would promote the underground press – *International Times* and *Oz* and *Peace News* – advertise gigs and happenings, champion new bands, go on endlessly and often mawkishly about hamsters and sparrows, read out poems, and play far too many songs with lyrics that went, "I had a tree in the dream hills where my childhood lay."

By 1967, Radio London was the grooviest thing there had ever been:

bang in the centre of the pop world, bang in the centre of the alternative society, as deep into underground as it was possible to go. If you were young, had ears to hear and hated your parents and everything they stood for, it was essential listening. Where else were you going to hear the Royal Guardsmen's version of 'Snoopy And The Red Baron' *and* Captain Beefheart's 'Dropout Boogie', an advert for Top Deck and a soppy poem about a hamster?

Of course, it had to be stopped.

The pirate ships had sown political confusion on both sides of the House.

The Tories, as Conservatives with a large C, had favoured commercial television as a good thing, in keeping with monopoly-busting, competitive, entrepreneurial free enterprise, Capitalism and all that sort of thing. Their support for commercial radio, therefore, went without saying. But as conservatives with a small c, they deplored what commercial radio meant in practice: rock'n'roll, hooliganism, bum-freezer jackets and Italian hair.

The Labour Party, on the other hand, under Harold Wilson – Keep Left socialist – had a gut revulsion towards the proliferation of advertising or indeed anything to do with market economics or freebooters. On the other hand, they were desperate to present themselves as forward-looking, the party of youth, and like an uncle dancing at a wedding, tried to be identified as 'hip to the kids'. Wilson himself, for instance, had mucked about with the Beatles, when he presented them with their Variety Club of Great Britain 'Silver Heart' awards – "Thanks for the Purple Hearts," said Lennon.

Both sides feared the pirates' popularity. It was the sort of issue that, more surely than fisheries quotas or even devaluation, could swing an election.

"This explosion of music and fashion and teenage excitement, the lid had been kept on it for so long," says DJ Johnnie Walker. "So when it burst, it really burst, and it did scare the government. They didn't understand the half of it, but they did understand the unifying power of music."[35]

In 1964, Labour had come to power with a majority of just four seats and although Anthony Wedgwood 'Tony' 'Wedgie' Benn, the Postmaster General and thus the man in charge of the airwaves, huffed and puffed about the pirates, whose existence caused particular offence to his left leanings, nobody was prepared to risk valuable votes on anything so ultimately trivial. Unable effectively to govern with such a small majority, Wilson called a second election after just two years and on March 31, 1966 was returned with a majority big enough to take risks and get something done.

Battle lines were drawn. The pirates prepared their defences.

Still, in the end, the spur that really kicked the government into action wasn't principle or psephology. It was murder.

Screaming Lord Sutch and his band, the Savages, had had a minor hit in 1963 with 'Jack The Ripper' ("when the lights go down, that's the time he starts his – uh – chop around") produced by Joe Meek and predictably banned by the BBC.

Sutch was a dedicated self-publicist whose stage act began with him emerging from a coffin and whose everyday street wear often included top hat, Dracula cloak and leopard skin tights.

Not long after the launch of Radio Caroline, he started a station of his own, Radio Sutch, broadcasting from the south tower of Shivering Sands, a WWII sea fort in the Thames estuary and assumed to be, although a court later ruled otherwise, outside the three-mile limit.

It was a delightfully ramshackle rig. The transmitter, originally salvaged from a Halifax bomber, was powered by car batteries. Very little thought had been put into programming and although there were plans to hire Mandy Rice-Davies, call-girl star of the Profumo sex-spies-and-Tories scandal, to read extracts from *Lady Chatterley's Lover*, they never came to much. Anyway, before long, Sutch got bored with playing with his radio station, so sold it to Reg Calvert, his manager.

Reg renamed it Radio City and put out a few programmes, casting himself as DJ, but soon realised that better equipment and an injection of capital would be required to put the operation on a proper business footing.

So he approached Oliver Smedley, director of Radio Caroline and the great theorist of pirate radio. Oliver was an extraordinary eccentric: a proto-Thatcherite who, in a 1965 monograph published by the right wing Institute Of Economic Affairs, advanced the notion that pirate radio facilitated the free-flow of information and ideas, and represented a Free Market model which all businesses should copy. Don't get the wrong idea, though. Major Smedley (retd.) was no pointy-headed desk-bound intellectual. He was an action man, an ex-paratrooper who won himself an M.C. during the Normandy invasion and remained ever-prepared to back up mind and mouth with muscle.

Smedley advanced a loan and had a new transmitter delivered to Shivering Sands.

A few weeks later Reg defaulted on the debt repayments. Negotiations broke down. Threats proved futile. So Smedley, accompanied by his moll, the dauntless Kitty Black (who was also an esteemed translator of Sartre and Anouilh, Samuel Beckett's British agent and an accomplished knitter), and their henchman Big Alf Bullen, boarded Radio City. Having overwhelmed formidable opposition, they made their way to and disabled the transmitter, silencing the station.

No James Bond film had been released since *Thunderball* the year before and the world would have to wait another year for *You Only Live Twice*. In the press, the story of Calvert and Smedley filled the void. History does not record details of Smedley's taste in Martinis, but it's not hard to guess.

Calvert played the Blofeld role to the hilt. Furious at Smedley's impertinent incursion, he threatened to remove the boarders by bringing in air support to spray the fort with a special nerve gas he'd invented. Smedley called his bluff and in a show of insouciant self-confidence, left the fort three days later, leaving only a skeleton garrison behind.

On June 21, 1966, Calvert turned up at Smedley's home armed with a pen-sized 'nerve gas gun' and forced his way in. Major Smedley produced a shotgun and, at close range, shot Calvert dead. Police were called. Smedley was taken away.

Though, incredibly, Smedley was subsequently acquitted on the grounds of self-defence, the incident galvanised the government into action. Those who had claimed all along that unrestrained pop music was the first step on the road to mayhem and murder felt utterly vindicated.

On February 17, 1967, Parliament held a great debate. The pirate signals were, claimed Mr Edward Short (the new Postmaster General) interfering with those of the emergency services. "Recently, I had a very strong complaint from the Royal National Lifeboat Institution that its services had suffered," he said.

To which Mr Raymond Dobson (Lab., Bristol North East) added,

"In one year, 750 ships could have had their transmissions jammed by pirate radio stations. *I know that it did not happen* [our italics], but I say, 'Thank goodness that it did not.'"

Mr Short went on to complain that the pirates didn't pay any copyright fees (neglecting to mention that Caroline and Radio London had both offered to but the various collecting agencies had refused their money, fearing that it might somehow put them on the wrong side of the law).

Other complaints were that they operated in breach of the Copenhagen Convention of 1948, which divvied up the available broadcasting frequencies between the countries of Europe (neglecting to mention that so did 17 whole countries, including Spain and Portugal, who'd never agreed to the convention), that they could be used as a mouthpiece for Communist or Fascist propaganda, or extol the joys of sexual promiscuity, drugs and lounging around, and that their effect on the advertising revenue of legitimate newspapers and broadcasters could be ruinous.

Paul Bryan, for the Conservatives, while agreeing with the main objections to the pirates, drew an obvious conclusion: "The socialists will not tolerate commercial radio, but the success of the pirate stations means that people want commercial radio in addition to the BBC and there is no reason why they should not have it. It would have been perfectly possible to set up local commercial radio stations at no great cost. A great opportunity has been lost."

Early on February 24, 1967, visitors arrived at the *Galaxy*. The tender came alongside and Kenny, Tony Blackburn and the other pirates helped Johnny Beerling, a BBC producer, Jonathan King and Chris Denning aboard.

Chris Denning, the *Galaxy* DJ who had since landed himself a legit job with the BBC, had arranged the visit. Jonathan King had had a minor hit in 1965 with 'Everyone's Gone To The Moon' and had since become a mover and shaker in the pop business, producing, managing and so forth. He too was now working at the BBC.

(Both Denning and King were subsequently imprisoned for child sex offences. Other of Kenny's colleagues and acquaintances, most notoriously Jimmy Savile, have been accused [in Savile's case posthumously] of similar charges. Before any hint of guilt by association can begin to form, let it be said now and let it be said loudly that Kenny

Everett was only ever attracted to grown-up women and big strong men.)

Denning and King were presenting a BBC Light Programme Saturday afternoon show called *Where It's At*, a mix of pop gossip, star interviews and music. Beerling, its producer, though still not quite 30 years old, had built himself a formidable reputation around the BBC as a man with his finger on the pulse of this youth thing that people talked so much about these days. The show borrowed heavily – as far as BBC conditions would allow – from the relaxed style of the pirates. Beerling wanted to know more, particularly about the technical aspects. Enthusiastic tape-recordist and gizmo-nerd Kenny was the man to show him.

The great innovation of the pirates – an innovation in the UK anyway – was the self-op studio. The DJ sat alone. He (and at this point they all were 'he') cued up his own records, operated his own faders, slammed in his cartridges for jingles and sound effects, lit his own cigs, fetched his own tea and made his own editorial judgments about the suitability of content on the fly. No producers, compliance officers or programme controllers came near.

The studios were ergonomically designed to put everything the DJ might need immediately to hand. To Beerling – inured to the BBC chains of command and proliferation of men in nylon shirts who turned the knobs and watched the dials to make sure that every sound that left the building was of 'broadcast quality' – self-op was revolutionary.

The visit was covert. Although it was widely rumoured that the BBC was planning some sort of Big New Thing – an alternative or replacement for the pirates – the Corporation certainly didn't want anybody to know it actually needed guidance. Somebody snitched on Johnny Beerling, though, and embarrassing stories were leaked about his consorting with pirates in search of talent for the Big New Thing.

The Big L wasn't too pleased, either. Alan Keen, the programme director, was furious with his ex-employee Chris Denning for inviting the BBC to come snooping.

One of the upshots of the visit was that Kenny himself was talent spotted and was given a gig doing bits and bobs on the BBC's *Where It's At*.

Having got a foot in the impressive BBC double doors, he immediately made it his business to become part of the furniture. He discovered, for instance, that if you were carrying something under your arm – anything would do, clipboards could be effective, although he favoured a 10-inch tape spool and a stopwatch – no one challenged your right to be there. He would sit in the BBC canteen and have himself paged regularly, ensuring he was announced as "Everett – with two T's".

Meanwhile, in back rooms, where the still-to-be-announced Big New Thing was being planned, the relative merits of many DJs, pirate and otherwise, were being hotly debated. In the BBC archives sits a shameful report, compiled by an unknown who signs himself (or herself) 'T.S.G', which could be a name (Thomas Stanley Grubb?, Theresa Susan Goebbels?) or could be a job title (Talent Spotter General? Taunter of Suppliant Guttersnipes?).

'T.S.G', having heard a tape of a couple of his Big L programmes – *The Kenny Everett Show* and *Miners' Record Show* (sponsored by Miners 'softlysheenylipsensation' cosmetics) – seems to be in favour of hiring Kenny while at the same time making it clear that he or she wholeheartedly disapproves of everything he says, does, stands for and is.

All typos and spelling errors are here faithfully reproduced, as is the layout. The centred and underlined repetition of YES, one fears, was intended to be a demonstration of T.S.G.'s with-itness; an indication, perhaps, of his familiarity with the graphic style of these newfangled colour supplement thingies they'd not long started having in the Sunday papers.

"A pseudo – (?) American Voice. Sounds experienced – but will do 'voices'. Seems to fancy his luck.
YES
"Kenny Everett Show": – by far the most original of the young d.j.'s. I found the style in bad taste, but with suitable restraint and encouragement K. Everett could be one of the BBC's best d.j. "Miner's Record Show": –fluid introduction, full of good gimmicks.
YES
Without the "hard sell" and the occasional phoney American accent, a good pop d.j.. Must be made to curb the 'funnies' and voices.
YES
Gimmicky, commercial, fluent competent.

<u>YES</u>

A competent experienced d.j. I found the continuous changes of voice irritating and his personality supercillious [sic] but he certainly has some talent. Should be available but would need very firm production.
<u>YES</u>"

At the bottom of the memo, J.E.Grant and Jack Dabbs – both senior producers in the Popular Music department – have appended: "A competent and experienced pop D.J. Would need <u>very</u> firm production to curb his non stop 'funny' voices, which he changes every few seconds. With the right encouragement he could be an asset to the Corporation."

A much greater asset, one can't help thinking, than the bunch of self-important, impertinent prigs who thought it their right to pass patronising judgment on his talent. Anyway, on Saturday May 20, Kenny's Beatle connection made him even more of an "asset to the corporation" than T.S.G., J.E. Grant or Jack Dabbs could ever have imagined.

A few days after first hearing the record at George Harrison's house, Kenny, along with "every single person in the universe", went to the *Sgt. Pepper* launch party at Brian Epstein's fancy pad in Chapel Street, just over the wall from the Queen's back garden. All four Beatles were in attendance, "dressed in bows and beads".

"I remember them standing up against the fireplace, bonkers, they couldn't string two words together," says Kenny. Lennon in particular, "was on Mars!"

A few days earlier, however, the Beatles had managed to string more than a few words together for Kenny's tape recorder, which, together with tracks from the new album, constituted an important chunk of that week's edition of *Where It's At*.

This was the official BBC preview of *Sgt. Pepper*, for many an event of greater importance than, say, a Royal Wedding or a papal visit, and the man given the responsibility of reporting the occasion with due import and dignity was the young upstart with the "irritating" changes of voice and "supercillious" (sic) manner.

Kenny played at least a sample of every track. The BBC had banned the closing masterwork of the album, 'A Day In The Life', just the day before, because of the line about going upstairs on a bus, having a smoke and going into a dream, which the Corporation deemed to be a drug reference. This confused the general public who assumed that, while practically every other line on the album was something to do with drugs, this line was most definitely a working man's Woodbine reference. The ban did, however, mean that Kenny had to reduce his selection from that particular track to a few instrumental highlights which of course included the great orchestral climax.

Kenny was fanatical in his praise of the album and – always the tape recording nerd – adored its cutting edge production as much as its musical or lyrical virtues, commenting on the wild stereo panning on 'Being For The Benefit Of Mr Kite' and the "odd sound effects" on 'Fixing A Hole' – "not sound effects as we know them, but sort of phased distortion on the voices. This is where they get two of the same sound and push it through hundreds of machines and it comes out of the other end sounding electric."

He summed up the album with: "I don't think ever in my experience as a disc jockey, I've ever heard a sound as beautiful and superb as this new album. It's an achievement of our modern age of genius, an advancement in the recording technique, the Beatles!"

Paul McCartney returned the compliment.

"This is James Paul McCartney, Upper 5B, saying that Kenny Everett is just about one of the finest disc jockeys in the world, as disc jockeys go, aren't you Kenny?"

A week later, two days before the official release of *Sgt. Pepper*, "one of the finest disc jockeys in the world" was invited to another Beatle party, this time at the country retreat that Mr Epstein had bought a few months earlier at Kingsley Hill in Surrey.

John, George and Ringo were there with their wives – Paul, much to Mr Epstein's chagrin, was otherwise engaged – together with the cream of pop's glitterati including Mick Jagger, Marianne Faithfull, Lionel Bart (composer of *Oliver!*), Klaus Voormann, Derek Taylor (the Beatles' erstwhile press officer) and Peter Brown. The acid was top quality, from a batch specially commissioned from one of America's most experienced underground chemists and smuggled in by a film crew. John lurched around with a teapot, making sure everybody got dosed, then retired to the womb-like back seat of his psychedelic Rolls Royce, listening to Procul Harum's 'Whiter Shade Of Pale' over and over again. Cynthia,

John's wife, tried to throw herself out of a bedroom window. One of Brian's assistants threw up in some shoes.

Kenny, also ever so slightly suicidal, joined a circle of George Harrison's acolytes, lying at the great man's feet. On the perimeter of that circle sat a 30-year-old blonde called Lee Middleton, industriously rolling joints. Lee was the long-time girlfriend of Billy Fury, the rock idol of the early sixties and still a 'face' on the scene. While George, heavily into the task of explaining the meaning of life to the confused and slightly morose Kenny, pontificated, the joint rested too long between his fingers for Lee's liking. A spat ensued and George strode off with a rattle of beads and a jingle of bells. Kenny had never met anybody who dared stand up to a Beatle before. To say he knew at that moment that one day he would marry Lee Middleton would be not so much a romantic exaggeration as a barefaced lie. But nevertheless, reader, one day he would.

★   ★   ★

The official announcement was made on July 27: "The BBC yesterday gave details of their answer to the pirate radio stations and announced the new names for its four networks," said *The Times*. "Light, Home and Third are to disappear, and in their place come four numbered services." Radio 1, 2, 3, and 4, it said, would enhance and replace the old stations. "Of these, Radio 1 is the truly new service, with pop programmes much in the pirates' style taking up most of the day." Robin Scott, Controller of the Light Programme – nicknamed, in honour of his hair colour and a TV ad for Ajax bathroom cleaner, the 'White Tornado' – was appointed the first Controller of Radios 1 and 2.

"It would be foolish to pretend we are not using some of the techniques of the commercial stations," he said. "Jingles, slogans and internal publicity for the station will be going on between the records and that sort of thing. But we want to avoid the mid-Atlantic style they have created. I am sure there are good British disc jockeys who will create their own style."

Kenny was a "good British disc jockey" who had already created his own style without any help from the BBC. With his "just about one of the finest disc jockeys in the world" stamp of Beatle approval, he further proved he was an "asset to the Corporation" by taking an important consultancy role in the planning of the new channel (originally called not Radio 1 but '247'). In meetings with Johnny Beerling and Robin Scott, he explained the set-up and workings of the self-op studio.

Self-op was possibly the most terrifying hurdle the BBC had to negotiate, not just technically but politically and philosophically. Not least of the problems was dealing with the Association Of Broadcasting Staff, the BBC's Trade Union. It was going to take some fancy footwork to get an agreement to cut staffing levels down from five or so – the norm for such a show would have been something like DJ, producer, production assistant and at least one technician, more likely two, to spin the discs and work the faders – to just one. (In fact, as it turned out, no Radio 1 DJ ever worked entirely alone.)

Over lunch at Verrey's restaurant, Kenny told Scott and Beerling the facts of life about jingles. Between the three of them they figured out that home grown jingles using, say, the Mike Sammes Singers backed by Sounds Incorporated, could never cut the mustard because

a) they wouldn't sound right, and

b) under existing agreements the performers, composers and musicians would have to be paid every time the jingle was used, resulting in ruinous expense and mountains of paperwork.

Kenny told them about PAMS in Dallas – where British agreements held no sway – and a suite of jingles was ordered, many of them identical to the Big L jingles except for one word: "Wonderful Radio London" became "Wonderful Radio 1".

Beerling also commandeered a tiny room, a couple of tape decks and a mixing desk and set Kenny up in what he called his 'Wireless Workshop', where, happy as a pig in shit, he put together trailers and promos for the new station. "And now, here's some news about the new BBC channel called... (SINGS IN THREE PART HARMONY TO THE TUNE OF 'I HAD A LITTLE NUT TREE')... two, four, seven on your radio / music on the wireless wherever you go."

July had been the warmest on record since 1959, but the picture had grown more unsettled in August. On the 8th a record-breaking 117 mm of rain fell in just 90 minutes on the Dunsop Valley in Lancashire.

The Marine and Broadcasting (Offences) Bill became law on August

14 making it illegal to work for or to bring supplies like food and oil to the pirate ships

In an interview on March 16, Ronan O'Rahilly explained the consequences of the Bill: "Most of the thinking people in Britain are unaware of what the Marine Offences Broadcasting Bill will do to us. If a British shopkeeper sells cigarettes to a Radio Caroline announcer, he [the shopkeeper] becomes a criminal. If the Archbishop of Canterbury or Cardinal Heenan or the Chief Rabbi gave a sermon on Radio Caroline, they would become criminals, too. If a journalist writes a newscast or talks on Radio Caroline, he becomes a criminal. If a British advertiser advertises on Radio Caroline, he becomes a criminal. If, on the other hand, the Pope were to write a sermon for Radio Caroline, he would not be a criminal, nor would any foreign figure who wanted to use the medium to voice publicly something he wanted to say. In other words it is stifling the freedom of speech of the British subject."

Radio London shut up shop at 3 p.m. on the afternoon the Bill became law. There were heartfelt messages from many of the station's fans, including Mick Jagger ("We're very sad to see you go"), Lulu ("I feel awful"), Dusty Springfield and Cat Stevens. Surprisingly, Ringo was the only Beatle to send a goodbye and it was muted in its sentiment, "It's a bit of a pity and the radio will never be the same, but it's one of those things."

Kenny's goodbye message was the longest ("It's just been a gas and I won't forget it. Hope you won't, either"). The last record that Radio London played was 'A Day In The Life', the *Sgt Pepper* track that the BBC had banned. The tears that began with the opening notes, "I read the news today, oh boy" had, by the song's second and final orgasm, grown into chest-heaving sobs.

The DJs came ashore.

"On the last day," says Ed Stewart, "the customs kept us there for nearly two hours going through every bag in case we were trying to bring some drugs or alcohol back. That's why we were late back into Liverpool Street. When we got back there were nearly 3,000 people waiting for us."

The DJ's train was mobbed. Banners were paraded – "Freedom Died With Radio London".

Eleven days later, on the Friday before the August Bank Holiday weekend, Peter Brown, Geoffrey Ellis and Brian Epstein drove down to Kingsley Hill for a long weekend in the country. Brian had invited a few 'boyfriends' down and, when they didn't show up, he drank heavily and decided to drive back to his London house in his Bentley. After he left, the expected guests turned up and Geoffrey and Peter partied hard all night.

On the Saturday, Peter rang a very woozy Brian and tried to talk him into coming back down to the country. Brian refused.

On the Sunday, Brian's Spanish butler and one of his friends broke the bedroom door down and found Brian lying dead in his bed.

The inquest found the cause of death to be 'incautious self-overdoses' of the sleeping pill Cabitrol. Peter Brown, shattered by the loss of his friend, turned for comfort to Tommy Nutter, the outrageously talented Savile Row tailor. He and Kenny drifted apart.

And the Beatles turned to the Maharishi Mahesh Yogi, "the giggling guru", and his spiritual regeneration movement. "He told us not to get overwhelmed by grief," said Lennon, "and whatever thoughts we have of Brian to keep them happy, because any thoughts we have of him will travel to him wherever he is."

In most parts of the country, the schools re-opened on September 4 and the weather turned unseasonably cold. The great Summer of Love was over. At the end of the month, just as everybody was certain that the flowers, bells, beads, madness and fun had all been safely put away, that the last guest had definitely left and the lights had been turned out, Robin Scott, the new controller, came on the air just before seven in the morning, and announced the birth of Radio 1. At seven on the dot, there were jingles, then Tony Blackburn: "And good morning everyone. Welcome to the exciting new sound of Radio 1." He pushes up the fader on his sig tune, Johnny Dankworth's 'Beefeaters', and pops in a cart to instigate the barking of the imaginary dog he'd brought with him from the *Galaxy*. "Yes, indeed, we've even got Arnold back. Hello everyone. Welcome to the first of the Tony Blackburn shows. I shall be waking you up every morning except Sunday, between 7.00 and 8.30. So let's away – (Thunderclap) – if this one doesn't wake you up then nothing will. This one's number three this week in the Radio 1 Fun Thirty, from the Move it's called 'Flowers In The Rain'."

And, appropriately, outside all the flowers that had brightened that glorious summer lay drenched and battered.

After 'Flowers In The Rain', Tony Blackburn said something else and played the Bee Gees' 'Massachusetts', but history had stopped caring by then.

CHAPTER FIVE

Kenny usually gets credit for first calling the BBC 'the Beeb'. Old timers will tell you different. They remember using 'Beeb' along with 'Nonsense Factory', 'the Gingham Corporation' (small cheques) and a host of harsher epithets back in the forties and fifties. They'll also tell you how the BBC – along with most other broadcasting organisations – is structured. "There are essentially two groups or sections," they'll say. "On the one hand there's a small band of talented, dedicated individuals whose job it is to make programmes. On the other hand there's a much, much, much larger band of equally dedicated individuals whose job it is to stop them."

A marriage between the BBC and Kenny Everett was never going to work. He was blessed with a mistrust of authority, exacerbated in his case by bullying (real or imagined) in the playground, the classroom and the workplace. Timid by nature, he found the line between self-esteem and arrogance hard to identify. He had secrets, too; sexual feelings he could hardly bear to acknowledge, much less talk about. Secrets breed paranoia, sensitivity, chippiness, and in his case a tendency to overcompensate by shooting his mouth off about things of a less personal nature – like BBC policy. As it said on his file, he would need "very firm production".

The other partner in the marriage, BBC Radio, was more than 40 years old and settling comfortably into middle age. It looked back to its glory days when it delighted millions in World War II with a heartwarming mix of wholesome comedy, jolly tunes, improving talks and grave but inspiring news. Who'd want to change such a winning formula?

To be fair, the BBC's inability to compete with the pirates in the cool, hip and groovy stakes wasn't entirely the result of institutional stodge. The pirates were free-floating; the BBC tied down by its history, its obligations to the licence payer, contracts with its staff and a thousand agreements with trades unions and the various copyright organisations. The biggest constraint as far as fans of Big L-style Top 40 radio were concerned was 'needle time'.

In the twenties, when it first got going, radio had spread panic in the record industry, the assumption being that if punters could hear music on the wireless all day they'd stop buying records entirely. Accordingly the record companies' trade organisation, PPL (Phonographic Performances Ltd.), negotiated a limit to the number of hours per week the BBC could devote to playing records – 'needle time' – and a fee payable for each record played. By the fifties, PPL had realised that its panic had been misjudged: that far from damaging record sales, airplay was a vital form of advertising – something to be coveted, fought for, paid for, even. Get your record on a couple of key shows and it will be a hit.

Perhaps needle time would have been abolished there and then were it not for the existence of a third party in the negotiations. The Musicians' Union's job was to protect the working conditions, rates of pay and employment prospects of its members. Needle time forced the BBC to rely on live – or at least BBC pre-recorded – performances. As well as several orchestras to play the classical stuff, it employed a string of what amounted to house bands to take care of the pop: Bob Millar and His Millarmen, Arthur Greenslade and the G-Men, Bernard Herman (no relation to the Hitchcock film composer) and the NDO (Northern Dance Orchestra). They were good, but not that good. Though there was an evens chance that they might make a credible stab at Petula Clark's 'Downtown', the chances of their recreating the raw, driving power of, say, the Kinks' 'You Really Got Me' were negligible. Although no corroborating evidence has ever come to light, John Peel, the late DJ, used to swear he once heard the NDO have a crack at Jimi Hendrix's 'Purple Haze'.

These 'house bands' provided steady and lucrative employment for scores of Musicians' Union members, which the union was understandably keen to protect. So, by the early sixties, a strange impasse had been reached whereby the BBC and PPL, which had originally imposed needle time, wanted it abolished, while the MU, knowing that abolition would mean job losses for its members, wanted to keep it in place. And since the MU was bolshie, and a musicians' strike – particularly if the other entertainment unions came out in sympathy – would have been a pain in the arse for everybody, it seemed easier to stick to existing arrangements than stir up a horn-player's nest.

So while the pirates could play records all day and all of the night, Radio 1 started life with an allocation of just seven hours' needle time in 24. Non-stop Top-40 pop was never even on the cards.

There was also the BBC's 'position' to consider. It was widely considered to carry as much if not more responsibility for the nation's moral welfare as the Church of England and it usually took the blame for any perceived decline in standards. The shocking moral decline that, according to many *Daily Express* readers, assailed Britain in the sixties was, if the letters pages of that same *Daily Express* were to be believed, mostly caused by bad language in *Steptoe And Son* and the mini-skirted Gojos (the precursors of Pan's People) on *Top Of The Pops*. A misplaced areola – never mind an actual nipple – one too many 'bloodys' or, God forbid, a rogue 'fuck' such as the one that theatre critic Kenneth Tynan had wilfully positioned in an episode of the BBC's late-night satirical show *BBC3* would provoke a jammed switchboard, a flood of letters, questions in the House and doubts cast on the Corporation's continued right to exist.

The *Policy Guidelines For Writers And Producers Of Variety Programmes*, the notorious 'Green Book', published in 1949, was almost universally ignored, but like the Ten Commandments, still set a sort of standard, variations from which might be tolerated but never condoned. "There is an absolute ban on jokes about lavatories, fig leaves, prostitution, ladies underwear (e.g. winter drawers on), animals habits (e.g. rabbits) and marital fidelity," it said. "Extreme care should be taken in dealing with references to jokes about prenatal infusion, e.g. his mother was frightened by a donkey..."

Pop music had long been regarded with the same wariness as prenatal infusions. The BBC didn't know how to do teenagers and when it tried it came over all gauche and awkward. *Six-Five Special,* its flagship TV pop show of the late fifties and early sixties, was presented in a healthy, scout-hut atmosphere, with the lights most definitely on, by Pete Murray and Josephine Douglas, your chirpy youth leaders whose smiling enthusiasm tried somehow to neutralise, like a cold shower, the snarling sexuality of the rock boys.

It wasn't just a product of a more buttoned-up age. Over on the other Channel, *Oh, Boy,* ITV's answer to *Six-Five Special,* was all about snarling sexuality. When Cliff, spotlit in a pitch-black studio, curled his lip, grabbed his upper arm, and looked up at camera – head down, liquid eyes only – even dads sometimes felt a groinal stirring.

BBC wholesomeness infected radio, too. There's nothing wrong with a few foot-tapping ditties, boys and girls, as long as you please remember to *keep the hormones securely in their glands.*

Saturday Club, presented by 'Your Old Mate Brian Matthew', was the sort of thing a benign English teacher might have cooked up to keep the unsavoury elements occupied in the lunch hour. It was never Mr Matthew's fault, of course, he's earned the respect he commands a thousand times over, but he was playing the cards he'd been dealt in what was, before the advent of the pirates, the only game in town: a game in which there was just no place for whoop-snoggling moonshine-swilling swamp-worrying lasso-me-lord-I-got Satan-in-my-Levi's rock'n'roll.

Kenny believed that radio should "give me the feeling that Radio London gave me whilst driving along in an open-topped car, when the wind was blowing and the sun was shining and you heard somebody enjoying themselves on the radio. They really enjoyed themselves – you could hear it in their voices; they had a happy edge on their voices and you knew they were enjoying themselves and were putting out a nice, entertaining programme. It made you feel better."[36]

Pop on the BBC Light Programme rarely made you feel better. At times, it could even induce an edgy anxiety, the way a street trader does: "Here's some nice shiny trinkets, but get ready to scarper if the law comes, all right?"

Worse even than the BBC's responsibilities as Guardian Of The Nation's Morals, was its stewardship of All That Is Cultured. It was an age when the division between High and Low Culture was so rigid that some terrible junk that Haydn plagiarised would *always* be considered superior to, say, an angelic trumpet solo by Louis Armstrong or a Cliff Gallup guitar lick. The link between culture and morals was unquestioned: High Culture promoted virtue: Low, vice. Good boys listen to Beethoven (and that is what makes them good), bad boys listen to Buddy Holly; and girls should be kept away from culture altogether because it's liable to excite the passions, promote free-thinking and cause unwanted pregnancies.

The overweening problem was one of understanding. The BBC brass didn't 'get' pop and neither did the politicians responsible for banning and licensing.

During the big parliamentary debate on the Marine and Broadcasting (Offences) Bill, Mr Edward Short, the Postmaster General, addressing the subject of a possible new BBC service to replace the pirates, said, "My colleagues and I are in no doubt that there is a wide demand for continuous *light* music [our italics] and that it would be right to meet this demand... I do not think that it is a demand for non-stop *pop* [our italics]. Clearly the housewife who is at home during the day – and some still are – likes to hear something like 'We'll Gather Lilacs' and that sort of nostalgic music. She likes a rather different kind of light music."

He was wrong in every way imaginable. The demand for pop had reached the clawing, desperate stage. Nobody under the age of 40 – 'housewives' included – wanted 'light music'. They barely knew what it was. 'We'll Gather Lilacs' was a massive hit for Ivor Novello in 1945.

In this world, seething with misunderstanding, mistrust and misgivings, Radio 1 was born.

Robin Scott, Johnny Beerling and a few others were given the job of picking the roster of DJs and presenters for Radios 1 and 2. In BBC terms it was a massive responsibility.

Like all the Light Programme DJs, Alan 'Fluff' Freeman, who, since 1961, had brought such excitement to the *Pick Of The Pops,* worked off a script, with every 'Not 'arf', 'Awright' and 'Stay bright' neatly typed on special cloth-based paper which rustled more quietly than wood-based. These scripts would have been vetted by at least one producer before transmission.

The new order at Radio 1, it had been agreed after considerable debate, would take the radical step of abandoning scripts and letting the new DJs make it up as they went along, just like they did on the pirate ships. The obvious fear was that thus unsupervised the wrong sort of chap could launch a tidal wave of filth or Communist propaganda on the nation before anybody more responsible could reach the 'off' button. So, if Scott insisted on indulging this folly of unscripted banter, he had better make sure that his chosen DJs were indubitably 'the right sort of chaps'. And while he was at it he'd better make sure they didn't behave like animals in the canteen, either, tipping back the chairs, making ladies blush and mocking the turn-ups of their superiors.

One of Robin Scott's colleagues, Mark White, was given the job of interviewing Tony Blackburn.

"One of the first things he asked me," says Blackburn, "was, 'Which school did you go to?'

"'Millfield,' I replied, silently thanking my father whose wish it was that I attended one of the top fee-paying schools in the country. A public school background counted for a lot at the BBC back then. I clearly remember wearing a suit for the interview, and referring to Mark as 'Sir'. ..."[37]

"When I went into my interview at Radio 1," said John Peel, "the guy was very nervous. He probably thought I was going to rub drugs into his hair or something. During the interview, I said something about public school in some context and he brightened up. He said, 'Oh, do you know someone who went to public school?' And I said that I had in fact gone to public school. He said, 'What one of those schools on the South Coast?' And I told him, no, it was Shrewsbury, actually. 'How's old Brookie?' he said. And as soon as he knew I'd been to Public School he relaxed and I knew I was in."[38]

Tony Blackburn was hired straight away, months before the launch of Radio 1, given a job hosting the Light Programme's *Midday Spin* and earmarked as a safe pair of hands in which to place the eventual launch of the new station and its flagship breakfast programme.

The full list of chosen ones was published on September 4.

"Taking the pirate radio cutlass firmly in their teeth," said *The Times*, "the BBC yesterday unveiled their array of disc jockeys who will broadcast on Radio 1, the pop station, from September 30."

A few of the new guard – Pete Murray, Alan 'Fluff' Freeman, Jimmy Young – were the same as the old guard but the majority were from the boats. They showed up for work wearing "orange slacks, bearskin coats, gold embroidered jackets". The BBC handed them lapel badges saying 'I'm A Radio 1 Upman' and 'Ring-a-247-Ding' to pin on their bearskin coats and gold embroidered jackets. Some wore them. Some wore them, but in an ironic way. Others merely glanced at them and dropped them in the nearest bin when none of the bosses were looking.

The suspicion that the BBC had opened its sacred portals to the thieves and infidels who'd rub drugs in your hair at the drop of a hat died hard.

Though not yet working for the Corporation, 'Whispering' Bob Harris was a frequent visitor to Radio 1's first home, the Aeolian Hall, an incongruously august temple to aesthetics.

"A more Victorian building and atmosphere it would be hard to encounter. I remember the looks of disapproval I got just wandering around wearing my slightly hippie gear – oh my God – talk about being looked down your nose at. It was absolutely that kind of atmosphere. In a way I kind of liked it because it made me feel more rebellious. It encouraged us all to be rebellious."

Kenny Everett never needed much encouragement to be rebellious. He had proved himself an 'asset to the Corporation' by helping with studio design, jingle making and so on, but still had the dread words 'would need <u>very</u> firm production' on his file. So, while Blackburn (Millfield) revelled in his hour-and-a-half of daily prime time, featured in every newspaper story about Radio 1 and had his picture in *Radio Times,* Everett (St. Bede's Catholic Secondary Modern) in addition to his contributions to *Where It's At* – which survived the regime change – was given a measly one hour of airtime a week, taking his turn with four other DJs on the revamped Radio 1 version of *Midday Spin.* It rankled.

"We met up again at Broadcasting House," says Wilfred De'Ath, the man who'd first launched Kenny's radio career three years earlier. "He came over to dinner again. We didn't like him as much then. We thought he'd got rather big headed, which was fair enough as he'd had a lot of success. At that age, three years is a long time. He spent the whole time moaning about Tony Blackburn. He didn't like Tony Blackburn and he thought Tony Blackburn had had too much publicity."

Kenny's contract specified that he would be paid £30 – around the national average wage for a week's work – in recompense for fulfilling his duties *viz* "to introduce at the microphone a selection of records chosen in collaboration with the producer from the BBC gramophone library."

The imposition of a producer rankled, too. Out at sea, the DJs didn't have producers. They were alone with their jingles and nausea.

But as it turned out the producers were a godsend. Bernie Andrews, Johnny Beerling, Doreen Davies and the rest acted as a buffer between the jocks and the clumsier side of BBC management without which the jocks – wide-eyed saps staring into the multiple, gaping maws of the Beast With Seven Heads – would either have been eaten up and spat out or found themselves somehow manipulated into reading Youth Club scripts and playing 'We'll Gather Lilacs' on an endless loop.

Kenny's producer, Angela Bond, became his champion and trusted confidante. Whenever, throughout his career, Kenny took it into his head to sound off about the BBC – which was pretty much all the time – he never once expressed anything but unstinting praise for Angela. "If I have to have one [a producer] at least I've got the best."

Kenny and Angela were both Northerners – Angela was from Hull – and her dad was a sea captain so they had vague seafaring connections in common, too. She had been a disc jockey herself in the early sixties over in Hong Kong and along with Johnny Beerling, Derek Chinnery and others, had worked on the 'manifesto' for the launch of Radio 1 (rumour has it that she was delegated to type up the thing – knocking on the head somewhat the notion that the BBC was in the front line of the feminist vanguard).

She nurtured and encouraged, facilitated and enabled, and, on the rare occasions it was required, exercised with tact and guile the 'very firm production' his file said he needed. She also dealt with the bureaucracy. Without a producer, the BBC paperwork would have drowned Kenny more effectively than the sea ever managed. The running order and script notes had to be typed. Every record or tape played had its details logged for the PasB (Production as Broadcast) report which went into the BBC files and provided the basis for the returns made to the Performing Rights Society (PRS), the Mechanical Copyright Protection Society (MCPS), Phonographic Performance Ltd. (PPL), the Musicians' Union (MU), Old Uncle Tom Cobbleigh And All (OUTCAA).

One of the advantages of *Midday Spin* to BBC management was that it was, technically at least, a record review show: a useful wheeze because 'reviews' were not included in Radio 1's allocation of seven hours' needle time, and so, like rusk in a sausage, could eke out the rations nicely. The downside for Kenny was that all the records had to be new releases and he had to top and tail them with a token review, "and that's on the Pye label, catalogue number H–231, and it's quite good," which could cast something of a pall over his natural exuberance and limit his chances of proving his worth.

Luckily he had bigger fish to fry. Indeed, he was frying, on a regular basis, the very biggest fish in the pond.

Though Kenny's affair with Pete Brown had cooled, he remained a trusted Friend of The Fabs. On September 6, just a few days after Brian Epstein's death, the Beatles were back in the studio recording songs for their proposed film *Magical Mystery Tour*. In a session that went on till three in the morning, Paul recorded his solo piano and vocal demo of 'The Fool On The Hill' and they laid down the basic rhythm track of George's 'Blue Jay Way', but most of the time was devoted to recording take after take of John's vocal for 'I Am The Walrus'. Kenny was there. At one point John broke off to chat to him, reminding him about the day they'd spent, stoned out of their gourds on Weybridge Golf Course – the inspiration, he told him, for the reference in 'Walrus': "sitting in an English garden waiting for the sun / If the sun don't come you get a tan from standing in the English rain."

The song was released as a double A-side with 'Hello, Goodbye' towards the end of November and again, a couple of weeks later as a track on the *Magical Mystery Tour* double EP. Kenny was still doing bits on *Where It's At,* now in its new Radio 1 slot at 2 p.m. on a Saturday afternoon, and fronted a *Magical Mystery Tour* special.

He wasn't supposed to. From the tapes it sounds as if the original idea was that he'd share the Big John Lennon Interview with Chris Denning.

As if.

His scorn for Chris Denning was always played as if it was a joke, a bit of good old DJ joshing, but sometimes genuine venom bleeds through.

In a little dialogue between two characters, both played by Kenny, he asks: "Why are you sitting in the dark?"

"Because I'm listening to the radio."

"Is that against the law?"

"I don't think so, but I wouldn't want the neighbours to know I'm listening to Chris Denning."

In a jingle for *Where It's At* he sings: "Kenny Everett and (MUMBLES QUIETLY) Chris Denning (NORMAL VOLUME) all together on the wireless machine."

Chris Denning's questions to John are, there's no two ways about it, lame. The out-takes reveal that Denning kept banging on trying to get John to record a personalised message he could use in his Wednesday show.

"Shut up... Chris Denning and his bloody Wednesday show," says Kenny.

Kenny and John have a chat about phasing. "We can cut in some examples at the edit," says Kenny.

Obligingly, John leans into the microphone and says, very slowly, "I am being phased."

"Ooh," says Denning. "We could put phasing on that."

"That's what I did it for," sneers Lennon, as only Lennon could sneer, the exasperation and contempt informing every syllable.

Denning continues to behave as if he's in the Two Ronnies *Mastermind* sketch, dealing with the question before last.

Kenny and John have an extended conversation about the possibility that the Beatles might go into a studio, record a few hours of just them chatting together, cut it down to something manageable and release it.

"Have you ever thought of doing an LP of just talk?" Denning asks.

In the end, he gets the message.

"Shall I make a cup of tea or something," he says.

Kenny and John gag around. They do voices. They flirt.

"When are *you* gonna do a wireless programme?" asks Kenny.

"Well we had thought of looking into the wireless," says John, impersonating Kenny's slightly camp Crosby refinement. "'Cos there's a lot of possibilities, you know. So it's quite possible that we would do something, you know. 'Cos it's so much fun, as you yourself know, Ken, being on the other end of the microphone."

Paul improvised a little song for the programme, based closely on the chords of the band's newly released single 'Hello, Goodbye'.

"While sitting at my piano one day

A magical thought came my way

To write a number for the BBC
Kenny Everett and Chris Denning
All together on the Wireless Machine ..."
The *Where It's At Magical Mystery Tour* special went out on November 25. It was indisputably Kenny's show and billed as such. Chris Denning took over the 3–5 slot immediately afterwards. At the handover there was banter...

"Listen you," said Chris.

"What?" replied Kenny.

"When we did that interview with John Lennon, I was there too. Why was I not just on the wireless with you two talking?

"You, Chris, are lying on the editing floor."

"Oh."

On December 9, *Where It's At* transmitted its last programme and a week later Kenny took over the Sunday morning 10–12 slot; his own BBC show at last, with a guaranteed lunch-cooking/homework-avoiding audience, to do with as he wished. And a sympathetic producer who'd help him do it.

Angela chose the music, went to all the meetings and plundered the BBC archives for the sound effects, snippets of dialogue and snatches of atmospheric music for Kenny to use in what he termed his 'fiddly bits'. Untrammelled access to one of the world's finest sound collections was another tape recordist's dream come true. Kenny would spend days – sometimes as much as three days for one show – dubbing, editing and mixing, the mad scientist in his Wireless Workshop, creating the ten and 30 second symphonies of nonsense, the boings that kept the show bouncing. No DJ ever put so much preparation into a programme.

His church choir background is everywhere in evidence. He constructs baroque cathedrals of sound, overdubbing track after track, singing all the parts; rules of counterpoint and harmony, which others might spend years learning at music college, intuitively absorbed; the sound engineering skills acquired through trial, error and the many instructive articles in *Tape Recording* magazine. The studio was his home. Watching him at work was like watching Fred Astaire or Muhammad Ali, an object lesson in elegance, rhythm and precision, the octopus arms moving from cart to fader to deck, press this, adjust that, keep talking, watch the timing, and this comes in *here*.

Kenny's show was followed by *Family Favourites*. Bang on 12 o'clock, the relay transmitters would be deployed and the exclusively British audience that could listen to Kenny would be joined by listeners as far flung as Cologne, Hong Kong, Dunedin and Kuala Lumpur. *Family Favourites* at that time was presented by the urbane charmer Michael Aspel. Knowing that Aspel had the grave responsibility of being the voice of the BBC to the World At Large, it became Kenny's chief mission in life to make him giggle.

"Oh, here she comes," Kenny would tell his audience. "Oh, look a new handbag. Oh, how camp, new earrings, seamed stockings. She's sitting in front of the microphone and now the final touch of eyeliner."

The people in Nicosia and Kuala Lumpur heard none of this. If Aspel had responded to it or referred to it, they would have been worryingly mystified. The consummate professional, he remained upright as stone. Not a giggle, not a snort, not even a sudden intake of breath was heard. Until the occasion of Kenny's last day in the pre-*Family Favourites* slot, when Aspel announced to the world, "Ladies and gentlemen, I must tell you there's this small person who's on before me and for the last 12 months he's been taking the merciless pee out of me." Long term residents of Hong Kong, Cologne and Dunedin reading this book will, no doubt, be glad at last to know that the small person Mr Aspel was referring to was Kenny Everett

The invention of characters to people Kenny's show developed haphazardly, and continued to do so throughout his career. An old man – who never seems to have acquired a name but was sometimes referred to as 'Granddad' – would now and then take a trip with shuffling feet and many groans, to the echoing depths of the BBC archive to drag up some treasure. Granny, a nymphomaniac pensioner, would importune anything and anybody. "Granny is 300 years old and a victim of a disease called living. When the series comes off, probably in about three months' time we'll have to think up an end for Granny. Of course, she could be strangled by her sewing machine."[39]

Kenny played all the parts himself except for one. In the BBC canteen one day he and Angela encountered Brian Colville, an actor blessed with a mellifluous baritone and a sly sense of humour. In diction, pace, manner and class, he was the opposite of Kenny. Angela suggested hiring him to play Kenny's butler. Money was found and contracts signed. The surname 'Crisp' seems to have arrived spontaneously. The first names, 'St John Montague' and the ex-army background, developed over the following weeks. "Crisp wakes me up every morning and we climb into the pram and are away to the studio." Crisp ironed Kenny's scripts. When Granny grew too troublesome, Crisp was summoned and told to put her away. "Get back in your cupboard, Granny."

GRANNY: I'm just a feeble female.

CRISP: Oh, dear. Oh, dear.

GRANNY: (SALACIOUSLY) Crisp, come into the corner with me, I'm feeling a little *blue*.

CRISP: (TREPIDATIOUSLY) Yes?

GRANNY: I've just developed the blues.

CRISP: (WITH DUTIFUL SYMPATHY) Give me your hand, dear.

GRANNY: (WITH AN ORGASMIC SHUDDER) Oh, Crisp.

As was Kenny's way, an epic cast of less specific characters was conjured with a switch of accent or intonation, sometimes four or five of them in the space of one sentence, commenting on each other, taking the piss, turning thought, meaning and register into a wild, mercurial mess. A constant presence was the posh voice of a BBC executive type, repressive and repressed, humourless and out of touch, the sworn enemy of fun, noise, mucky talk and Kenny.

By Christmas, Radio 1 had swelled the number of listeners to the old Light Programme by 22%. Glasses were raised, backs patted. Mention that the 'triumph' owed more than a little to the government's great kindness in wiping out every last trace of credible opposition was by general agreement deemed impolite.

Kenny's Sunday morning show had undoubtedly contributed to the numbers and had found itself an audience that neither *Melodies For You* over on Radio 2 nor even *The Archers Omnibus* on Radio 4 could ever hope to steal.

Celebrity visitors came to his studio. With a pencil he drew an ornate frame on the wall and invited the guests to sign. The suits were not pleased by this desecration of BBC property and had it erased at the first opportunity.

He was a success. He made a princely £250 for TV advertisement voice-overs. He bought a little red Fiat 850 and could afford to be so flash with his cash he soon ran up £21's worth of unpaid parking tickets. Success, and the confidence that came with it, made his customary and heartfelt need to bite the hand that fed him all the more pressing.

In March 1968, he gave an interview to *The Londoner* magazine[40]. It ran it over a double page spread under the headline "THE FRESH AIR THE BBC CAN'T KEEP OUT".

"The BBC has as little to do with pop as cement," he starts, as a warm up. Then he goes on to criticise the management, "it's all geared to outmoded ideas"; the manning levels, "there are 20 people to do one man's job"; the censorship, "sometimes they tell us to be so careful it's ridiculous, we can never talk about the news for fear it may be interpreted as a policy statement"; his colleagues, "none of the Radio 1 disc jockeys can be bothered to spend sufficient time preparing their programmes"; the "hideous" equipment, "pirate stations left the BBC standing equipment wise – cartridge machines we used on Big L were way ahead of those we are still having to use at the BBC"; the transmitters, "Radio London even had better reception, Radio 1 tends to fade away too easily"; the Musicians' Union for their support of needle time, "although they seem to be cutting their own throats by this rule, they insist on sticking to it"; and public service broadcasting in general, "There should be free radio with advertisements and records."

To prove he wasn't in the habit of being negative about everything in the world, he added a few words in praise of drugs. "I don't really go for alcohol. It's the sloppiest drug around. People on 'pot' have a different mentality. They are calm, peaceful and get things done. Nobody's ever done anything useful on alcohol. It only leads to violence. Personally I've been experimenting over the last year or so with 'acid' and 'bombers'. Now I'm back to smoking pot and grass. But you have to take these things before you see their faults, don't you? Anyway when I joined the BBC they knew I was an acid head."

He mentions that he'd already been reprimanded once for mocking the BBC's laggardly progress in the introduction of stereo. "If I said anything too critical now, I could be immediately suspended."

"What would he do," asks *The Londoner*, "if indeed he left the Corporation? 'Either commit suicide or join Radio Manx. Preferably commit suicide, I think."

It's hard to know whether the *Londoner* provided an outlet for a lot of long pent-up feelings, whether Kenny believed that mouthing outspoken anti-establishment views would buy him credibility, or whether he was just back on the bombers again. Most likely it was a combination of all three. Kenny was, by nature, nerdy, needy, weedy, anxious and afraid, but now he was also a famous celebrity, loved by millions, envied by his peers, pally with the Beatles and an asset to the Corporation. The occasional display of gauche arrogance is only to be expected. Especially if you've been doing bombers.

Authority at the BBC was, in those days, exercised chummily. Bucking it was a sport enjoyed by all. But when push came to shove, for goodness' sake, ranks jolly well closed, teeth gripped pipe stems more firmly, references to cricket and sportsmanship were bandied and the hierarchy became as rigid as that of the Civil Service or the Armed Forces.

The *Londoner* hit the newsstands on the Thursday. On the Monday Kenny was summoned to the office of Robin Scott, Controller of Radios 1 and 2, and given a stiff verbal warning, after which Scott, hoping to pre-empt the anticipated demands for real blood, fired off a 'done and dusted' memo.

"I was shown this article when it appeared, and was naturally horrified. Everett is a brilliant disc jockey... who I was quite determined to persevere with, because he is far ahead of his fellow disc jockeys.

"He was given the peak Sunday morning Radio 1 programme in the full knowledge that he was a tricky character to deal with and this is not the first time he has had to be called to order

"His drugs stories (largely apocryphal) and his stated views are most embarrassing – and highly inaccurate. His ingenuousness is only matched by his stupidity. In fact he has been served by the production and engineering team in an exceptional manner – and many a rule has been bent to help him

"I have given him one last chance to mend his manners.

"Robin Scott."

The Unions were not so easily placated. Tom Littlewood, General Secretary of the Association of Broadcasting Staff (ABS), took great umbrage at Kenny's comments about manning levels.

"Phrases like 'There are about 20 people to do one man's job'," he wrote, "are seriously resented by my members."

"There is no doubt that material of this kind being published by a member of the permanent staff would result in suspension and possibly dismissal. Could you let me know whether there is anything in the contract of individuals like Mr Everett which permits him special licence to publish libels about his working colleagues and criticisms of his employers? Would there be any objection, this being the case, to an amendment to the BBC's permanent staff agreement of service, to provide that not only the contract staff but permanent staff should have equal rights?"

The implicit threat being that if Kenny gets away with it today, every single employee will be slagging off the BBC tomorrow, and that's a promise.

When the *Daily Mail* picked up on the story and repeated some of Kenny's more inflammatory remarks, including more complaints about needle time, Hardie Radcliffe, General Secretary of the Musicians' Union, sax player and fierce trade unionist (named after proto-socialist Kier Hardie), the man who arguably achieved more to defend the rights of British musicians than any individual in history, fired off a letter to the BBC's Director of Administration Mr. J.H. Arkell CBE. Words were not minced.

"We are unwilling to tolerate Everett's sniping any longer. If you *really* can't tame him *we* must do it: and it would not surprise me if, when our Executive Committee meet early in June, they will feel the most effective way to do this would be to withdraw the services of our members from broadcasting.

"Whether this new 'personality' you have acquired should be allowed to thumb his nose at the Corporation is of course your affair... I feel very strongly that, if you really cannot lose this nuisance, you are under an obligation yourselves to disassociate the Corporation from his irresponsible ramblings. I regret to say that, until you find some way to do this, I shall be unable to maintain correspondence with the Corporation."

In other words, fire the bastard or we'll not only strike, we won't even speak to you any more.

It could have been a repeat of the Garner Ted Armstrong debacle were it not for the fact that the BBC brass was made of sterner stuff than pirate chiefs. In those days all English schoolboys, grammar or public, were trained for Imperial Service. Nobody wanted war with the MU or ABS over the Everett Affair, but any sign of weakness, the brass knew, could bring the enemy streaming over the ramparts and into the compound where their demands for more pay and shorter hours would be unsupportable. Sheaves of memos flurried, all couched in diplomatic euphemisms, with words like 'strike', 'threat' or even 'demand' carefully avoided for fear of spreading panic and despair among the lower ranks and womenfolk.

The boffins in contracts and the legal department were consulted. More memos were drafted. Heads were put together. Eventually a compromise was reached. Kenny would not be fired, but he would be gagged.

A meeting was arranged after which Frank Gillard, the Director of Radio, who as a BBC war correspondent had worked under fire in North Africa, Sicily and on the D-Day beaches, wrote:

Dear Mr Everett,
This is to record that at our meeting this afternoon you agreed:
1. that during the period of one year from the date of this letter you would:
a) not write for publication or speak in public (including the giving of interviews to the press) about the BBC or its affairs or about Radio or Television without first obtaining the BBC's permission
b) not include in any performances for the BBC remarks or interjections of a type which the BBC had told you to avoid
2. that if you were in breach of the agreements in 1. a) and b) above, the BBC would have the right to cancel any contract which the BBC might then have with you.
If the above correctly reflects what was agreed, will you please sign the form of confirmation below and return this letter to me. A copy is enclosed for you to keep.
Yours sincerely
Frank Gillard

There was nothing empty about the threat to 'cancel any contract'. In that first year of Radio 1, the schedule was given a shake-up every couple of months or so. The latest plan was to take Kenny off the Sunday morning show and give him a *daily* 45-minute show every evening at 6.45. On the one hand it was a huge accolade, recognition of his value to the station and the confidence management had in him. But it was also a juicy carrot which, unless he toed the line, he'd never get to taste.

Kenny put off signing the gagging order. Then put it off some more. On June 9, when he broadcast his last Sunday show, there was some lingering doubt – certainly in the minds of his fans – whether he'd ever return to the BBC. To prove his worth, he made his last show a good one.

The Beatles were at Abbey Road, making what would become *The White Album*. To the chagrin of Paul, George and Ringo, Yoko Ono, by now a permanent presence, had taken to lying on a mattress underneath the piano, shouting John's name. Far from annoying John, this seemed to please him, although it must be said that John had, by this time, made his farewells to coherent thought. Kenny popped down to see them, taking his tape recorder along.

"Is there any particular record out at the moment that you like?" asks Kenny.

"Oh, yeah, let me think," says John. Then he sings to the tune of 'Cottonfields', "When I was a little bitty baby, my mother would smash me in the cradle."

After several more mumblings and stumblings about the Beatles' recent sojourn in India with the Maharishi, Kenny asks, "Have you got anything to say that our listeners would understand?" When John clearly hasn't, Kenny invites him to ask the questions.

"What are you doing?" says John.

"Well, at the moment, I'm having a daily show come on soon," says Kenny, brightly.

"Really? So they haven't sacked you? I was getting you a job with the Isle of Man. I put in a word for you with Ronald Manx," said John, clearly flatteringly *au fait* with Kenny's interview for *The Londoner*.

Kenny asks whether the success of *Sgt Pepper's Lonely Hearts Club Band* had set the bar too high for future recordings.

"It only got high 'cause everybody said how high it was," Lennon replies. "It's no higher than it was when we made it." And it all goes back to la–la land.

"If that's what India does to you," Kenny tells his listeners, "I'm staying with Bognor Regis."

At the end of the interview, the Fabs improvise a jingle. "Goodbye, Kenny," Ringo sings, "it's good to see you back. Goodbye Kenny, we hear you got the sack."

Next day, just in case Ringo had heard something he hadn't, Kenny signed the gagging order, adding, "I feel somehow a little uncomfortable about signing this thing. However if refusing to sign it puts me in danger of losing radio work in the future, as you gave me the impression it would, I can see no alternative than to sign it."

He had six weeks off. Time to put into operation the most bizarre and unrealistic scheme of his life. Kenny Everett had decided to become heterosexual.

CHAPTER SIX

These days the very suggestion that anybody who wasn't born that way could 'become' heterosexual would be greeted anywhere except rural Alabama with raised eyebrows and derisory snorts, but it must be remembered that in the late sixties the whole world, at least in its attitudes to sexual orientation, was rural Alabama. Though Britain had come a long way since 1861, when gays could still be strung up, the decriminalisation that came in 1967 did not immediately bring about universal respect and understanding.

Homosexuality was generally regarded, even by sympathetic commentators, as at least a 'social problem', if not a 'mental disorder'. It was still included in the International Classification of Diseases (ICD) as recently as 1992. Luckily, properly qualified doctors could give you something for it, including: "Oestrogen treatment to reduce libido; psychoanalysis, and religious counselling; electroconvulsive therapy; discussion of the evils of homosexuality; desensitisation of an assumed phobia of the opposite sex, hypnosis, psychodrama, and abreaction. Dating skills were sometimes taught, and occasionally men were encouraged to find a prostitute or female friend with whom to try sexual intercourse."[41]

A common belief was that the 'homosexual phase' was something many men went through during adolescence. Unfortunately some men stayed like that. A nudge of some sort – maybe a 'prostitute or female friend with whom to try sexual intercourse' – should have them right as rain in no time at all.

Others reckoned it was the result of excessive mother-love and was nothing a spell in the army (or more bizarrely, the navy) couldn't fix. One learned paper suggested it wasn't a 'disease' at all or even a 'condition' but a 'social role' that "did not emerge in England" (can you believe this?) "until towards the end of the seventeenth century".[42]

There never seemed to be any doubt in anybody's mind that the opposite of homosexual was 'normal' and the universal epithet for it was 'queer'.

'Queer' and 'camp' were of course entirely different things – a distinction resulting from the shroud of secrecy imposed by public opinion and the law. Noel Coward, for instance, was amusingly 'camp', but no *Daily Express* reader believed – or wanted to believe – that he was actually 'queer'. He was friends with the Queen Mother and Lord Louis Mountbatten, for God's sake. He was a patriot. If a man like that found he had urges like that he'd shoot himself, it stands to reason. Even after decriminalisation, Coward was worried about disillusioning his more sheltered fans. When asked why he didn't come out, he replied, "There are still a few old ladies in Worthing who don't know."

Liberace, the fifties piano star whose diamanté suits, spangled hair and lisping poems about his mother and his brother George made rows of frilly pink tents look positively butch, sued the *Daily Mirror* for implying that he was gay and, more incredibly still, not to mention unjustly, won his case.

There were even people, admittedly few in number, who thought that Kenneth Williams was just a theatrical chappie, putting it on a bit (sometimes a bit too much) for comic effect. They seriously believed that one day they'd read of his engagement (Joan Sims? Barbara Windsor?) or a paternity suit, perhaps.

Secrecy made role models for gay people practically non-existent. Those that did emerge set the bar unreachably high. In *The Naked Civil Servant* (published 1968), Quentin Crisp ("one of the stately homos of England") showed the world how to be gay and defiant, but role models for those who wanted to be gay and humdrum didn't arrive for ages.

Colleagues took it for granted that Kenny was gay. "I knew within seconds of meeting him that he was homosexual," says Wilfred De'Ath, the producer who first put Maurice Cole on the wireless. "I remember saying to my wife, I'm sure he's homosexual and she agreed with me. I mean don't get the wrong idea, we didn't condemn him, we just thought it was interesting that he hadn't realised it himself."

Everybody on the *MV Galaxy* knew too. "The most complicated colleague on board," says Tony Blackburn, "was 'Edith'. You'll know him better as Kenny Everett... He was something else: super quick, crankily creative and one great big jumble of confusion. Leading a double life as the most exciting DJ in the country was probably more than enough for such a slight, incredibly shy man. But that wasn't all he had to deal with. Most of Kenny's younger days were spent covering up the fact that he was gay. I'm afraid for all their permissiveness, the sixties weren't ready to embrace homosexuality. Kenny fought it, too, for a while."

There is no evidence to suggest that his sexuality proved any impediment to his career. He was in Light Entertainment, for God's sake, a field in which it often seemed that heterosexuals were the 'queers'. A nervously repressed homosexual was never going to frighten the horses. One story suggests that being gay may actually have helped his career...

A star producer at Radio 1 was Bernie Andrews. It was he – just one of many achievements – who gave the Rolling Stones their first broadcast, despite their having failed a BBC audition, by hiring them as backing band for Bo Diddley and inviting them to record a few of their own songs, which he then smuggled into the schedules to great acclaim. In the early days he was John Peel's great champion and advisor without whom Peel would almost certainly have been out on his ear after the first blast of Spooky Tooth.

Every Friday night, Bernie would host a party to play and discuss the latest additions to his record collection. "It was a massive record collection," says Bob Harris. "It filled the house and it was all vinyl back then. Vinyl is heavy. So heavy that the house started sinking. The whole house was sinking under the weight of this collection and so eventually Bernie sold it as a job lot to Elton John."

Kenny was a regular at these Friday night soirées, as was Richard Kerr, the composer who later went on to write hits for Barry Manilow, Dionne Warwick and Roy Orbison.

"Every Friday night we used to go round there," says Richard. "Bernie had a whole stack of the new singles and albums or whatever and we'd all start just chatting and drinking. I used to just drink milk. I was into my milk phase. Everybody else drank Mateus Rosé. Mateus Rosé was the tipple of the day – horrible stuff but the bottles made lovely table lamps. They were evenings when we'd just listen to the new releases and talk about them in a half-hearted way. I remember Junior Walker & the All Stars' 'How Sweet It Is'. That stayed with me for a long time. Kenny was there more often than not. It was at least a year later we [Richard and his pal Jonathan] realised we were the only straight people there. Bernie had a word with us and said he wanted us to stop going because we were cramping their style. It never struck me as significant that women never went there and it was all male."

Kenny may have dabbled in man-on-man action with Peter Brown and maybe at Bernie Andrews' soirées, but repression, Northern working-class Catholic guilt, fear of parents' reaction and so on, made sure that there was never at this stage in his life a chance that he'd come out, come clean, own up.

It's also important to remember that being gay in the sixties – aside from the annoyances of discrimination, disapproval and the law – was also bloody inconvenient. Not, perhaps, as awkward as being a wheelchair user in that age when ramps were a rarity, but a good bit worse than being left-handed. Your culture was 'sub'. Your preferences 'specialist'. And if, as one read in the papers every day, being gay was just a 'phase' or a 'condition' or an 'affectation', how hard could it be to give it up? Surely no harder than giving up smoking. And then how much easier life would be.

Kenny seems to have thought, or hoped, that heterosexuality might be an acquired taste, like avocados or Nick Cave, and all he had to do was acquire it. Years later, after he'd come out, he was interviewed by Sue Lawley on Radio 4's *Desert Island Discs*. "I just thought I would one day wake up and I'd go, 'Oh, I get it'. The shape and the lumps and the softness would all fall into place. I realised a lot later you are what you're born. If you're born gay then you're gay forever."

But in 1968, the strategy seemed to be something more along the lines of "If you can convince everybody else you're heterosexual, you'll *be* heterosexual."

"He was always boasting about how many women he'd had," says Wilfred De'Ath, "and the more he went on about it the less I thought he was heterosexual. We met for a drink at the Hilton Hotel and he was with an incredibly beautiful girl. We had a drink and I think he was stoned – in fact, I'm sure he was stoned. I was really unsympathetic because I've always disapproved of drugs and what they do to you. There was a coolness between us then. I really fancied this girl myself and I remember her saying to me she'd twigged – everybody had twigged – he clearly wasn't interested in her in a sexual way."

The nameless arm-candy was not, however, the only blonde in Kenny's life. Lee Middleton, the woman he'd first encountered at Brian Epstein's Kingsley Hill party a year before, had gradually become an indispensable companion.

Lee – proper name Audrey – was a Sheffield girl, who had married young. On the day that rock'n'roll came to town she ran off with Alex Most (Mickey's partner in the Most Brothers) to London, where she worked as a hostess and showgirl in London clubs. Over the next few years, she lost Alex Most to Lionel Bart, the *Oliver!* composer, released three records under the name Lady Lee, briefly took up with sixties rock idol Duffy Power and then began a longer term relationship with even bigger sixties rock idol, Billy Fury.

She loved animals. So did Billy – a keen bird-watcher. At their house in Ockley, Surrey, Lee and Billy assembled a sizeable menagerie and hosted parties for the great and the good of the pop world at which the drugs were always of the finest quality. Nearly six years older than Kenny, she had – has – a pretty, friendly, no-nonsense face, a wide-open smile and understanding eyes that invite you to tell her everything, now.

Kenny encountered her for a second time, this time with Billy Fury, at a mutual friend's house. After a good few joints had been smoked, Lee invited him down to Ockley and one summer's afternoon he took her up on the offer. Richard Kerr, was there too, and Bernie Andrews, and some very special acid.

"I remember it so clearly," says Richard. "The word was going round this was JL's stuff [John Lennon's]. It was on blotting paper at the time. I only ever took the stuff twice because it had a very bad effect on me. But I remember Kenny was there and Bernie was there and it was a very warm afternoon and Bernie was wrapped in a blanket lying in the corner of one room. It was a very strange time."

In *The Custard Stops At Hatfield,* Kenny distinctly remembers everybody turning into pineapples.[43]

Other weekends at Lee and Billy's followed, with acid an essential part of the entertainment. On one occasion Kenny became paranoid and decided that suicide was the only logical course of action. Lee didn't indulge him. "Look if you are going to kill yourself, could you do it outside? We've just bought this new carpet, you see...."[44]

Kenny was charmed.

Lee and Billy's relationship was a little complicated. Her friend Judith Hall had supplied Lee with an alibi when Lee went off on holiday to Tunisia with the Decca promotions man, Tony King. But Judith had always fancied Billy. So she told Billy what was going on. Lee and Billy split up at Christmas 1967. Judith moved in with Billy. All very sixties.

Much to the surprise of all their friends, many random passers-by and most of all Kenny and Lee themselves, Kenny and Lee became an item. He had talked (he rarely stopped) to her about how disgusted his feelings about men made him feel. They started knitting and made a rug together.

That summer, during his six-week vacation from the BBC, the two of them drove through France and Italy and back through Switzerland and Germany in Kenny's little red Fiat. It was an erratic trip. In her autobiography[45], Lee tells how they were lucky to get back to England in one piece. They spent a lot of time stoned and, thus preoccupied, hit a deer in Switzerland. Then they had to fly back to England after a set-to with an E-Type Jag just outside Marseilles.

Kenny had stipulated throughout the trip that the hotel rooms should have single beds and was very put out when they had to share a bed at one hotel in Italy. Lee, under no illusions about Kenny's proclivities, took it all with patience and good humour.

His bid to 'become heterosexual' was clearly a long-term project.

The new Radio 1 show, called *Foreverett,* was five days a week of panic and slog. He was used to spending two or three days preparing a two-hour show. Turning out one a day could only be done by either forgoing sleep or tolerating lower standards. Worse still, the BBC had taken Angela

Bond, his producer, protector and friend away from him and given him instead a team of producers who took turns trying to apply the 'very firm' hand.

By the second week he was knackered.

Things got infinitely worse when he was offered his first TV show by Granada, the Manchester-based company that held the ITV franchise for the North West of England.

It was something of a miracle he got the gig at all. When the producer phoned his agent, she told him that Kenny was unreliable and suggested they ask Tony Blackburn instead. Kenny switched agents soon after.

So, on top of the five days a week slog on *Foreverett,* once a week Kenny was driving up to Manchester to make some telly. He found himself part of an ill-assorted bunch of people, some of whom would one day achieve distinction. John Birt, the show's producer, would go on to become the Director General of the BBC. Bill Podmore, one of the directors, would produce *Coronation Street* during its glory years.

Germaine Greer, one of Kenny's co-presenters, was an Australian academic, one of the first women to storm the previously all-male bastion of Cambridge Footlights, and had edited and posed nude for both the English underground magazine *Oz* and its Dutch equivalent *Suck.* Two years after *Nice Time,* she'd go on to write *The Female Eunuch,* a key text of the feminist movement. Jonathan Routh, the other presenter, also Cambridge educated, had already made a name for himself on the TV prank show *Candid Camera.*

It had an impressive roster of writers, too. Michael Palin and Terry Jones (before their success in *Monty Python's Flying Circus*), Graeme Garden and Tim Brooke-Taylor (before their success in *The Goodies*), Clive James, Chris Allen and Gillian Reynolds all worked on the show.

"*Nice Time* was a celebration of working-class humour and popular culture, which used real people to entertain," says John Birt.[46] "It began each week with a musical item: a choir of George Brown lookalikes singing 'My Way'; or a percussion group of teeth tappers; or some George Formby impersonators with ukuleles singing 'I'm leaning on a Lamp-post' or an ensemble of ventriloquists' dummies mouthing 'The Legend Of Xanadu'."

'The Legend Of Xanadu' with its whip-cracking chorus was a number one hit for Dave, Dee, Dozy, Beaky, Mick and Tich.

"Every week Jonathan, Kenny and Germaine visited the markets and fairgrounds of Bury, Bolton, Blackpool and other Northern towns and asked fat ladies in bloomers to tell us about their first kiss; or gentlemen pensioners to improvise a western shoot out; or a group of holiday makers to march and to whistle 'Colonel Bogey'; or men in a pub to strip naked a shop window dummy."

The big moment came at the end of the show when Kenny might say, "If you live in Gas Street, Bradford, look out of the window and you'll see a big removal van. Go and bang on the door and a big brass band will march out and play for you for an hour!" They would go out. They would bang on the door. The band would come marching. It was the telly. It had the power to make such miracles happen.

Kenny sang and wrote the lyrics for the signature tune. The music was by Richard Kerr. They released it as a single, with another song they'd put together, 'And Now For A Little Train Number', on the B–side. Both songs were whimsical, but clearly not made as comedy records. Like Tony Blackburn and other DJs who'd probably rather not have their efforts remembered, Kenny fancied his chances as the goods on the turntable.

"I suppose I am a frustrated pop star," he told the *Dee Jay Book*[47]. "I love going to the Beatles' sessions, because you can see them sitting there playing, getting all the twiddly bits right."

Kenny, from his long hours in the Wireless Workshop, knew all there was to know about twiddly bits. Indeed, if all there had been to being a Rock God was getting the twiddly bits right, there's no doubt that Kenny would have been bigger than the Beatles, but sadly the job description makes other demands.

He'd previously released two covers of Harry Nilsson records, 'Without Her' and 'It's Been So Long', neither of which had forced record shops to buy bigger tills. Though he did make more records ('Snot Rap' went Top 10 in 1983), 'Nice Time' was his last serious shot at proper pop. His determination to get the twiddly bits right might, however, have been its undoing.

"I heard it as they were putting it down in the studio," says Richard Kerr. "It sounded a pretty good arrangement to me. Then I didn't hear it until the record was released. It was different. Apparently, Kenny had gone into the studio, unbeknownst to the producer of the record, a guy called Wayne Bickerton, and put all these sound effects on and in doing so he'd erased the bottom half of the bass guitar. Bickerton was absolutely furious. There wasn't much he could do about it because the record was out."

The lyrics were toytown psychedelia, so *Sgt Pepper*-drenched it's a wonder there were no letters from copyright lawyers.

"Have tea on the Nice Time raft
Help the fat gentleman take off his tie
Help the fat lady eat her marmalade pie
Sit down and enjoy a Nice Laugh
(Ha ha ha ha ha ha ha ha ha)"

There's more …

"Mrs Sefton leads the band
Aspidistra in her hand
Come on dearie, pull up your skirt
Have a nice dance and grab hold of Bert"

The B-side, 'And Now For A Little Train Number', is loads better.

In November 1968, Kenny had hands-on experience of helping the Beatles "get their twiddly bits right".

Every Christmas since 1963, the Beatles had produced a flexi-disk – a record with the grooves cut into a cheap bit of floppy plastic – to send out free to fan club members. The early ones were usually recorded as an afterthought to a regular session at Abbey Road. The lads would improvise a few gags, read out 'thank you to all our fans' statements written for them by their press officers ("Did you write this yourself?" "No, it's somebody's hand-rota"), shout their Christmas greetings ("Hello, this is John speaking with his voice"), and maybe mangle a chorus of 'Good King Wenceslas' ("Brightly show the boot last night, on the mosty cru-el").

The later ones are more elaborate, with specially composed songs, ('Christmas Time Is Here Again') and stories ("Podgy the Bear and Jasper were huddled around the unlit fire in the centre of the room…").

For the 1968 record, the Beatles asked their favourite DJ to use his skill with the twiddly bits to make their Christmas flexi sound happy.

He had his work cut out. 1968 had been a rough year for the band. The studio sessions for *The White Album* had been fraught with spats and sulks. At one point Ringo left the band altogether. Paul and John both had a go at playing the drums. In the end they coaxed him back by covering his Ludwigs in flowers.

All the same, by Christmas, the Fabs were barely on speaking terms, so, rather than gathering around a mic and gagging it up together like they usually did, each of their contributions was recorded separately.

Paul, in his house, plays random chords on piano and guitar and sings random words: "I'd like to wish everyone a happy Christmas, this year of 1968 going on '69."

Ringo's contribution, according to the sleeve notes, was recorded in the back of his "diesel-powered removal van Somewhere In Surrey". He conducts an argument with himself:

"Fourteen and six,"

"Nineteen and fivepence ha'penny, if you don't mind."

"Yes."

"Don't you say 'yes' to me. I'm telling you."

"It's a private line, you know."

"Private line!? I've been on this line for two years."

One sincerely hopes that at the time of recording he was at least drunk.

George phones in his message, most probably from the home of Nat Weiss, the Beatles' US representative, in New York. He doesn't sing anything himself but introduces Tiny Tim, the falsetto ukuleleist, who plays and sings 'Nowhere Man' in the worst possible way.

John makes the biggest impression. He contributes two stories/poems written in the style of *In His Own Write*. His love for Yoko was at its most obsessive.

"Once upon a time there were two balloons called Jock and Yono," he maunders. "They were strictly in love, bound happened for a million years. They were together, man, unfortuna-timetable they seemed to have previous experiences which kept calling them one way or the other. You know how it is... But they battled on against overwhelming oddities including some of their beast friends ..."

The 'beast friends' against whom they were battling being, presumably, Paul, George and Ringo.

As John chunters, in the background somebody tinkles tunelessly on a piano. Somebody else blows aimlessly on a recorder. One would like to believe that it's perhaps their respective children, Kyoko and Julian, but more likely it's Yoko.

Kenny does his best to make something of it – not to make sense of it, because that would be unfeasible, but at least he imbues it with some sort of 'Revolution No. 9' feeling of arty aleatoricism. He cuts in bits of opera, a speeded up version of 'Helter Skelter', some early synthesizer music from Perry and Kingsley (the Vanguard Visionaries), sound effects and applause, and generally does his best to reassure the Fab Four's fans that everything is still relatively fab in their lives.

"Non-Beatle Kenny Foreverett had a Nice Time mucking about with the tapes," say the sleeve notes, "and deserves to be called PRODUCER although this is an unpaid position."

Logistically and professionally, fitting in a weekly telly show, which involved filmed inserts as well as once or twice weekly trips up to the Granada studios in Manchester, with a five-days-a-week radio show and occasional unpaid producer jobs for the Beatles is a recipe for ab-dabs. When Granada decided they wanted a second series of *Nice Time*, Kenny threw himself on the mercy of Angela Bond.

He told her that the producers of *Foreverett* didn't understand him like she did. He told her all his troubles, doubts and fears about Lee. He told her he couldn't cope.

Kenny, when he was needy, which was a lot of the time, could bring out the mother in a serial killer. Angela was a pushover. She fixed it for him. She had words in the right places and negotiated a new role for Kenny in yet another schedule change.

A few weeks later, the *Melody Maker* headline screamed, "*Saturday Club* is axed for Everett".

Saturday Club, since its beginnings as *Saturday Skiffle Club* in 1957, had become a fixture in every teenager's life. Despite over-reliance on favourite hits being given the BBC treatment by Bernard Herman and the NDO (with Vince Hill on vocals) there was always a chance of a live performance by a visiting American – the Everly Brothers, Jerry Lee

Lewis, Eddie Cochran and Gene Vincent all cropped up at one time or another – and the best of British, including the Beatles. Its axing, at the beginning of 1969, didn't cause street riots, but all the same it was a hard act for Kenny to follow. But he had help. Angela was back, and Crisp the Butler, and Granny. How hard can it be to slip into an old pair of shoes?

When, in March 1969, *Nice Time* swung into its second series, the regime was still punishing but doable.

In April, the *Daily Mirror* ran a feature about Kenny and his new girlfriend, Lee (referred to throughout by her real name, Audrey). At breakfast tables all over the country, wives must have turned to their husbands and said, "There, I told you he wasn't."

"Kenny's girlfriend Audrey," said the *Mirror*[48], "has stopped watching him film those zany stunts that he does each week for ITV's *Nice Time* show.

"It was just too much for her seeing Kenny's frail five-feet-five enduring such hazards as stepping into the ring with Henry Cooper (I was supposed to knock him out, says Kenny, but he wouldn't lie down. He said 'Only world champions ever defeat me'), chasing Jonathan Routh through Manchester on a horse and cart, or being hoisted high in the air by a tower crane in a bandsman's uniform with a balloon tied to his head."

Granada was paying him £300 a week to fight Henry Cooper, tie balloons to his head and share the presentation of a half-hour show – filming inserts on Monday and Tuesday, then up to Manchester for rehearsals and recordings in the studio on Wednesday and Thursday. The Gingham Corporation meanwhile gave him £45 a week for a two-hour show which involved a day or so in the Wireless Workshop doing the twiddly bits.

"'If *Nice Time* is bread then the Beeb (his Radio 1 show) is 'like a hobby' said Kenny."

The "heterosexual by 1970" project was going well. In Manchester, he often stayed with his producer, John Birt, with whom he shared his hopes and fears.

"He gradually came to appreciate that he was attracted to men," says Birt, "but his upbringing made him uncomfortable with this. Like me, he hadn't known about homosexuality when he was growing up. (When as a teenager I first heard words like 'queer' and 'poof' and 'faggot', I recognised they were disparaging but didn't understand what condition they referred to). Kenny saw his homosexual feelings as an affliction. He took LSD and pronounced himself cured: he proclaimed he now found women attractive."[49]

Research into the use of LSD in this context was still in its early stages, and the exact dosage required to make homosexual become heterosexual a matter of some speculation.[50] So, to make sure, Kenny just took a lot. It became his custom, when the Saturday show was over, to turn into a pineapple.

"I took acid every weekend for about a year or two," he later told the *Daily Mirror*. "For me, in those days, it meant 'Instant Party Time'. It probably got rid of half my brain cells… but it hasn't, fortunately, got in the way of my career. You don't need a brain to be a DJ… I had the insatiable impulse to try it all – to do everything. When I was on it, I could never understand people who just didn't want to try it. Looking back it was like a world war going on in your head. My dad – and lots of other men – saw a real world war. For most of them it was an amazing experience… Taking LSD is a potted version of having a world war going on inside your head. You do see dreadful things, horrible things. You see ecstasy as well."[51]

To summarise: according to the Everett thesis, taking so much acid that you believe you are taking part in the Battle of Britain and the D-Day landings, 'cures' you of homosexuality. The exact medical details of how this happens are still something of a mystery.

Against all the odds, though, would you believe it, the 'cure' did seem to have its effects. During one of his acid trips, in the middle of the night, Kenny was moved to have *actual sexual intercourse* with Lee. Next day, like an adolescent boy after his first grope, he was on the phone to all his mates. The first thing he said to Angela Bond when he got into work was, "I've done it!" and one assumes that by 'it' he meant not just doing it, but the whole shebang of 'becoming heterosexual'.

He threw himself into the twiddly bits of heterosexual life with the same enthusiasm he gave to his radio programmes. He and Lee rented a flat in Holland Park for £6.50 a week on a promise to do it up. Kenny had one of the rooms soundproofed and built a studio, filled with state-of-the-art equipment, so he could work in the domestic bliss of his'n'hersness.

There was no doubt that Kenny and Lee were in love, but the possibility that some aspects of their heterosexual domesticity might have been for display purposes only was suggested by their answering machine message which announced: "This is the Maurice and Audrey Show, why don't you sing along with us". The rug they'd made for the loo was similarly inscribed "The Maurice And Audrey Show".

Rug-making (not, as some have suggested, a euphemism for 'drug-taking') was, in the version of the story Kenny told the press, how they met. "She was making the rug from one end and I started from the other. We eventually met in the middle."

They liked animals, too, and filled the rented flat with a cat, three kittens, a chihuahua, (which was the spitting image of Kenny), a blue and gold macaw and a Great Dane called Bosie, the nickname of Oscar Wilde's lover, Lord Alfred Douglas.

They had flat, pets, rugs and joint answering machine message. Inevitably the distant tinkle of wedding bells soon became an insistent clang.

The proposal came one day when they were round at the flat of their old friend, Don Paul (former member of the Morton Fraser Harmonica Gang and the Viscounts, who had a hit with the British cover of 'Who Put The Bomp [In The Bomp, Bomp, Bomp]', later a record producer). Kenny asked Don whether he thought he should marry Lee. Lee was sitting next to him at the time. Don thought it sounded a good idea. Kenny took Lee out into Don's garden, stood her under a magnolia tree and made a formal proposal.

She was a June bride dressed in a table-cloth. No dress fabric came up to scratch, so they bought a lacy table-cloth and had it adapted ("Bride's Dress Seats Eight!" screamed the headlines). Lee accessorized the table-cloth with a floppy hat and their chihuahua. Kenny wore an Edwardian suit with a pink cravat and carried a single long stemmed rose. Bucking custom, they held the reception first. A chef called George who was in the process of becoming a chef called Lorraine did the catering. S/he turned up in net, chiffon and stubble chin and was suspected of spiking the punch with speed. Either way, the guests, including Germaine Greer, John Birt and best man Don Paul, were pretty much off their heads by the time they were ferried, in a specially chartered London bus, over to Kensington Register Office for the ceremony. Lee and Kenny went sedately in a carriage drawn by two white horses.

In the street outside the register office, they were mobbed by press. There was more drama inside when the registrar read out Kenny's name and mum, Lily, unaware that her boy had changed it by deed poll from Maurice Cole, shouted, "It's not legal!"

A couple of Kenny and Lee's gay friends, anticipating civil partnership by 35 years, stood behind them to share the vows.

The honeymoon was in Jersey. Kenny fell asleep as soon as they arrived so Lee spent her wedding night chatting with Don Paul and Tony King who'd tagged along.

They rented a weekend retreat, 'Laudate' in Newdigate, Surrey. It was the country home of Peter Asher, formerly half of the singing duo Peter & Gordon and brother of Jane Asher, the celebrated actress probably then better known as Paul McCartney's ex-girlfriend. Boasting an impressive layout – the Japanese-styled house and swimming pool were set in eight acres of grounds – rumour had it that, before Peter Asher's time, it had been used as a hide-out by one of the Great Train Robbers. Derek Taylor, the one-time Beatle press officer who'd lived there for a bit in 1968, described it as 'an acid-head's dream'. John Lennon, floating through the eight acres, had dreamed up 'Happiness Is A Warm Gun' there.

There was, however, something unsettling about 'Laudate'. "The house had the strangest vibrations," says Derek Taylor[52]. "I don't think there was a day we didn't feel… that we were being watched by odd men and funny women."

The vibrations touched Lee, too. One weekend she and Kenny had friends, including Bernie Andrews, down to stay. They held a séance and scared themselves silly. The occasion triggered Lee's lifetime involvement with psychic studies.

★   ★   ★

The gagging order Kenny had signed with the BBC was never going to have much meaning. "Radio is a very instant medium. All that adrenalin zooms around when you're in a position of danger, that's what radio is."

The first hiccup came when he linked into the news with some half-hearted attempt at a jokey reference to the Californian band Jefferson Airplane: "And now here's the news read by Peter Jefferson with his airplane." The lead story was of a horrific plane crash with great loss of life. There were complaints.

The first rule for any BBC employee is 'you don't mess with the news'.

In December, he was shooting his mouth off again, this time in the *Sun*,[53] under the headline 'What I'd Do With Radio 1.'

He described Radio 1 as 'dull' and banged on about needle time. "I'd start a big battle with the Musicians' Union over this business of needle time. I'd have to do something about that."

He slags off his fellow DJs, too: "I'd keep Blackburn. I like *What's New* with Dave Symonds. They have it in for him you know. John Peel? I think he's gone a bit overboard. If only he would put a pop record in his shows every now and again."

He says that, apart from *What's New*, he never listens to Radio 1 anyway. He's more of a Radio 4 sort of person. He's a particular fan of *Woman's Hour*. "It's not really a woman's programme at all. It's like a sort of *Late Night Line-Up* [BBC2's arts and culture show] without being so tedious."

Once again, the memos flew, the first from J.H.Arkell, Director of Administration, to Douglas Muggeridge, who'd taken over from Robin Scott as Controller of Radios 1 and 2: "Reading page 17 of the *Sun* at breakfast this morning, I decided to have a word with you about Kenny Everett since this was a delicate moment for the Musicians' Union to be irritated more than is necessary. Even before I had dictated it, I had Ratcliffe [general secretary of the MU] on the telephone..."

Douglas Muggeridge replied: "I think we have to be careful here and decide now whether we mean this to be final or not and also what action we take if he transgresses again. If we really mean to terminate his services then we should say so without any ambiguity and be prepared to act on it. At least this is how it seems to me. I cannot recall whether we have done this before, but I rather think that we have given a final warning in the past."

Having already been given one last chance, in other words, Kenny was being given another last chance – only they really meant it this time.

He blew this last chance just a couple of weeks later, when he broadcast a remark so potentially defamatory that even now it would be legally ill-advised to mention the name of the actress involved, or that of her husband at the time, or that of the alleged father of her child/children.

He was given a third, final, final, definitely, really mean it, final warning and this is not a joke. This time though, Angela Bond had a bit of a go at him, too. Kenny took this as a betrayal, decided she was on the side of the 'suits' and refused to work with her. Two other producers were sent in, taking turns to exercise "<u>very</u> firm production".

Quite aside from his prodigious talent, Kenny's ability to commit career-stopping crimes without getting fired was enough to spread rumours of Superpowers. Teflon man. Watch the shit just slide off. It provoked awe.

"As I was getting more involved in the music scene in London, I used to go over to David's occasionally," says Bob Harris, 'David' being fellow DJ David Symonds. "I guess this would be '68 or '69. He was managing a band and invited some people across to his house to listen to some of their new recordings – Dave Cash and Jeff Griffin my producer, maybe 10 or 12 people. And I remembered when Kenny arrived, it was like the king, or god or someone had walked through the door, because the hushed reverence was absolutely beyond belief. He was revered."

Even the Beatles looked on him as some sort of saviour, at least of their next Christmas flexi. If the 1968 record had been put together in an atmosphere of mistrust and discord, the '69 offering was made in a war zone. In many ways it's touching that under the circumstances they were still trying to present a united front for their fan club as they crumbled apart.

Miraculously, this time Kenny managed to get all four together round a mic, at least for the intro. John is the cheerleader, trying to inject a bit of Christmas joy into the proceedings.

"Lads," he says, "if you'll just shout Happy Christmas into this tape!"

"Whuh ... Happy Christmas?" asks Paul, sleepily.

John and Yoko are then recorded wandering around their Tittenhurst Park estate.

"What will Santa bring me?" says Yoko, playfully.

More than half the disc is given over to John and Yoko's cooing and giggling. Yoko sees the coming decade as one of "peace and freedom and everything…" which will see everyone "flying around", temporarily forgetting that aeroplanes had been invented some time before.

"Merry Christmas," she warbles in her squeaky operatic voice. But even that isn't half as disturbing as John, the wild man of pop, the Working Class Hero, addressing Yoko as 'mummy'.

Kenny cut from John and Yoko to Ringo chanting, "Merry Christmas, Merry Christmas, Magic Christian, Magic Christian," *Magic Christian* being the title of the forthcoming film in which Ringo co-starred with Peter Sellers. "It's just a plug for the film, Ken," he says. "Try and keep it in."

On this one Kenny's enigmatic credit reads, "This flexi-disc was forged by the Iron Wrist of Maurice Cole."

It was the last ever Beatle Christmas disc. Paul had already acknowledged in an interview with *Life* magazine that the group had in effect disbanded. Christmas 1970 was spent with the four of them suing each other's arses off.

To the Beatles and to his fellow DJs he may have been the Messiah, but to the BBC management, increasingly, he was just a very naughty boy.

The last straw came on July 18, 1970.

It was a slow news day. The UN Security Council was trying to block British arms sales to South Africa. There was a dock strike. But otherwise so little was happening that Princess Anne's new wristwatch, described as 'mod', made many front pages.

Radio news was hit by the same story-drought. By its last story, it was scraping the barrel. "Finally," the newsreader announced, "Mrs Mary Peyton, wife of the Transport Minister, has passed her advanced driving test first time."

"She only passed," said Kenny, off the cuff, "'cos she crammed a fiver into his hand. I know these people." And on to the next record.

With admirable economy, Kenny had messed with the news, perpetrated a potential slander and upset the Tory party which was in government at the time. Not only that – perfect coincidence – just to top the crime with whipped cream and sprinkles, on the very same day, the *Melody Maker* published an interview:

"BBC's Radio 1 is awful – really revolting," Kenny told them. "It's only the people who are so nice – gentle tea drinking chaps all very civilised, ex-Air Force and so on. They serve tea every half-an-hour. But that's all I really like about the Radio 1 programmes. Very good people to work with. Just that. Radio 1 people themselves agree that it's a mess. They try to do pop programmes, but it was doomed before it even started. The programmes are all in very good taste, but they all add up to a large percentage of horror – except for a few exceptions."

In the subsequent flurry of memos, Douglas Muggeridge reckoned a sacking was inevitable. Johnny Beerling put in a bid to have the punishment mitigated to a suspension ("... if Georgie Best misbehaves on the field, the Football Association does not sack him and permanently damage the Manchester United team. They suspend him for a month or two"), but by this time Ian Trethowan, Managing Director of Network Radio and never a Man U fan, had weighed in, pointing out that if a final warning appeared to mean nothing there was a danger of all the other DJs running riot.

In his defence, Kenny said, "The remarks were said humorously. Obviously I didn't mean them seriously." But it made no difference. Sentence was passed. Messiah or not, he was out.

The protests even made it into *The Times* letters page.

"From the Reverend Roy A. Clements

"Sir – I see that the BBC has sacked the one disc jockey with any real talent for entertaining. Some of us consider the level of humour from the average DJ to be abysmally low, the one area of relief being the Kenny Everett Show. He at least is funny, and it is easy to tell that he intends his humour. Consequently you would have to be pretty obtuse to misconstrue the remarks which the BBC have found apparently so objectionable.

"The BBC claims that it likes to allow its DJs as much freedom as possible, but it is obviously afraid to let them use it, no matter how mildly they attempt to do so. Please tell Aunty that the revolution is simmering in the very corridors of the establishment, and every now and then she helps it along magnificently."

Gerald Kaufman, Labour MP for Manchester Ardwick, miffed by the recent Conservative return to power and eager to attribute blame, cites the sacking as yet another example of anti-Labour BBC bias.

"In a letter to Lord Hill of Luton," *The Times* reported, "about the dismissal of Mr Kenny Everett, the disc jockey, he [Kaufman] said he was interested that the BBC taking the view it was wrong for personal attacks to be made by broadcasters on their government or their families, should take this stance so soon after a change of government. 'I recall that personal attacks of extraordinary virulence, though often couched in humorous terms, were frequently made upon members of the Labour Government.'"[54]

The Free Radio Association, which in 1967 had marched from Trafalgar Square to Fleet Street in support of the pirates, resorted to threats:

"Dear Sir or Madam,

"Due to your shocking irreverence in promptly dismissing Mr Everett from Radio 1 for what was only a joke, which you, sir, must admit, we are lodging an official note of protest against this decision and will be forced to commence jamming Radio 1 and also BBC TV for the whole South West from Bristol to Lands End, using Polden Radio (near Bridgewater) (which will be taken by force) and a portable transmitter near Exeter, *UNLESS by 3rd August 1970* you reinstate him in his former position."

Kenny launched a publicity offensive of his own. Jonathan King and publicist David Block arranged for a posse of reporters to interview him at his Holland Park flat. The ladies and gentlemen of the press were plied with champagne and the next day's papers painted Kenny as the victim of small-minded bigots at the BBC.

"Mostly my mouth works faster than my mind," Kenny told the *Daily Mail*[55], "so at times things came out sounding like an insult quite unintentionally. That's why I relied on the British sense of humour to work it out for me."

"It's very difficult when you're sitting in that little soundproof room – like a lunatic without a straightjacket – trying to cue up a record, wind on a tape, check the cartridge machine to see that the right jingle comes up, keep an eye on the clock and endeavour not to put the entire Beeb off the air by pressing the wrong button."

"I'm sure that if I said 'hello' I'd get indignant letters from the Abolition of the Word 'Hello' or something equally unlikely and unfunny. If I ever get a radio show again it's going to be totally silent."

For the time being, though, it looked as if the chances of Kenny getting even a silent radio show were slim. Why should he worry? The week before the sacking, he'd started a new TV series. It paid infinitely more than the £45 he was getting from the BBC and better still, unlike *Nice Time*, it was *his* show with *his* name in the title.

CHAPTER SEVEN

"Whereas people like Tony Blackburn, John Peel and myself, would go into radio as a career that we wanted to build on," says Bob Harris, "Kenny was much more of a moth round the flame. I don't think that Kenny had any concept of a 'career'. The word didn't compute with Kenny at all. He'd been dropped into heaven. He's got a workshop. He's got studio equipment. He's got three tape machines. And he has all these achievements – the radio shows, the TV, Beatles connections – but I don't think he would feel any sense of consequence about anything. And I don't think he thought much of the other DJs either."

Ask anybody whether Kenny Everett was 'ambitious' and they smile indulgently, amused by the idea of Kenny being a networker, a go-getter, a mover or shaker. Never having to bother with all that stuff is one of the great luxuries of being so markedly good – not to say the best – at what you do.

As Bob says, Kenny didn't think in terms of achievements. He had no sense of consequence. No career. Success arrived like an unplanned but welcome baby. He enjoyed it. Most of it, anyway. For now. He quite liked having money. He saw advantages to being famous – getting nice tables in restaurants, the recognition and respect of colleagues and employers. And he loved public acknowledgement that he was good at what he did.

By all accounts, he lurched from one job to another. People made offers. He said 'yes', unless his agent, Jo Gurnett, told him otherwise.

"Obviously there were times when I told him 'no' and he accepted that," she said. "If anyone contacted him direct and he thought it would be difficult to say 'no' he told them to ring me so that I could say 'no' for him and I could be the bearer of the bad news. He certainly wasn't filled with huge ambition – he just was grateful and happy with what he was doing and certainly never thought about the future too much – he was doing radio and TV and the work was constant."

The ease with which, on leaving, or being fired from one job, he'd walk into another, usually better, job, does sometimes make it look as if some grand strategy is being played out, but there's no evidence or testimony suggesting that there was. Kenny was sought after for his talent, he didn't need to scheme: and any luck he had was the Keatonesque luck of the innocent.

As Keith Skues put it so concisely, "Kenny couldn't give a monkey's, basically."

After Radio 1 dropped him, Kenny rattled around in TV for a while, making programmes that could have been, and probably should have been, career killers.

Barry Took was a comedy writer and producer with a string of successes to his name. With Marty Feldman he wrote the oft-repeated and still-funny radio series *Round The Horne* which, week after week, tore up the *BBC Variety Programmes Policy Guide For Writers And Producers,* chewed up the pieces, spat them out and used the resulting mush to make papier-mâché models of inappropriate body parts.

As 'comedy advisor' at the BBC he was instrumental in launching the megastardom of Dame Edna Everage and encouraging the first series of *Monty Python's Flying Circus.* In the USA he wrote for the incredibly successful *Rowan And Martin's Laugh-In,* NBC's bid to make comedy for the Beatle generation. When he returned to England to become Head of Light Entertainment at London Weekend Television, as well as commissioning Chesney and Wolfe's new sitcom *On The Buses,* he addressed himself to the problem of transferring the talents of Kenny Everett from radio to TV.

He had three goes at it all together.

The Kenny Everett Explosion was set off on July 10, 1970, just a week and a day before Kenny was fired by Radio 1. It ran at 7 p.m. on Friday nights (other times and other days in other parts of the country) for 10 30-minute episodes. Like the radio show, it featured Kenny, Crisp the Butler, running gags and lots of music – and there lies the problem.

There were two schools of thought about putting pop on TV. The first went for the club or dance hall approach; largely successful in *Ready Steady Go!,* less so in the always slightly naff *Top Of The Pops.* The second went for the concert approach; again largely successful in *Oh, Boy!,* less so in *Thank Your Lucky Stars.*

TV executives looked at the straightforward simplicity and downright *cool* of radio's approach – a bloke (or, by this time, Annie Nightingale) talking about stuff or doing stuff, interrupted quite frequently by records – with envy, and wondered 'How can *we* do that?'

The problem – obviously – was pictures. Having the band play live or mime in the studio ramped up costs and, unless the band made a bit of an effort, could be dull. Eventually bands would learn to co-operate by producing their own videos and MTV would be born, but until then what could you do?

One solution, eagerly grasped by *The Kenny Everett Explosion,* as it would be a year later by *The Old Grey Whistle Test,* was old film clips.

As *Whistle Test*'s Bob Harris says: "There were no videos at that point – we used old cartoons. If you had, say, a Steve Miller Band track, there was no film from America, no video so what do you do with this track? Mike [the producer Mike Appleton] gave it to Philip Jenkinson who was the great film archivist – he had rooms full of old movies. He'd be playing the Steve Miller track and opening up cans of film and going through the images and then cutting it all to the beat of the music. He had an amazing instinct for matching the right track with the right film. The combination of 'Tubular Bells' with old film of skiers on the white, white snow was always one of my favourites. Funnily enough, the early rappers started doing this later."

Old cartoons had a special appeal. A twenties *Felix The Cat* or *Betty Boop* could be recycled at a knockdown price and in the minds of the target audience, came ready-drenched in whimsical chic. In pre-internet, pre-video days, that old cartoon grammar of the stretches, eye pops and sweat drops was largely unfamiliar and seemed surreally reminiscent of the works of Robert Crumb or Gilbert Shelton, heroes of underground comix. Paired with Pickettywitch's '(It's Like A) Sad Old Kinda Movie', it could be charming. Paired with Captain Beefheart and a four-skin spliff it was a glimpse inside the mind of God.

All the tapes of *The Kenny Everett Explosion* have been lost or wiped. Rumours that one tape (some say it was a whole episode, others just the opening titles) had been excavated under the floorboards of the old LWT Wembley studios when they were demolished in 1993, appear to have been something of an exaggeration.

The memories of those who saw the show and those who worked on it also seem to have been wiped, or at least gone hazy. Kaleidoscope animation (popular on *Whistle Test* too) gets mentioned, as does a filmed insert – stunningly inappropriate to modern sensibilities – of Kenny dressed as the Pied Piper leading either mice, rats or, most likely, children into a maze accompanied by Smokey Robinson & the Miracles' 'Tears Of A Clown'. There was a door in the set which, when opened, might reveal King Kong snarling outside, or a Ray Harryhausen Cyclops, or the stampeding chariots from *Ben Hur*. And then some people remember Kenny's overweight friend, Vee, disco dancing in a cage. And there might have been a bean bag or two.

One memory most people share is that the show wasn't very good, really.

Kenny told the *Daily Mail* that the real reason he had made *The Kenny Everett Explosion* was to repay a £2,000 loan he'd raised to equip the studio at his Holland Park flat, his pride and joy and the place where he could still indulge his first love, radio.

"I wanted to do trails and things for the BBC at home," he says. "The two tape recorders cost £600 each. And I was able to record lots of my interviews for myself for my radio show. Television's nice but I really love radio. Television's such hard work but it's all right if you want to get the perks."[56]

The cruel irony was that now he'd got the studio, he had no radio show to make 'trails and things' for.

The last echoes of *The Kenny Everett Explosion* died away on September 11. It was replaced, a week later – same slot – with another show, *Making Whoopee*, hosted by none other than Kenny Everett.

Making Whoopee was a showcase for Bob Kerr's Whoopee Band, a trad-jazz/novelty song outfit, vaguely in the tradition of the Bonzo Dog

Doo–Dah Band and Spike Jones. Mr Kerr was himself a former member of the Bonzos, and singer with the chart-topping New Vaudeville Band. At the time of writing, the band is still gigging.

The show was recorded at the Half Moon pub in Putney and seems to have consisted of little more than Kenny compèring and sometimes joining in with the band's mix of "surreal humour with hilarious musical gags and twenties jazz on amphetamine".

Halfway through the run, in an attempt to gee up the ratings by acknowledging that the show was probably more suitable for children than grown ups, it was moved in the schedules to 6.15 on a Saturday. Still it failed to set the world alight.

But it kept Kenny's cash-flow healthy. He and Lee, on the lookout to find a more permanent country retreat than 'Laudate', came upon a derelict smallholding in Cowfold, Sussex – parts dating from the 12th century, with stable-block, barn and piggeries, no kitchen or bathroom to speak of – on the market at £19,250. Kenny took out a mortgage, borrowing the deposit from his sister's husband. They moved in and started renovating.

The previous occupant had left a letter warning that the back bedroom was haunted. In the course of renovations, they found a child's ancient leather shoes in the inglenook chimney (less ghoulish than it sounds, shoes were often concealed in houses as good luck and to keep witches away). As an unending source of fascination for a psychic investigator like Lee, Cowfold, her very own haunted house, couldn't be bettered.

As soon as *Making Whoopee* came to the end of its run, it was immediately replaced, again in the 6.15 Saturday slot, with another new show simply called *Ev.*

This was essentially a revamp of the *Explosion* with more comedy, more guest stars and less music. Crisp the Butler was present as were various characters played by the granite-faced actor Ronnie Grainge. Guests included the Bee Gees, Agony Aunt Marjorie Proops, The Tremeloes, Cyril Fletcher, Ray Davies of the Kinks, romantic novelist Barbara Cartland, the flamboyantly bewhiskered Conservative politician Sir Gerald Nabarro and – could any show be complete without her – the posh cookery diva and celebrated drunk, Fanny Cradock.

For the last episode of *Ev*, LWT hired an open top bus and staged a mock-up of Kenny and Lee's move into their new Cowford house. Marc Bolan joined them on the bus and sang 'Ride A White Swan' as they all rode into the village. Ted Moult, the celebrity farmer and star of double-glazing adverts, came with them, too, and a 'top interior designer' to help the happy couple choose colours and fabrics. Ted Moult inspected the soil and gravely announced that the house was built on a bog. Nothing would ever grow there. The 'interior designer' then wandered around their lovingly restored property with its 12th century period features advising them to rip out the inglenook fireplace and install false ceilings to hide the oak beams and perform similar desecrations.

In the end, the couple were told the whole thing was a huge prank. They laughed. Ted Moult laughed. The 'interior designer' – actually an actor – laughed. And then they all enjoyed a good old singsong around the open fire.

And, as you can imagine, *Ev* wasn't very good, either.

Luckily, the BBC, even with the pirates gone, was still not quite the only radio station in town.

By the autumn of 1970, Kenny had landed himself a half hour show, sponsored by Esso, on Radio Luxembourg. In the spring of 1971 he appeared also to have some connection with Radio Monte Carlo (not to be confused with several other Radio Monte Carlos or, indeed, with Radio Geronimo, a British pirate station which, around this period, used the Radio Monte Carlo transmitter) for whom he recorded a very strange interview with John Lennon.

In the previous year, Lennon had released his first proper solo album (i.e one that didn't just consist of him and Yoko, heartbeats and feedback). Called *John Lennon/Plastic Ono Band*, it was heavily informed by the primal therapy sessions John had been attending with the therapy's originator, Arthur Janov. The basic idea of primal therapy is that repressed childhood trauma can be released and dissipated through physical and emotional catharsis. It usually involves a lot of screaming.

The album is raw, ragged and bleeding. The first track is about the death of John's mother. So is the last track. Along the way he also mentions that "God is a concept by which we measure our pain". It is as far removed from 'Yellow Submarine' as *One Day In The Life Of Ivan Denisovich* is from *Noddy's Funny Kite*.

Sales were respectable by normal standards – it made number eight in the UK album chart. But John was used to Beatle sales, and, besides, Ringo's first solo album had gone to number seven, Paul's to number two, and George's all the way to the top.

Kenny Everett was a trusted pal who had given admirable service in the promotion of all the Beatles' albums since *Help!*. If anybody could breathe life into the dying sales, it was him.

Like so many others, Kenny had taken the Beatles' break-up as a personal tragedy. A huge fan of Lennon the funster, Lennon the gagster, soulful Lennon who wrote moody melodies with killer hooks, he wasn't at all sure about primal John.

On March 27, 1971, he went out to John's place at Tittenhurst Park at Ascot in Berkshire and sat in his newly built studio. Neither John nor Kenny were ever straight talkers and it's hard to spot what level of irony they're working at. John certainly seems to have given up irony entirely, but there's also an alarming possibility that Kenny's given it up, too, and genuinely believes that he can dispel John's surliness with a brisk talking-to, pull him together, stop him moping about pain and God and get him back into the studio singing those lovely close harmonies with George and Paul.

"Well," says Kenny, "tell us about your LP, John. It seems not to be as jolly as your last ones."

"Jolly as what?"

"Well, as the rest of them."

"Well, such as?"

"*Revolver, Sgt Pepper* ..."

"Ah, well that was a group effort, you see."

"Do you reckon yourself the sad member of the group?"

"Well, I wouldn't say they're all particularly much happier than me. But, they might emphasise the happier side, that's all."

"Are you thinking of doing a jolly album?"

If you spent weeks trying to come up with the most inappropriate question to ask the man who'd just released a song, recorded alone with acoustic guitar into a cassette recorder called 'My Mummy's Dead', you could not do better than, "Are you thinking of doing a jolly album?"

They go through the album track by track. The subject of dead mothers has, eventually, to be addressed. John talks about the way in which his feelings of abandonment afflicted his adult life. Kenny stubbornly sticks to his guns.

"But you should be the happiest man of the century," he says.

"Why?"

"I mean you've been through all that hell and damnation of being dragged up by the heels to the heights of stardom. And now, you've sort of secured yourself in your own little studio, in your own huge house, in 70 acres of delightful scenery. So let's have a jolly LP, John!"

It gets worse. They talk about politics. John's latest single was 'Power To The People.' Unlike John, Kenny is in broad agreement with the idea of government, democracy, capitalism, the status quo and so on.

"I mean," he says, "they've been at it for hundreds of years, they must have it right by now."

"You think they've got it right?"

"Well, as right as you can get it on earth."

"Well, that's the only chance you get. If you don't get it right on earth, where are you expecting to get it right?"

"Yeah, but you've got to have bad bits to make the good bits stand out."

A month or so later, Kenny discovered that somebody had left a back door open at BBC radio. He snuck in.

BBC Local Radio was started at around the same time as Radio 1 partly as a response to criticism that the Corporation suffered from a metropolitan bias. By 1971, 20 or so stations – Radio Leicester, Radio Leeds, Radio Stoke and so on – were bubbling away.

The local radio producers, working with tiny budgets, were, of necessity, a resourceful bunch. Towards the end of April, one of them, Roy Hayward from BBC Radio Bristol, approached Kenny and asked whether he would be interested in doing a little programme for them, no names, no pack drill, six and a half quid. He reckoned with a bit of fancy footwork he could clear the paperwork before anybody noticed that Kenny was officially banned from the BBC. The scam worked. The memos didn't start flying until a full 10 days after the transmission.

"19 MAY 1971
KENNY EVERETT
A Bristol producer (Roy Hayward by name) recorded a programme (*Pets And People*) on Monday 26th April in which he used the above named artist. The transmission took place on Sunday 9th May. He started off a Talks Requisition Contract on the following day (10th May) and this filtered its way through the regional Booking Office and Talks Bookings, London, eventually ending up in this section where it belongs, yesterday.

Would you say that we have little alternative but to complete the contract (at the figure of £6.50)? I have asked Contracts and Finance Executives to point out to Mr Heywood the sins and omissions for which he is responsible."

BBC Radio Bristol didn't take a blind bit of notice. They'd bagged Kenny Everett and weren't about to give him up. A month later, they got another stiff memo from the Contracts Dept.

"You will know of the 'Stop' on the above artist (and you will doubtless be aware that a high level decision was taken before his use as a relief disc jockey for Local Radio in your area). Of course it's not easy for every one of the Corporation's 20,000 odd employees to be aware of such a thing and the only way 'control' can be maintained is if staff conform to rules and regulations whereby booking procedures follow the proper course.

"Without wishing too slavishly to conform to the aforementioned rules and regulations it does seem to me a little odd that for a recording that took place on July 5th and a transmission that took place on July 16th, the Talks Requisition contract was only typed on July 19th and received here on July 21st."

Other stations caught on. Soon Radio Brighton, Radio Merseyside, Radio Nottingham, Radio Solent and Radio Medway were boasting shows hosted by the Wireless Wizard, Cuddly Ken.

Kenny made most of the shows at the new house in Cowford, where he'd had yet another studio installed by an engineer from the old Radio London days, equipped with two big Studer tape recorders he called his 'tanks'.

Everything was a rush job. Lee would act as his runner. As soon as he'd finished a programme she'd scoot the tape down to the Red Star

Office for express delivery to the relevant station. Often they'd be sent off only partially edited. Producers would find themselves transmitting the first half while hacking away at the second half with a razor-blade. At the same time, they had to listen out for words or phrases that might need bleeping. Kenny could rarely be bothered with self-censorship. Takes all the fun out of it. Sometimes whole links would have to be removed and extra records incorporated to fill the gaps.

He used his Radio Merseyside shows to provide answers to the questions his mum had raised in her letters,

"Yes.

"No.

"Not likely.

"And would you like a three-legged Great Dane for Christmas?"

Working for so many stations, and with much of the material recycled and syndicated, Kenny was earning nearly as much from local radio as he would have made working for Radio 1: enough, at least, to carry on the renovations to the house. Lee reckoned he'd have done the radio work for nothing, anyway.

By the middle of 1971, a banned DJ flaunting the rules was the least of the BBC's problems. In June, the *News Of The World* had published the first allegations that led to the Janie Jones payola scandal, a murky story of Radio 1 producers and DJs getting free holidays, prostitutes and orgies in return for plugging records. Janie Jones, a miner's daughter from County Durham who'd won a clog-dancing competition at the age of five and never looked back, wasn't brought to trial until 1973. Fifteen individuals were eventually implicated. For two-and-a-half years the BBC was crippled with pain and embarrassment as new details of the scandal emerged: tales of two-way mirrors, of 'lesbian acts', sex-slaves, whippings and worse.

The court heard how Mr Y, 'a television producer', might have made a 14-year-old girl pregnant and could therefore be blackmailed. Mr X later answered questions about a cheque for £100 he gave to one of the girls but said, in his defence, that he didn't know she was a prostitute. 'I thought she was much too young to be involved in anything like that,' he said in court. Like that makes it better.

Under the circumstances, the BBC big wigs – the ones that weren't too busy looking through two-way mirrors – decided that Kenny's crimes were perhaps not so grave after all.

Kenny wouldn't have understood payola. It's a fair certainty that if he'd been offered so much as a cream bun to plug a record he'd have boasted about it on air the following day. Anyway it seemed stupid for the BBC to continue applying a ban that was so flagrantly being defied – and not just by local radio. The telly, BBC2, wanted Kenny for a new late-night satire show called *Up Sunday*.

To regularise the situation, Ian Trethowan, Managing Director of BBC Network (MDR), agreed to lift the ban with the proviso that, in future, all Kenny's radio shows should be pre-recorded and vetted. On February 8, 1972, Douglas Muggeridge, Controller of Radios 1 and 2, made it official: "Further to your memo of 1st February, and confirming our recent phone conversation, MDR has now agreed that the ban on Kenny Everett can be lifted."

If Kenny, or anyone else, was expecting that this would herald the immediate offer of a plum spot on Radio 1, he was disappointed. It would be 18 months before he'd make any showing on Radio 1 at all. But he was on the telly.

Up Sunday, a satirical 'last look at the week', was first aired on February 6, two days before Kenny's ban had been lifted. Kenny made his first appearance a week later, on the 13th.

It was the last knockings of the satire boom that had started life 10 years earlier with *That Was The Week That Was* and *Private Eye,* and featured many of the usual suspects – John Wells, Willie Rushton, John Fortune, along with poet/critic Clive James, grizzled journalist and campaigner James Cameron and stellar guest appearances from Peter Sellers, Sir John Betjeman, Spike Milligan, Adge Cutler & the Wurzels and others.

It was august company for Kenny. His colleagues bristled with Oxbridge degrees, public school gloss and royal honours, but the weed from St Bede's, whose only qualification was an ABC Cinemas award for skipping, more than held his own. The show ran for two years, and Kenny appeared in 11 of them, providing fluff and filth (John Wells called the show "TV for dirty minded insomniacs") to leaven the stick and the scathe.

Like *Film Night* and *The Old Grey Whistle Test, Up Sunday* was a spin-off from the BBC2 chat and culture show *Late Night Line-Up*. "*Late Night Line-Up* was this developing arts strand on BBC2," says Bob Harris. "It just grew into this fantastic strip of programmes and stars came out of it, like Joan Bakewell and Philip Jenkinson. They would have a cinema review one night, an arts review the next night."

All the *Late Night Line-Up* shows came under the umbrella of the Presentations Department rather than Light Entertainment or Arts and Documentaries and had to crammed into Presentations' tiny studios.

"*Old Grey Whistle Test* was in Presentation B – 4th floor at Television Centre," says Bob. "We shared facilities with News Reading. Weather, I think, was in Pres A. The studio was hardly bigger than my living room. We only had eight microphone points. The whole thing was very creative. And I think the feeling was, you know, let's just let them get on with it."

Up Sunday had the same licence to "get on with it".

To stay topical, the contents and running order were kept fluid. On many occasions, the performers kept fluid, too, most notably at Christmas 1972, when celebrity alcoholic and former *Bonzo Dog* frontman Viv Stanshall emerged from a Christmas hamper bearing a large one, fell over, broke the glass he was carrying, cut himself and sprayed blood all over the studio.

The all-white studio (which made Stanshall's blood so spectacular) and the use of technical marvels of the time like chroma key (sometimes called CSO or green screen – even though *Up Sunday* used blue) give a such a strong hint of the visual style used to great acclaim a few years later in the first *Kenny Everett Video Shows* that the temptation among the *Up Sunday* production team to say "remember where you saw it first" must be unendurable.

Kenny's first foray into national radio after the lifting of the ban was not on his natural home, Radio 1, but on the middle-brow talk channel, Radio 4. This was a weird one. During term time, three or four hours a day of Radio 4's schedule were given over to Schools Radio with shows like *Discovery*, an attempt to make science interesting, *España Es Diferente*, an attempt to make Spanish interesting, and *Human Physiology*, an attempt to make human physiology interesting – more successful inasmuch as it sometimes made its target audience think of words like 'breast'.

During the school holidays the lack of these programmes left a hole in the schedule which had somehow to be filled. Since there's a limit to the number of improving documentaries and phone-ins an audience can take, for the 1972 summer hols a producer named Richard 'Dickie' Gilbert made a revolutionary proposal: to keep the kids entertained and the adults smiling what Britain really needed at 9.35 on a Wednesday morning was half an hour of madcap comedy. "I think you might be onto something," said the powers that be stuffing shag into their briars, and *If It's Wednesday It Must Be…* was shocked into life.

The core cast consisted of the humorist and controversialist Kenneth Robinson, then in his late forties and a Radio 4 regular, playing irritated uncle to Viv Stanshall, the man who bled on *Up Sunday,* and Kenny. It was a mash-up of bits and bobs, some repeated from other projects, some just nicked from elsewhere. Kenny, for instance, imported Rock Salmon (Masked Accountant) and Chris P Bacon from his Radio 1 shows. More thrillingly, he brought – possibly for the first time and almost certainly the last – jingles to Radio 4: the equivalent of bringing a vuvuzela into the British Library.

"What is the station our nation is yelling for more," he sang. "There's no denying the station is Radio 4. Giving out the good work, I could listen for days, serials and concerts and plaaaaaays."

Meanwhile, Stanshall would play selections from his extensive collection of old 78 rpm records, make up stories and generally arse around. It's here that he first told some of the stories that would eventually become the stage show, album and movie *Sir Henry At Rawlinson End.*

The guests were equally bizarre. The dour Scottish performance poet Ivor Cutler, who sang to the accompaniment of a hand-pumped harmonium ("Go and sit upon the grass and I shall come and sit beside you, while we talk I'll hit your head with a nail to make you understand me") was a regular, as was Ron Geesin, the "electro-melodic sound painter", Benny Green, saxophonist and anecdotalist, Jeffrey Bernard, columnist and alcoholic, and DJ Annie Nightingale.[57]

Kenny never flinched from asking the big questions:

"Can I say bum on the BBC?"

"Just a minute, I'll check. Can he say bum on the BBC?"

The question echoes down the corridors of Broadcasting House.

"Can he say bum on the BBC?"

"I'll check"

"Can he say bum on the BBC?"

Finally Kenny gets the OK and launches into a song to the tune of 'When I'm Sixty-Four':

"Bum, de-de-bum, bum bum de-de bum ...
Never be naughty, cuddly Ken
Keep it to yourself
If you want to say a naughty paragraph
It's not worth it just for a laugh
Better be careful, watch what you say
Auntie's not asleep,
Oh no, if you've got something naughty to say
Cover it with a BLEEP."

"I am now in a position," wrote *The Times* radio critic David Wade after hearing the first transmission, "to complete the puzzle posed by the title *If It's Wednesday It Must Be...* The concluding words are: ... Time to do the Shopping, or Hide in a Cupboard, or Shoot Yourself, or in fact Any Old Thing at all so long as it Prevents You Tuning In at 9.35."[58]

A few weeks later though, the same critic saw fit to recant his hasty judgment and wrote: "Mercifully there has been a marked improvement in the tone and content of this programme and I have heard the last two offerings with a relatively steady pulse and normal blood-pressure... *If It's Wednesday...* does all right as an accompaniment to making the beds, clearing the breakfast or doing a spot of weeding, although Kenny Everett's one-man adventures of Rock Salmon will stand rather closer attention."[59]

If It's Wednesday It Must Be... ran for three series – one in the summer hols, one at Christmas and one at Easter.

Rock Salmon was a hero in the Captain Kremmen mould. In one episode his arch-enemy Loongland (that 'malodorous git') and his henchman Legiron have imprisoned Rock and his camp sidekick, Aubrey.

LOONGLAND: Legiron, wrap them in this aluminium baking paper.

ROCK: Curses – foiled again!

LOONGLAND: Strap him down on this table with a circular saw. That should cut him down to size.

SFX: BUZZ SAW

LOONGLAND: What's this writing on the inside of his leg? It says 'Brighton'. What's the meaning of this?

ROCK: Don't you know? Rock is lettered all the way through.

LOONGLAND: Is this some kind of joke?

ROCK: We just did it for a laugh.

LOONGLAND: Well, two can play at that game. Legiron – dismember Salmon's arm.

ROCK: You swine, you wouldn't …

LOONGLAND: We will make the master accountant quite 'armless.

NARRATOR: Has Rock gone to pieces? If he pulls himself together will he be a self made man? How much more of this rubbish can you stand? Try to miss next week's ordeal.

Having got away with saying 'bum' during the summer, for the Christmas edition Kenny gave blasphemy a whirl.

"Hello. Kenny Everett here. Did you know it's actually my birthday on Christmas Day? It really is. December 25, 1944, the front room of our house in Liverpool. I have often been tempted as a result of this to believe that I'm the Second Coming. Last time I thought this, George Harrison came along and tried to tell us *he* was, but I knew he was an imposter when he sang" (blast of George singing *My Sweet Lord*) "'I really want to see you, Lord …'. He wouldn't write that about himself, would he? He wrote it for *me*. Jesus and I are both Capricorns, you know. Not only do we have that in common – we both have a lovely nature and an acute desire to be loved. And a beard."

Kenny's Radio 4 appearances became an audition tape/plea for an end to his exile and the return of his proper job back on his rightful channel Radio 1. Lee was recruited in a supporting role as his co-petitioner and accomplice.

"Why won't the BBC give me my job back? Ever since his cruel demise from the BBC, Cuddly Ken has been living in a rat-infested mansion in the Sussex money belt. Lee?"

"Yes, dear."

"Is there any food in the fridge?"

"No, dear."

"Then pass me another ice cube."

Kenny sings – to the tune of 'The Blue Danube': "No food in the fridge (boo-hoo boo-hoo), no heat in the pipes (boo-hoo boo-hoo), no dough in the bank (boo-hoo boo-hoo), oh golly oh cripes (boo-hoo boo-hoo), my fame is alas (boo-hoo boo-hoo), a thing of the past (boo-hoo boo-hoo), I'm just a poor soul, on the dole, at this merry Christmas time."

"I had the great British Public eating out of my hand," he said. "When I said [squeaky voice] 'Hi folks, this is Cuddly Ken,' the world listened. When I played a record it stayed played… Send money to Squalor Mansions, Rat Alley, Cowfold."

★ ★ ★

Towards the end of 1972, Kenny's marriage wobbled. It was the renovations at Cowfold that did it.

One day a young carpenter called Charlie came to mend the windows. His wife, Sonya, kept horses and gave riding lessons. Lee and Sonya eventually decided to go into business together, breeding and training horses.

Kenny was much given to crushes. A man of a certain kind – usually practical, capable and inappropriately heterosexual – would walk his way and Kenny's heart would leap out of his chest, thumping.

Lee and Sonya were away for long hours leaving Kenny and Charlie alone together. When Charlie took a break from the sash-cords, he and Kenny liked nothing better that to retire to the studio, listen to music and drop some acid. Before long, poor Kenny was in love.

Lee grew suspicious and confronted him. He denied his feelings for Charlie but rows and mistrust flared. Lee took comfort in the arms of an old lover for a while, and Kenny took comfort in pharmaceuticals.

"One morning I woke at 6.00 am to find him missing," says Lee in her autobiography *Kinds Of Loving*[60]. "I rushed round the house but he wasn't there, so I looked outside for his car. At this time we had my Mini, his BMW and also a Land Rover for the horsebox. To my horror and confusion not one of those vehicles were on the premises."

Kenny, in a 'sleeping pill haze', had gone for a drive, slewed into a ditch, walked back for another car with which to pull the first out, slewed that into the ditch too, walked back for the third car with which to pull the first and the second cars out of the ditch and, as that one careened into the ditch, too, began at last to see some sort of pattern emerging.

Lee and Sonya's success with horses tempted them to have a go at proper farming. In February 1973, the five of them, Lee, Kenny, Sonya, Charlie and Sonya and Charlie's new baby, moved to a 60-acre hill farm near the biblically named village of Babel in Carmarthenshire, Wales. It was the full early-seventies back-to-nature self-sufficient Good Life Whole Earth Manual idyll. There were cows to milk, wood to chop, veg to grow, chickens to be raised, fences to be fixed, mud to be crossed, health to be had. According to Lee, Kenny spent a good deal of time drunk or stoned with Charlie.

In April, BBC Radio had another schedule shake-up. It was decided that rather than being transmitted simultaneously on Radios 1 and 2, *Family Favourites* – the 'what's the weather like in Kuala Lumpur, Bill?' forces request programme that Michael Aspel had presented so stoically in the face of Kenny's attempts to corpse him – should henceforth go out on 2 only, thus freeing up two hours of Radio 1 airtime, one of which was given to Kenny.

The continuing insistence that his programmes be pre-recorded and vetted now worked to Kenny's advantage. Rather than face the 200-mile commute from Babel to Broadcasting House, he converted one of the outbuildings into a studio and made his programmes there, just as he had the local radio programmes at Cowfold.

When done, he'd drive the tape down to the station at Swansea and, just as they'd done with the local radio programmes, send it Red Star to Paddington. A BBC minion would pick it up from Paddington and take it to Radio 1, where it would be heard, considered, edited and, when all was well, transmitted. In practice the tape often arrived with minutes to spare and, again as had happened with his local radio shows, split into at least two reels so that the second could be edited while the first was being broadcast.

There was no Crisp in the new programmes but the fiddly bits went rococo. Whereas previously he seemed to be working on the assumption that unless something new happens every 10 seconds the audience, and more importantly he, will lose interest, now the attention span was down to about two seconds.

The one-minute intro he provides for David Bowie's latest release ('Life On Mars') starts with a manic build-up intercut with sitcommy woodwind, then, for no particular reason, Kenny's voice goes slo-mo and deep. He plays the start of the record at half-speed, too, "David Bowie's gone butch," he says in his camp San Francisco voice. As the last notes of the song die away he says, in adland American, "David Bowie, modern genius", then switches to trouble-at-t'-mill Lancashire for "writes all his own stuff", then in a different Lancashire accent that – with characteristically intricate attention to detail – appears to have been recorded on a different track so that the two can slightly overlap "really, ooh?" Then something indistinct, then half a bar of piccolo hornpipe, then something else indistinct, then in posh English, "and more power to his elbow", then a 20 second jingle in at least four part harmony to introduce his "give it a spin" spot... and so it goes on.

Outside the comfort zone of his outhouse studio, the Babel soap opera continued. Charlie's wife found out about Kenny's feelings for Charlie and walked out. Charlie followed her. They made it up but agreed to move out of the farmhouse and into a cottage nearby. Kenny threw himself into hand-milking cows and discovered he had the knack. Like rug-making and tape editing, it became one of his skills.

His return to Radio 1 put him back on the *Top Of The Pops* roster. Between April and October 1973, he presented the programme six times at £65 a show. For the last of these, on October 11, he played up to his new country yokel image, appearing in battered tweed hat and smock-frock, with straw in his hair and a couple of teeth blacked out. At one point he turns to a bemused female audience member and remarks, "I bet you've got a fine set of udders, my dear." Many people in 1973 were still unaware that sexual politics had been invented.

Elton John sang 'Goodbye, Yellow Brick Road', Slade sang 'My Friend Stan', Status Quo sang 'Caroline' and the whole place was awash with tank-tops, baggies and lethal platform shoes.

After the recording, still in his yokel costume, Kenny was interviewed by two charming middle-class teenagers for an insert into a *John Craven's Newsround* precursor called *Search*. The kids seem a great deal more relaxed about the whole thing that Kenny.

"What kind of music do you personally like?" the kids ask.

"The last movement of Mendelssohn's Violin Concerto."

The kids titter.

"No *seriously*," he replies.

"Where do you get your ideas from for your zany effects?"

"Tony Blackburn."

"Do you think *Top Of The Pops* overdo the special effects and don't concentrate on the groups enough?"

"Whichever answer won't get me fired."

It's an odd answer from a man with one foot out of the door. This was to be his last *Top Of The Pops* for some time. His last Radio 1 show for a while had gone out a week and a half earlier.

Six years after the pirates had been shut down there was, once again, another game in town. Commercial radio was back and this time it was perfectly legal.

CHAPTER EIGHT

The Conservative Party manifesto for the 1970 General Election pledged to introduce local commercial radio stations to mirror the success of commercial television. They won a surprise victory. More surprising still, they met their manifesto promises – one of them, anyway.

The Sound Broadcasting Bill was given its first reading in the Commons at the end of 1971. It became law on June 12, 1972. There would be new stations in Birmingham, Manchester and Glasgow, and two in London: one for news, another for 'General Entertainment'. Twenty-one other locations were earmarked for stations in the near future. Contracts were put out to tender, but anybody who was planning to revive the glory days of Big L or Caroline got a slapped wrist. Contractors, it was made clear, "would not be allowed to play pop music all day" but would be expected to provide "a truly public service fostering a greater awareness of local affairs and involvement in the community". Fun-lovers scanned the small print for some reference to chalk up the nose or hanging DJs over the side by their heels but found only more requirements "to present balanced programmes, to cater for all sections of the audience and to retain broadcasters of high quality".

It was not a propitious time for bold, expensive new ventures. By the end of 1973, the economy was going down the toilet, inflation was at 9% and rising, the Arab oil-producers had quadrupled their prices, petrol was rationed and there were strikes by civil servants, dockers, gas workers and firemen.

Eight bids were submitted for the London 'General Entertainment' contract from various consortia involving newspapers, banks, politicians and ex-politicians, sly-faced crooks and Hughie Green, the grinning, winking host of TV's *Double Your Money* and *Opportunity Knocks*. The winning bid came from a company originally called Radio Capital and later Capital Radio, set up by the euphoniously named 23-year-old property magnate David Maule-ffinch and his even more extravagantly-named father-in-law, Barclay Barclay-White, who ran a chain of dental surgeries. They had assembled a team of big hitters including movie moguls Richard Attenborough and Brian Forbes, Beatles producer George Martin, theatrical impresario Peter Saunders and top TV writer and former Secretary General of the Young Communist League, Baron 'Ted' Willis.

Capital could never have been a pirate-style station any more than Radio 1 could. Apart from all the stuff in the contract about "balanced programmes to cater for all sections of the audience" and "a greater awareness of local affairs and involvement in the community", it was also hampered by Kenny's number one bugbear: needle time. At the launch, nine hours a day was all they were going to get. And with no 'house bands' of the kind that Radio 1 had at its launch to fill the hours with ersatz pop, this would mean a lot of talk.

Capital's programmes director, Michael Bukht, believed that radio could be used as a "fulcrum for change" and set about fashioning a truly community based service. The station planned to provide a flat-share service, a job finder, a consumer watchdog, the Capital Helpline, Help a London Child, agony aunts and the Flying Eye – a plane to spot traffic blackspots and broadcast reports right from the cockpit – as well as an interactive soap opera, the plot of which listeners could influence, drama serials and comedy shows. For pirate fans this did not sound promising at all: less Big L, more Radio 4 meets Radio Leicester meets the well-meaning tweedy lady from Social Services.

The new station acquired a home in Euston Tower, then the tallest office building in London, and started wiring up studios. Ads, it was announced, would cost £120 at peak time, but after midnight the price would drop to just £6 for a 30-second slot. Two months before the launch, the sales department was already receiving enquiries from "romantic young men" eager to fork out six quid to serenade their sweethearts.

The search began for "broadcasters of high quality". By June, Capital had signed Dave Cash, velvet-voiced actor Gerald Harper, classical buff Robin Ray, lyricist Tim Rice and Radio 1's Nicky Horne. In September, Aidan Day, who'd just joined as Director of Music, approached Kenny, offering him two two-hour programmes on Saturday and Sunday afternoons, no collars and ties, no <u>very</u> firm production, no Garner Ted Armstrong. Kenny didn't need asking twice.

On September 21 Jo Gurnett, Kenny's agent, informed the BBC that Kenny would not be continuing his Radio 1 programme. He broadcast his last on September 30. The *faux* sentiment of his goodbye to the BBC was a thing of smoke and mirrors. Is he sad to go or delighted to get shot of the lot? Oh, the ambiguities.

KENNY: At this point, ladies and gentlemen, I shall have to say goodbye.
JOLLY MUSIC
KENNY: In fact I've come to the end… because that's all I'm doing for the BBC. It's (SNIFF) been wonderful being with the BBC: all those portals and corridors and typists and… I mean portals and corridors and producers. I'll have to run through my old producers, you know, because I owe them a debt of honour or something and they've looked after me and stopped me from saying (BLEEP) and such stuff like that. Like Angela Bond, who was my first producer for many years. She was great. Old Ange. Hello, Ange, how are you, love? She stopped me from saying (BLEEP) a lot, too. Then there was Teddy Warwick who's produced me right up to this day. Hello, Ted. Him and Derek Chinnery, you see, are the two most powerful producers in the Beeb. When they say something the earth rumbles (ECHO) the heavens darken and before you've got time to skim the gunge off your cocoa, someone's wheeling you off to casualty with fractured nerve-ends. So to those two power maniacs, I'd like to say, 'Thanks for having me, kids' and to all the people in the BBC it's 'Ta-ra'. Boo-hoo. I hate goodbyes, so for now I'll just say (BURP) and hand the wireless waves back to the BBC.
JINGLE: So till we meet again please keep a little smile upon your

face / Remember there's nothing quite as nice as being jolly all over the place / (RALLENTANDO) And any time you think of me, please try and raise a smile, and then / (FOUR PART HARMONY) remember the Wireless Wizard's name was cuddly ...

BIG SYMPHONIC CLIMAX, CUT IN LINE FROM MOVIE, "If this doesn't get 'em nothing will."

JINGLE: (ANGELIC FOUR PART HARMONY, A GREAT AMEN) Ken, Ken, Ken, Ken.

SCHMALTZY VIOLIN UP AND FADE.

The newly named Independent Broadcasting Authority (formerly the Independent Television Authority) slung a bit of wire between the chimneys at Lots Road Power Station in Chelsea, called it a transmitter aerial, and they were off.

At 5 a.m. on the morning of October 16, on 539m medium wave and 95.8 MHz VHF, the London Philharmonic Orchestra with the Royal Choral Society and the herald trumpets of the Welsh Guards conducted by Sir Arthur Bliss broadcast an over-the-top bells-and-whistles arrangement of 'God Save The Queen'. As the last echoes of the rumbling tympani died away, Richard Attenborough, actor, director, producer and Chairman of Capital Radio, announced – no doubt holding back a tear provoked by the magnitude and magnificence of the occasion – "This for the very first time is Capitol Radio". And straight into Simon & Garfunkel's 'Bridge Over Troubled Water'. "I'm on your side," sang Art, "when times get rough and friends just can't be found." When the last chord had died away, David Symonds, very quiet and dignified, back announced the record, then said, "Good morning from myself David Symonds, the time is nine minutes past five on the first day of Capital Radio." He then thanks getting on for everybody in the world, and pushes up a fader on Neil Diamond's 'Chelsea Morning'. After Neil's finished, David spends a few seconds thanking a few people he might have missed and then it's the Big One – adverts. And who's doing the voice-over on the second of those ads, for Nevada watches, the second ad ever to be legally transmitted on British radio? Of course it is.

Congratulatory telegrams poured in, some of them from celebrities: the Beatles bothered, and so, if reports are to be believed, did Frank Sinatra.

There were boobs and goofs. On the evening show, Nicky Horne had laryngitis. Monty Modlyn got hiccups in the middle of an interview. Dave Cash was puzzled by a phone call from somebody claiming to be Kenny Everett. Cash knew for a fact that Kenny was in Wales and doubted whether the bit of wire at Lots Road could carry Capital's signal that far.

Kenny in fact, stayed in Wales most of the time, Red Starring his painstakingly constructed programmes to Capital usually using the now familiar Just-In-Time system.

Unlike Radio 1, Capital broadcast in stereo – "Capital sounds, go round and round." While most programme-makers barely noticed this, and it didn't make a blind bit of difference to listeners still relying on the Decca Debonaires they'd had since 1959, to Kenny the sound-sculptor stereo added a vital new dimension to his art. He delighted in providing little gifts for fellow-audiophiles who'd spent time and money setting up some proper equipment. Jingles and sound effects would zoom around the room. "And this week's show," he would be sure to mention, "is in stag-g-g-g-g-e-r-r-r-ring ster-r-r-r-reo" with both words bouncing between the speakers, "so be sure to listen with *both ears*."

It all took more time. Often, the sun would be rising by the time he emerged from his outhouse.

"My wife is a wireless widow," he told the *Daily Mail*,[61] in a profile that went on: "Apart from trips to London for the live shows and the odd foray into nearby Llandovery for supplies, Everett is self sufficient. Power comes from his own generator and water from his own spring. A farm manager and Lee run the place while he tapes the programme… Everett has always tried to keep his ties with the pop world to a minimum 'I've never got involved in the scene. It's a phoney world. I'm happy on the sidelines.'"

The attractions of log fires and spring water were beginning to wane… "To hell with all that," he told the *Mail*. "I'm 29 and need me comforts." Kenny's passion for Charlie was on the wane, too. According to Lee, a distant fascination lingered, but the glorious gloss of new love had largely drowned in the mud.

By the winter of 1973, conditions in London weren't much less austere than they were on the farm. Fuel supplies were running low. The Arab oil-producing nations punished America and its friends for supporting Israel by refusing to sell them oil. Meanwhile, British miners had decided their importance to the economy should be recognised in their remuneration package and, when this was refused, imposed an overtime ban. The power stations were down to reserve stocks and the government did what it could to conserve electricity. It rationed supplies.

It was a cruel Christmas. Stores were allowed to switch on their lights for just five days a week. The rest of the time shoppers had to rummage for gifts by gas or candlelight. The giant Christmas Tree in Trafalgar Square, an annual thank you from the people of Norway for British support in World War II, usually a blindingly glorious blaze throughout the season, was lit for just three days over the holiday, and then only by special intervention by the Environment Minister who was afraid of being dubbed an absolute Scrooge.

The oil crisis had affected even the LPs in people's stockings. To conserve vinyl – an oil-based product – they'd got thinner. The substantial slab of the pre-1973 LP had given way to a scrap of nothing, something halfway to a flexi-disk. The keen-eared could hear the difference.

Capital's backers shared the general gloom. It had cost a million and a half to launch the station and it would need a million a year to keep it up and running. Although it claimed a million listeners in its first couple of months, other surveys suggested much smaller figures. One claimed it was less popular than Radio 3, the BBC's serious music channel. The possibility that punters might prefer Hindemith's 'Fünf Stücke für Streichorchester' to 'Chelsea Morning' and a flat-share service brought complaints from advertisers. £120 for a prime-time 30-second slot, they reckoned, was a rip-off.

There were grumbles about the channel's music policy, too.

"Sir," wrote a gentleman from RAF West Ruislip to *The Times*. "After listening to the music on Capital Radio during its first week, may I prayerfully request a return to test transmission recordings."

Top 40 fans complained that a lot of Capital's output was album tracks, oldies and 'less mainstream artistes'. Others complained that it was too 'middle-of-the-road'. Others still that it was 'too American'.

Even the DJs were confused. At the launch party, DJ Tony Myatt explained to a passing journalist that Capital operated a playlist system based, at any given time, on 73 records. Why 73? "I think it's because it's 1973," said Tony, and went on to describe the system of colour coding under which they were categorised: "Red is lively, blue is medium tempo, green is lush and white is... er... more green than blue."[62] There's a chance that drink may have been taken.

"Although one can say it now, one couldn't at the time," says Sir Richard Attenborough. "There were some weeks when the viability of the whole operation was in question and we might have had to close down. We almost didn't make ends meet."

Michael Bukht, Capital's Programme Controller, cast around for ways to boost the station's figures. He was an extraordinary man, admired by (ever so nearly) all his staff. A devout Muslim, he possessed a fierce temper and is said to have once karate chopped his way through a locked office door. Kenny described him as "the nearest thing to King Kong I've seen".

The Mighty Kong declared war on Radio 1 and decided that, rather than nibbling at the ramparts he would take its most strongly held defence, its very citadel, by storm. He set his sights on the *Breakfast Show*. (DJ's do actually think in these terms, by the way. It's not just whimsical hyperbole.)

Noel Edmonds was the *Breakfast Show*'s new incumbent on Radio 1. He'd been given his first break when he took over Kenny's show after Kenny had been given the boot and had since gone from strength to strength, eventually stealing even Tony Blackburn's glory. With his Wellie Stickers, his Silly Phone Calls and his Flynn The Milkman he was commanding formidable ratings.

Bukht knew that in Kenny he had an able and willing champion who'd acquit himself gallantly in any contest with Edmunds. But even better, he realised he had a second weapon in his arsenal which, combined with Kenny, could, like hydrogen and uranium, visit mass destruction on Edmonds' Wellie Stickers, his Silly Phone Calls and his Flynn The Milkman.

The order went out: "Bring me Kenny *and Cash*."

Dave Cash, as well as doing his own show, had been a frequent visitor to Kenny's Capital show. On November 24, the two of them had interviewed Paul and Linda McCartney while the top celebrity couple were out and about publicising their new *Wings* album, *Band On The Run*.

It was not the most auspicious visit to Capital. On their way into Euston Tower, Paul had been served with a writ – one of the many flying around between various ex-Beatles, the accountant Allen Klein and Apple at the time. He was being sued for £20m. It's the kind of setback that can cast a pall over a chatty interview, but Kenny and Dave managed, just, to keep everything relatively cheerful. The old magic, it appeared, was still there.

Their first proper outing since the *Galaxy* came on Kenny's birthday. *The Kenny And Cash Christmas Special Breakfast Show* did not, it must be said, prompt cheers in the House of Commons and neither did it cause the OPEC countries smilingly to relent, but to the millions (all right thousands) (all right hundreds) (let's go back to thousands) who fondly remembered the good old days of Big L, it brought a moment or two of cheer to that cheerless Christmas. Kenny and Cash were back at the microphone in London at least, Slade was at number one – "It's Christmaaaaaaas" – and Wizzard, at number four, sang "I Wish It Could Be Christmas Every Day".

In the New Year, Roy Wood's wish came true. The Capital breakfast slot, from 6.30 to 9 every weekday morning, was filled by *The Kenny And Cash Show*.

It was not a programme that could be recorded in a Welsh shed. Lee found a manager to milk the cows and endure the mud and she and Kenny upped sticks for the smoke. Capital rented them a London flat – slightly too near a railway line, so Lee rented another on Charles Lane in St John's Wood, a five minute walk from Paul McCartney's house in Cavendish Avenue, 10 minutes from Abbey Road Studios, just the other side of Regents Park from Euston Tower.

Kenny and Dave had both come a long way since *MV Galaxy*. They were pros. They had developed their own distinctive styles. Techniques they had pretty much invented were now commonplace. Old hat even. Jokes that had seemed so funny in the floating madhouse, now barely raised a smile. You had to be there.

Clive Warner, who now lives in Mexico, was, back then, a sound engineer working at Capital. "I was present during quite a lot of these *Kenny And Cash* shows," he says. "Usually it would be the end of a very long night running MCR (Master Control Room) and doing any odd jobs needed by the presenters, like fixing a mike or patching the reverb chamber into a desk.

"At first Kenny and Dave did a reprise of what they'd done on London, *The Kenny And Cash Breakfast Show*. It went down great."

But soon a disparity became apparent.

"Kenny was an inventive genius and continually churned out new and exciting gimmicks to use on his show, whereas Dave was more of the 'nice guy with a good voice' kind of presenter.

"Kenny was very much 'hands on' and lugged his stack of carts into the tiny DJ studio, where he'd cram a selection into the multiple-slot cart machines. He'd have nine carts loaded and ready to go. There'd maybe be a cart with applause, another with a scream, another with some weird stuff from *Monty Python's Flying Circus*, whatever caught his ear. Plus jingles he'd create himself. Kenny was versatile.

"So there they were sitting side by side in the tiny studio as the clock came onto the hour, and I ran the adverts, linked to the news presenter, out to the ads again, played the intro to *The Kenny And Cash Show*, and Kenny came out of the starting gate like someone had lit gunpowder under his arse, leaving Dave Cash wondering how the show had already been going for a while without him. Kenny basically would be at 500 mph while Dave was still obeying the 30 limit."

Even after the show was over, Kenny wouldn't ease off the throttle.

"Our open plan production office – called the Playpen – was where Ev ran wild on Fridays," says DJ Mike Smith[63]. "If you hadn't been soaked by Ev doing a run-by with the paint-sprayer, you simply were not part of the fun."

There were frequent attempts to reignite the old Kenny and Cash fire. Harry Nilsson was brought in as a guest, but sadly kept silent throughout the show, until right at the end when he said goodbye. For some pootling competition, they offered a Ferrari as first prize, neglecting to mention that it was a Dinky Toy. As an April Fool's Day wheeze, they pretended they were back on the *Galaxy*. Kenny simulated the noise of the tender bashing against the ship coming aside bringing them their weekly supplies of fish fingers and they played only records of that era. It was one of their most successful shows, and one of their last.

"Even as jaded as I was, as the weeks went by I began to see changes in Dave Cash," says Clive Warner. "Bags developed under his eyes. He seemed to lack concentration. Finally, the inevitable happened and Kenny arrived one morning by himself to run the show single handed, and it became the *Kenny Everett Breakfast Show*."

The partnership had lasted less than six months and though its ratings were more than respectable, it had failed quite to put the anticipated ginger up the arse of Capital's fortunes. Rumours had it that Richard Attenborough was selling the paintings off his walls to pay the wages bill. Another said that letters laying off employees had already been typed, and were waiting to be dispatched at a moment's notice. Eventually they were. "Job Axe Falls At Capital", said the headline. Twenty-eight people, including the entire newsroom staff, were made redundant.

Kenny was living in a wireless bubble. Every weekday morning he was up at 5 a.m., in the car, round the park to Euston Tower, on air at 6.30. He'd arrive back home, often with his producer Annie Challis in tow, at around seven and have breakfast. Some days he'd vanish into his home studio after breakfast and not emerge until dinner time. Otherwise there might be lunch with pals or a record plugger. With the labels frighteningly aware that their product was only one of 60 or 70 releases being launched that week into an unforgiving economic climate, these tended to be elaborate, boozy affairs drifting on to three or four in the afternoon. In the evening people would drop by for drinks. Kenny aimed for an early night, but found it easier to pour another drink than it was to excuse himself. Lee and the guests would end up carrying him off to bed. By this time, husband and wife were sleeping in separate rooms. Most nights he'd open his eyes and mouth long enough to drop a couple of Mandies. No harm in that. In the seventies Mandrax was a commonly prescribed sleeping pill that guaranteed quality sleep and lovely dreams. Only later was it discovered to be a drug which, if taken in combination with alcohol and/or cannabis, could be lethal.

Money flew out of their account slightly faster than it came in. Although the Welsh adventure and Kenny's feelings for Charlie were now history, the great British countryside still enticed. Without having sold the Welsh farm, he and Lee negotiated terrifying bridging loans and shelled out on a former pub, the Old Red Lion, once home of the actor Hugh Griffiths, in Cherington near Stratford-Upon-Avon and embarked on yet another of their fresh starts.

In September 1974, the *Sunday Mirror* ran a profile: "He carries his jingles – those jolly little snatches of music and chat between records – in something that looks like a businessman's briefcase. The cassettes of tape bear labels saying things like Hi HO, Betty Poos, Parrotty 'Ello and Cadunk."

It's impossible to know whether Kenny, by now, had just got used to feeding the press the clichés they wanted to hear, or whether the journalists made them up off their own bats.

"Like most funny men he is aware of the black side of life. 'I think a lot of people go into showbiz because they have been deprived of love early in their lives. In a way, audiences are a substitute. To some extent it's the same with me. My parents had to struggle to make ends meet – my father drove a tugboat – they were too busy with the necessities. Showbiz really is love between strangers. We disc jockeys try to make people go about their daily business in a happier mood.'"

It's a graceless way to talk about adoring parents but at least, as the piece goes on to explain, he's no longer wandering around with glamorous arm candy, claiming to be a wirier, jauntier version of Hugh Hefner, or Warren Beatty: "Kenny, although he is too much of a comic to be a sex symbol, still occasionally gets confronted by girls who would Do Anything For Him. He turns their advances away gently, not wanting to hurt them. 'I tell them that I'm married and an ex-Catholic and have to go home and say some Hail Marys.'"[64]

Hopeless love had once again come into Kenny's life. He had fallen for another unsuitably heterosexual man, this time one of the sound engineers at Capital (not, it must be said to avoid confusion, Clive Warren). As usual he poured out his heart to Lee.

Lee found solace in spiritualism. She became a regular at a spiritualist church that met every Sunday in a hired hall in Stratford-Upon-Avon and spent more and more time at Cherington. Kenny had to stay in London. His only solace was work.

"It became – for me at any rate – practically impossible to keep up with him," says Clive Warren. "What I didn't realise for a while was that hardly anyone would have been able to keep up, let alone the poor bloody engineer who had just been up all night making sure the station didn't fall off the air. One day one of the other jocks took me to one side and murmured to me that Kenny used to take speed before coming in to do his show, and then after it drive back home and drop a load of downers to counteract the speed and allow him to sleep. Before he left the station, Kenny usually went into the production studio with an armful of blank carts and worked like a maniac for an hour, then left with an armful of jingles and special carts to use in future shows."

By the May of 1975 the work schedule, the increasing estrangement from Lee, the uppers and the downers brought depression. He spoke often of suicide. Lee tells of an occasion when a plumber came round to fix a tap. "Do you like life?" Kenny asked him. The tap dripped for ages.

His hopeless love for the sound engineer turned into an obsession. Looking back, in 1986, he told the *Daily Mirror*[65]. "There came a time when I could control what I felt no longer. We were in a car together and I got familiar with him. It was dreadful. Instead of him saying: 'Sorry, I'm straight. And much as I like you I couldn't consider doing sexual things with you – or something kind like that – he panicked.'" The technician screamed at Kenny, telling him it was 'heathen and disgusting'. "I was left feeling dreadful... I was so upset I just didn't want to go on living."

Kenny continues the story in his autobiography.[66] "One night I took my usual couple of pills and, as they began to take effect and turn my brain into blancmange, it suddenly seemed like a good idea to take another one... then another and then another. After the first three, the reasons for staying alive seemed to get blurred..."

In his befuddled state, Kenny phoned Aidan Day, his boss and his friend at Capital, to say his final goodbye. Aidan called an ambulance. Kenny was rushed to the Royal Free Hospital in Hampstead. His stomach was pumped. His life was saved.

On Radio 4's *Desert Island Discs,* in 1993, he spoke of the incident to Sue Lawley.

"I didn't know how to approach people. I'd led quite a solitary life up to then. I mean the last thing you do when you fancy someone is go up to them and say, 'I really love you. Shall we get off together?' Because you tend to get a bunch of fives or a definite no and I got a definite no."

"But also presumably," said Sue Lawley, "it was upsetting because it had come at the end of 12 years or more in which time you'd been married and you perhaps were pretending you weren't homosexual – I keep saying homosexual because you don't like the word 'gay'."

"Gay to me means happy and jolly...."

Aidan phoned Lee to tell her what had happened. She came up the following day, and, with Kenny's agent Jo Gurnett, swooped down on the hospital and bustled Kenny out and back to the flat in Charles Lane.

The press laid siege. Reporters banged on the door and leaned on the bell until Jo Gurnett came out with a prepared statement: "It's ridiculous to say there are any problems between Kenny and Lee. They're a deliriously happy couple."

Lee told the *Daily Mail* that Kenny had been working hard, hadn't had a holiday for some time, got confused and mistakenly exceeded the stated dose with his prescribed sleeping pills.

"He does sometimes get depressed, but it's nonsense to say that he tried to kill himself or that what he did was a cry for help. He just did something daft and now he's very, very sorry."

Michael Bukht, at Capital repeated pretty much the same story.

To this day, Jo Gurnett maintains that it was all a mistake: "I totally refute that he tried to kill himself. He was having problems sleeping and just took too many pills. It really was just an accident as far as I'm concerned."

Lee took Kenny down to Cherington to convalesce. Richard Attenborough, Capital Chairman, sent him a loving letter telling him to take as much time as he needed to get better and not to come back until he was ready.

⋆ ⋆ ⋆

Down in the Cotswolds, Lee asked her Spiritualist Church for guidance. How could she help her husband? She was told a miracle would come in the shape of a book.

The next day, according to Lee's *Celebrity Regressions*[67], she went shopping and popped into the chemists to pick up Kenny's prescription for sleeping pills. On the counter she noticed a booklet with the title *Sleeping But Not Sleeping*. She bought it and went home, but had immediately to rush out again to attend to a wounded horse. While she was gone, Kenny found the book, read it and experienced some sort of epiphany. When Lee got back he sat her down and read the whole booklet to her, aloud, cover to cover.

Over the course of a difficult three months, he weaned himself off sleeping pills. His physical and mental health improved. So, for a while, did his relationship with Lee. They went off to Jamaica for a second honeymoon and even flirted with the idea of adopting a child.

Lee, in the face of Kenny's occasional ridicule, began to take more seriously her calling as a clairvoyant. She discovered, during a course of regression, that she and Kenny had known each other in past lives – in fact in two previous incarnations she had been Kenny's mother.

It all makes Kenny's occasional claims to have lacked maternal love in his life a bit rich. He had no shortage of mothers all eager to cherish and adore. Apart from his loving real mum, he'd had Lee fulfilling the role twice before and now she was up for a third crack at it: and, as if that wasn't enough Angela Bond at the BBC acted as a surrogate mother, as did Annie Challis at Capital, not to mention his agent, Jo Gurnett: "I always thought of him as my surrogate son," she says. "I treated him as such and cared for him always."

Spoiled for choice.

When he went back to Capital, Kenny gave up the breakfast show and resumed his two comparatively cushy weekend slots. Never quite content unless he was making radio, he also started packaging programmes in his home studio for Radio Victory, another of the new commercial stations, serving the Portsmouth and Southampton area. And he invented a brand new character.

On the *MV Galaxy,* listening to KLIF tapes with Dave Cash, Kenny had found that one line in particular from *The Charlie And Harrigan Breakfast Show* had stayed with him: "This programme is brought to you by the Kremmen Snuff Company who invite you to stick their business up your nose."

There were other influences, too.

When on Radio 4's *Desert Island Discs* he was, like all castaways, invited to choose, along with his eight gramophone records and one luxury item, a book other than *The Bible* and *The Complete Works of Shakespeare,* he went for an *Eagle* annual.

Dan Dare ennobled the front page of the *Eagle* comic every week. Together with his lovable sidekick Digby, Dan saved the world on a regular basis from the evil Mekon, green-faced, dome-headed ruler of the Treens, an alien race that lived on Venus. In the early fifties, Dan, played by Noel Johnson, had made radio appearances on Radio Luxembourg's *Dan Dare Pilot Of The Future* ("this programme is brought to you by the makers of Horlicks, The Food Drink Of The Night").

Kremmen Of The Star Corps, the World's Most Fabulous Man, was essentially Kenny's *alter ego,* the person he'd pretended to be while rushing around the playground at St Edmunds and who he'd dreamed of being while lying in bed at Hereford Road. At the same time he was Kenny's ideal boyfriend – his taste always ran to muscle-bound he-men.

Everything he wanted to be but could never be; everything he wanted to have but (or so he thought at the time) could never have. That was Kremmen.

The CV went:

Name: Captain Elvis Brandenburg Kremmen

Height: 6 foot 10

IQ: 498

Distinguishing features: Muscles of steel, legs like a gazelle, thighs like tugboats, X-Ray eyes, bionic blood, Saviour of the Universe.

Kremmen shared a birthday – December 25 – with Kenny, but was six years younger. Both were born in Liverpool.

Kenny had gone for a short while to St Peter Claver Junior Missionary School. Kremmen graduated from the Space Academy.

Kremmen's constant companion was the world's most voluptuous woman, Carla. Kenny's increasingly estranged wife seemed to find more comfort in the spirit world than with her husband.

The two-minute episodes of Kremmen that Kenny put together for Capital, though they delved into the usual stuff of sci-fi – alien wars, cloning, giant killer vegetables – were never, thank God, hampered by anything as pedantic as a real plot. For the most part the jokes could have come from mid-priced Christmas crackers (Sainsbury's, say, rather than Poundland):

"By the way, Captain," says Carla, "I just got a letter from my sister, you know the one in the circus with the trampoline act. She just gave birth to a bouncing baby boy."

Or: "Only yesterday a giant orange was about to attack the city of Chicago." "What happened?" "Fortunately it stopped just outside." "Why?" "It ran out of juice."

There were comedy names: Annie Mation, Arthur Itis, Minnie Scule, Molly Cule, Phyllis Stein and, everybody's favourite, Willy Heckerslike.

There were occasional glances towards the Kenneth Williams camp: "Kremmen," says the Commissioner, "I was looking at your file the other day…"

"Oh, you found it," says Kremmen. "Thank heavens, my nails are in a terrible state."

Or: "Hey, Doc," says Kremmen, "d'you wanna drag yourself up on deck?"

"Well, if it's all the same to you," says Dr Gitfinger, "I'll dress casual."

Or: "She smiled one of her smiles, tossed me a wink, cocked me a snook and shot me a glance. Having been shot, tossed and cocked, I grabbed my tranquilliser ray. (Fizz.) Ah, that's better."

There were extended sound effects. The take-off of a defective rocket, for instance, would be a little symphony of boings, booms, burps and blasters. And there was a constant bed of background music – carefully chosen fragments of Tchaikovsky, Elgar, Prokofiev, Stravinsky and Holst to match the mood and underscore the excitement.

Kenny, of course, played all the characters himself – with occasional help from DJ Tommy 'The Nightfly' Vance to provide deep-throat intros and outtros. More remarkably still, he produced the epics, singlehandedly, in his little home studio.

He shared details of his latest toys with readers of *The Capital Radio 194 Fun Book*.[68] "'I've got an instant phasing machine which phases my voice and makes it go all psychedelic. And then there's this twiddly knob called a varispeed control, that speeds my voice up or slows it down depending on which way I twiddle it.' Then, of course, there's the echo chamber. 'A very dangerous piece of equipment, that,' said Kenny. 'Many a good DJ has got lost in an echo chamber by turning it up too much. There's a chance that you might never come out…'"

He talks about some of his special Kremmen sound effects.

"There's that blood-curdling scream that is featured so often. 'That was easy,' said Kenny, 'I just stuffed my wife in the oven!'"

An even louder scream…

"'Another easy one. I just took the wife out of the oven and stuffed her up the mains!'"

Capital recognised a winner when they saw one and was treating listeners to four doses of Kremmen every day. Faced with having to churn out so much material, Kenny began looking for shortcuts. In one episode, Kremmen and the Commissioner walk from office to launch pad. There follows a good 15 or 20 seconds of echoey footsteps – a sixth of the two-minute show.

Finally, the Commissioner says, "You're very quiet Kremmen."

"Just trying to pad out the series," says Kremmen.

Kicking the sleeping pills turned out to be less of a life-changing epiphany than a temporary fad. Before long Kenny had a new crush on a new unsuitable man and tortured himself by inviting the new love, along with the new love's girlfriend, to Cherington just before Christmas. Not surprisingly, Lee was offhand with them. They left early. It was not a Merry Christmas.

He was also cultivating an expensive cocaine habit. "I got more and more interested in the drug and in partying," he said in his autobiography[69], "and less and less concerned about my work. I'd often snort a lot of coke, then go dancing and partying until the small hours." As his mother – or one of his surrogate mothers – might have said, "We know who to blame for *that* sort of behaviour don't we." Kenny had a new friend, you see, and he was a bad influence.

In 1974, when he was still doing the breakfast show, one of Kenny's guests had been Freddie Mercury, lead singer with the then relatively unknown band, Queen. The two hit it off. They had much in common. Both had a taste for the flamboyant. They shared a nerd's fascination with the process of recording and multi-tracking. They had a similar sense of humour, an uncanny sense of pitch, and could match funny voices, voice for voice. They both had religious upbringings, Kenny's Catholic, Freddie's Zoroastrian. And they were both living with women, even though for them 'the shape and the lumps and the softness' had never had the appeal it did for many other men.

Freddie remained devoted to his girlfriend, Mary Austin, until the day of his death and indeed left the bulk of his fortune to her in his will, but around the time he first got to know Kenny, he'd begun an affair with a male American record exec. He and Kenny later shared a lover, but never as far as anybody knows became lovers themselves – surprising perhaps, given that Freddie fitted Kenny's ideal of the muscle-bound, dark, moustachioed, Burt Reynolds-lookalike.

"I never thought Freddie and Kenny were lovers," says Paul Gambaccini. "Had they been, I would have thought that everyone in our circles would have known. The reason I never entertained the thought they were is because their sexual personae were too similar. Of course, that means nothing in terms of a one-nighter amongst two curious persons, but the idea just didn't gain traction in my head. To be blunt they were just silly together."[70]

Freddie had fun teasing interviewees who asked him about his sexuality. "Let's put it this way…" he'd say before launching into some long and cryptic generalisation. Maybe this encouraged Kenny to be a little – a very little – more forthcoming.

"I used to like fellas," he told the *Daily Express* in 1975. "I never considered women because I was not weaned on them. My world was taken up with chaps. There were a few men I got involved with. I think if I hadn't met Lee I would have developed that into an affair. Before I met Lee I never thought about women."

He talks about there being something all-male and cloistered about his upbringing, citing his time at Stillington and even on the pirate ships.

"Women are so busy making themselves attractive and vamping all over the place. They don't concentrate on being interesting or funny in a non-beautiful way. I'm mostly to be found with the guys because I find their company more entertaining."

Then he adds seriously, "If there's a sentence in this that will help someone along, I will be happy."[71]

And if these cack-handed, sexist remarks can be considered an attempt to be more honest about his sexuality, then Kenny should perhaps be applauded for taking the first tentative step on the road that leads to coming out. Otherwise feel free to sit on your hands.

A year or so after their first meeting, Freddie gave Kenny an advance copy of a track from their new album *A Night At The Opera,* mentioning that there'd been talk about releasing it as a single, but at 5'55", the record company feared it was too long to get airplay. Queen's manager

John Reid had suggested they shorten it. The song, after all, had different sections with different feels – ballad, hard rock, operatic. It would be no problem to get in there with a razor blade and pull a section or two out.

Kenny was inclined to agree with the record company. Long singles were never popular on radio. He changed his mind the first time he heard it. He loved it. He loved the mass multi-tracking, the pomp, the outrageous theatricality, Roy Thomas Baker's masterpiece production, the intricate engineering, the work and care that had been lavished on this little peep into an overwrought imagination.

The following day he played snatches of the track on his show, teasing the listeners over and over again, "Oops, my finger must have slipped."

Calls began to come in demanding to hear the full song. Over the next two days he played it, in its entirety, 14 times. 'Diddy' David Hamilton introduced it to a national audience as a *Hot Shot* on his Radio 1 show. Philip Drew, who ran the RKO stations in New York, brought it to the ears of America.

In the UK, 'Bohemian Rhapsody' went to number one and stayed there for nine weeks. At the time of writing, it is the third highest selling British single ever. On a Channel 4 TV show, it was voted best number one of all time.

'Bohemian Rhapsody' was one of the very few occasions that Kenny influenced – or even bothered with – the nation's musical taste.

Bob Harris, though his admiration for Kenny's wit, talent, innovation and production skills is absolute, agrees with most people that the actual music didn't mean much to him, not pop music anyway. "I don't think he had any sense of this being a good record or that being a bad record. He would just play stuff. He didn't have a really bad music filter. He would almost celebrate awful records, because they were as awful as they were."

In January 1977 Kenny began a strand that did exactly that. *The World's Worst Record Show* dredged through the mud at the bottom of pop's sparkling pool and subjected the toxic detritus to public scrutiny and a vote to find which song caused most pain. The winner was Jimmy Cross' 'I Want My Baby Back', a death song – written as a parody of The Shangri-Las' 'Leader Of The Pack' and Ricky Valance's 'Tell Laura I Love Her' – in which the grieving singer digs up his beloved's coffin, crawls in and sings the last chorus with the lid closed. Just because it's a parody, as Kenny's perceptive audience spotted, doesn't mean it can't still be terrible.

The application of Capt. James T. Kirk's weighty *Star Trek* inflections to Lennon and McCartney's gossamer whimsy made William Shatner's cover of 'Lucy In The Sky With Diamonds' another obvious contender, as was Eamonn Andrews' 1956 early experiment with rap, 'The Shifting, Whispering Sands'.

British singer and actor Jess Conrad earned the distinction of having three separate entries in the Top 30 – more than any other artist. One of them was 'This Pullover', a song which began life as 'Il Pullover', an Italian hit for heartthrob Gianni Meccia. To an Italian ear, the English word 'pullover' no doubt has a certain ring to it, a certain exotic chic lost on a British audience, especially when the word is featured in the couplet, "This pullover that you gave to me / I am wearing and wear it constantly." The shortcomings of the lyric aren't helped, either, by the vocal stylings of Jess Conrad, whose relationship with accurate pitch was never more than fleeting.

Jess loved the attention. As he told Spencer Leigh and John Firminger in the excellent *Halfway To Paradise,*[72] "Oh, it was wonderful. Kenny put it on a best-selling album, *The World's Worst Record Show*, which was on Yuk! Records and I had a hit all over again. The LP went into the charts and with all the publicity I got work and built my swimming pool as a result. It's done tremendously well for me in cabaret. In fact they won't let me off stage until I do 'This Pullover'. I don't mind at all. It's better to be regarded as the World's Worst Singer than not be noticed at all."

Yuk! (actually K-Tel records, rebadged for the occasion) released three *World's Worst Records* albums.

By the time the third one came out, Kenny had gone mega.

CHAPTER NINE

In 1978 Thames Television was on a roll. *The Sweeney, George And Mildred, The Benny Hill Show, This Is Your Life* were regularly doing 15–20 million viewers. The company had already poached Sooty from the BBC and was in negotiations to steal Morecambe & Wise. Its main studios on the banks of the Thames in leafy Teddington had a country club atmosphere with restaurants, bars, balcony overlooking the river and ample parking at rear. It was an infinitely more agreeable workplace than London Weekend's high-rise on the South Bank or the BBC's Ministry of Truth in Shepherd's Bush.

Jeremy Isaacs, the Director of Programmes, the man responsible for *The World At War* – the finest documentary series ever known – was a benign and inspiring presence, who understood programmes and programme makers. Indeed, give or take the odd dispute with the unions about the shop-floor's share of the company's considerable profits, everything was rosy down Teddington way.

One day Thames' Head of Light Entertainment, Philip Jones, eager to lasso the youth demographic, asked his 18-year-old son, "Who isn't on television who should be?" The reply was immediate, "Kenny Everett".

Kenny had done TV: *Nice Time* for Granada, three series for LWT and *Up Sunday* for the BBC. There had been other bits and bobs, too. Since

1975 he'd been working on *Celebrity Squares,* "the big box game of stars and cars" based on noughts and crosses and about as interesting. The show was hosted by Bob Monkhouse. Kenny was off-screen, doing the voice-over: "One of these celebrities is sitting in the secret square," he'd say, "but which celebrity is it? Is it Magnus Pike, Willy Rushton, Arthur Mullard, John Inman…" there were nine celebrities in all. The money was OK, but it was a dull, thankless job. Rumour has it that he whiled away the hours in his little voice-over booth playing Scrabble with his agent. He was often reported in the press proudly announcing that he'd never seen the show.

And as he'd discovered filming stunts and inserts for *Nice Time,* when telly wasn't boring it was a faff: hours in make-up and wardrobe, hours waiting for everybody else to get ready, then a cloud comes over the sun, or it rains, or there's a hair in the gate, or some passing kids stand in the back of shot flicking Vs. Then they make you do it twice, three times, 12 times because somebody didn't hit their mark or an aeroplane flew by. How much more satisfying it is to sit in your own studio, working at your own pace, and coming out with a finished programme? And now Thames TV was bothering him with promises of unimagined stardom.

"I told my agent to ask for a ridiculous amount of money so they would go away and forget it. But they said 'all right'."[73]

Philip Jones approached David Mallet, a director who'd been turning the comedy treadmill for nearly 10 years churning out sitcoms and comedy specials mostly for Yorkshire Television. But he had a heroic sense of adventure. He was up for anything.

David and Kenny had lunch and went for a walk. They talked about all the things you wished you could see on TV but never did. David sketched out a few notions, ideas for putting Kenny's radio show on TV in such a way as to retain the speed, energy, intimacy, spontaneity and technical wizardry. Digital video magic – usually known as Quantel effects, after the name of the company mostly responsible for developing them – was still in its infancy but already had the power to squash, spin, squelch, multiply and go Hall-Of-Mirrors-On-Acid. David talked of the opportunities the effects might provide. Kenny, the gizmo nerd, was intrigued.

Never has a marriage been more heaven-made. David went on to become the world's most sought-after maker of pop videos, working with Queen, Bowie, the Rolling Stones, Tina Turner, U2, Elton John and everybody else. If you want to know which of their videos in particular he was responsible for, the answer is always 'the best ones'.

Like Yul Brynner in *The Magnificent Seven,* Mallet began to assemble his team.

Barry Cryer is a scriptwriter, performer and rock god whose 1957 cover of Sheb Wooley's 'Purple People Eater' made number one in Finland. Since shortly after the Third Crusade, Barry had been providing top quality comic material for everybody from Jack Benny to Tommy Cooper and David Frost to Les Dawson. The Radio 1 producer Angela Bond had introduced him to Kenny a few years earlier with the idea of the two of them working together on a radio series. The series never happened but he and Kenny had kept in touch.

"I got the call to come in and talk about this new show for Ev with David Mallet, who I'd worked with on a show called *Joker's Wild* [a Yorkshire TV comedy panel game that Barry had hosted]. We sat round talking and we were going to do a segment of this show that was a miniature game show or something and David looked at me and said this is Ray Cameron stuff, isn't it?"

Cameron, a Canadian stand-up and writer, now probably best known as the father of comedian Michael McIntyre, had co-devised *Joker's Wild.* He knew about game shows.

"So Ray comes in for a chat and then David Mallet and I go for a pee and David looks at me and says, 'We want him on board all the way through, don't we?' And, of course, it was the best thing that could have happened. We just took to it like a duck to water. It was the Three Musketeers – me and Ray and Ev."

Mallet, Cryer and Cameron 'got' Kenny. They understood that transferring the appeal of his radio show to TV was going to take more than scripts, costumes and sets. They were making a new kind of show with a new kind of artiste so it made sense to do it in a new kind of way. Kenny wasn't and never pretended to be a stand-up comic or an actor. He was a DJ. He sat in a radio studio and with pretty much complete autonomy crafted his show. He had the freedom to be spontaneous, to work off his adrenalin.

A TV studio with a crew of perhaps 20 and hundreds of thousands of pounds worth of heavy equipment to manhandle does not easily lend itself to spontaneity. There were systems in place, too. A take started with a 30-second clock to give the tape time to run up. "Quiet studio please." The floor manager would count down with fingers... three, two, one. The performers would perform. "Reset, please, we're going again – Jerry can you make sure you hit your key light? And we're on the clock." Thirty more seconds of VT clock. "Quiet studio, please." And off again for take two.

Camera and sound crews wore soft-soled shoes. Sneezing off-camera resulted in a disciplinary hearing. Laughing was a sacking offence.

Kenny's show couldn't be doing with any of that. "We'd just run the tape all the time," says Barry Cryer. "We'd say to him 'This is just a rehearsal, Ev'. He was marvellous on a first take and then he'd get bored."

"We never knew what Kenny would get up to," says Ray Gearing, one of the cameramen on the show. "There was limited rehearsal, if any, and we learnt very quickly to add tons of cable to the cameras as Kenny did not confine himself to the studio but would suddenly exit out of the studio and into the scene dock and prop stores area. Yes it was 'kick bollock, scramble' but that was part of the show. If things went wrong, no one cared. David pushed the boundaries and lots of what you see on TV these days is only there because of David Mallet back then. He would not accept an engineer telling him he could not fade to white or do something technical that he wanted to do. He would just say, 'That's want I want to do... sort it.' David had a brilliant and refreshing eye for new ways to shoot things and guided the way for many pop videos that we see today. I liked his way of working."

Radio is an intimate medium. The DJ addresses his listener directly. TV comics nearly always worked with a studio audience acting as a sort of intermediary between the performer and the viewer. To try and get the intimacy of radio, for Kenny's show, they decided to jettison the audience and instead brought the studio crew in on the fun.

"There was no audience, but at the same time, nobody ever said 'Quiet!'" says Barry Cryer. "It's the only show I've ever worked on where if you heard any laughter it was the crew. We never asked them to laugh – that would have been insulting – but they just loved it."

TV executives had long resigned themselves to the fact that crew laughs were like band laughs – a sure indication that something filthy had been said, possibly some double-entendre understood only by the non-commissioned ranks. The viewer had got some inkling of this, too. Being invited to share the crew laugh made the audience at home feel as if they were in on some sort of private joke: something that only the performer, the chortling crew and they could understand. The result was instant intimacy, just like the wireless.

The newly emerging digital revolution gave the show not only the gizmos that provided its vocabulary of wizz-bang effects – which practically became a co-star – but also the luxury of editing. Video editing – the sort of thing you can do on a phone these days – was still tape-based, still clunky, but it was doable. It gave the show the freedom to try things, to mess around, to muck it up. If it didn't work, it didn't make the cut.

"Kenny's stated policy," says Barry Cryer, "was that the show would contain only 'silly bits, daft bits, outrageous bits and looney bits.'"

And naughty bits.

Arlene Phillips, from Prestwich in Lancashire, had been doing ballet, tap and modern since she was three. After school she moved to London and established herself as a teacher and choreographer. In 1974 she got a company together, schooled them in her own brand of jazz dance (kick, jump, roll the shoulders, Jerome Robbins, turn the knees, Bob Fosse, JAZZ HANDS), called them Hot Gossip and got them a gig at Maunkberry's night-club in Jermyn Street – 10 dancers, tiny floor, lurid cocktails with silly names, Grace Jones coming down the stairs on a motorbike.

One of the dancers, Roy Gayle, worked in a sex-shop and kept the company supplied with costumes. The line between fetish gear and dancewear has always been sketchy.

Three years later, despite several TV auditions, the company was still at Maunkberry's.

"I was coming to the end of my tether," Arlene Phillips told the *Radio Times*. "The comment I always got was: 'No, too sexy for TV'."

Originally Mallet had hired another choreographer for Kenny's show, but when one of the Hot Gossip dancers auditioned he was so impressed he fired the original choreographer and hired the whole company together with Arlene.

Dance routines and pop had never been comfortable bedfellows. Pan's People, the dance troupe on BBC's *Top Of The Pops,* were seen in much the same light as, say, the Trooping Of The Colour: a fondly regarded national institution that had little relevance to the modern world. On the plus side, they made *TOTP* more of a family show. While the teenagers thrilled to the music, their pervy dads could enjoy the choreography. The erotic promise that Pan's People merely hinted at, however, Kenny's show would deliver.

There were 11 dancers in the original Hot Gossip company, four boys and seven girls including Sarah Brightman, who later starred in *Cats* and *Phantom Of The Opera,* married Andrew Lloyd-Webber for a bit, and is estimated to be the wealthiest female singer in the world. Their costumes and Phillips' choreography did indeed make them, at least in the bulging, bloodshot eyes of *Daily Express* readers, 'too sexy for TV': especially for early evening TV when there might be children watching: and they would be watching because in its bid to be all-round family entertainment, the show even had a cartoon series.

In 1975, Thames TV had acquired an animation studio, run by Brian Cosgrove and Mark Hall and called, predictably, Cosgrove Hall. They set about animating Captain Kremmen. In keeping with the *alter ego* motif, their vision of The World's Most Fabulous Man has Kenny's tiny head perched on a collection of biceps, pecs and abs that strain his uniform like a condom full of walnuts. Carla is an unfeasibly chested platinum blonde with white thigh-boots and organ-stop nipples. Both are Essex-orange.

The plan was to transmit two three or four minute episodes per show and the budget was the sort of money Disney would have put aside for novelty pencil sharpeners, but Cosgrove Hall was nothing if not resourceful.

Lip-synch is rudimentary. Sometimes live action (a hand, perhaps, or a ticking clock) is spliced in. Where it's cheaper or easier, Claymation's mixed with the 2D. A spacecraft is a photo of a front-loading washing machine cut out of a catalogue. One episode ends with the ineptly printed caption: "Why does this animation reak [*sic*] of expensiveness? Find out in part two!"

Kenny's new show was scheduled to replace Hughie Green's long-running TV talent contest, *Opportunity Knocks*. Kenny was never known to be gracious in victory. In Kremmen's first TV outing, the brave Captain encounters a substance called Putron, a poisonous gunge of a colour described by Dr Gitfinger as 'Hughie Green'.

The first episode of the first series of eight *Kenney Everett Video Shows* was aired at 6.45 on July 3, 1978. It was music heavy, featuring Paul McCartney's Wings, Bonnie Tyler, the Electric Light Orchestra, Brian Ferry and the Steve Gibbons Band.

Hot Gossip, in a selection of fabric-skimping leotards that Arlene had designed herself – leopard-skin and nude accessorised with unusually placed strapping – writhed to the electro-disco beat of Cerrone's 'Supernature' (as they did it again later in the same series when David Mallet took them to the seaside to shoot a second version).

Kenny seems nervous, and unusually script-bound, but quite determined to get through this and make it work.

The reviews the following day were not universally ecstatic. "He's not as good as Monty Python, but he's a lot more amusing than Hughie Green," said the *Daily Express*.

The buzz around the show, however, suggested a huge hit – a feeling subsequently borne out by the ratings. And the buzz communicated itself to the crew and to Kenny.

"Those were the happy days," says Barry Cryer. "The joke at Thames Television was that Philip Jones [Head of Light Entertainment] must never find out what's going on downstairs. There were blank pages on the camera script. We'd think of something in the car going in. Everyone seemed to be having a whale of a time – Kenny was relaxed and spontaneous.

"The crews loved Everett – they fought to get on the show. One of the cameramen went and nicked a bike from the car park for a sketch once and then took it back again afterwards. What other show would a cameraman do that on?"

"Crews could not wait to see if they had been scheduled onto the Kenny Everett show," says cameraman Ray Gearing. "We probably would have worked on it for free but never let management know that. This was a time when the ACTT [the film and TV technicians' union] ruled. Kenny found out that if we were 'caught in shot' we could claim £9. If we were directed in shot it was even more and even more if we actually spoke, so Kenny would deliberately get us in shot or talk to us. We put the money in a kitty and we would have the biggest party at the end of series you have ever seen. We also got £9 if we could think of a joke for one of the characters."

On Ray Gearing's birthday, Kenny swung a camera round and got the whole studio to sing 'Happy Birthday' to him. He presented him with a 'cheap bottle of Japanese champagne' and a custard pie in the face. Ray got his own back at the end of the show – just before the end credits he snuck into shot and returned the favour with a pie of his own. Both incidents made the final cut.

"There were two sides to Kenny, the private side where he would just sit in the studio with us and just talk about everything and nothing like one of the crew, which is how he was treated, as one of the crew, but as soon as the red light went on he became this manic, brilliant little man."

That image of Kenny sitting in the studio and talking "about everything and nothing" perhaps gives the key to the show's success. This was a team effort based on mutual respect. Kenny, David, Barry, Ray Cameron, Arlene, Ray Gearing and the rest of the crew were all in it together.

It's often been said that Kenny would have been a great sound technician, working the faders, wielding the razor blade, going the extra mile to give the director more than he'd asked for, bubbling with gags to keep everybody's spirits up when the mood was in danger of turning ugly. He'd have enjoyed a private life with no fear of cameras, scandal or press intrusion. Maybe he'd have been happier.

As the series got into its stride, Mary Whitehouse, Nuneaton's self-appointed defender of wholesomeness and founder of the National Viewers' And Listeners' Association, was among the millions of viewers glued to the set. It was Mary's mission to purge the "poison being poured into millions of homes through television". She had condemned the Beatles' 'Please Please Me' as pornographic. She had railed against Mick Jagger's phallic use of the microphone and condemned the hideous and graphic violence in *Tom And Jerry*. Never slow to give praise where she considered it due, however, she also once congratulated Anglia television on a "truly delightful programme about the beaver".

sexy for TV, Hot Gossip at the BBC.

'£300 a week to fight Henry Cooper', *Nice Time*, 1968.
ITV/REX FEATURES

'I am a test card', *The Kenny Everett Explosion*, 1970.
ITV/REX FEATURES

...rsor of Spod, *The Kenny Everett Explosion*, 1970.

...cal activism, *The Kenny Everett Explosion*, TV 1970.

'Ev' with St John Montague Crisp (Brian Colville), 1971.
ITV/REX FEATURES

'Bring me the Head of Light Entertainment', Kenny with Rod Stewart (Rod's the one in leopard skin).
FREMANTLEMEDIA LTD/REX FEATURES

Billy Connolly in the toilet, *The Kenny Everett Video Cassette*.
FREMANTLEMEDIA LTD/REX FEATURES

...g the Pops with Tony Blackburn, Noel Edmonds, Beautiful Babs, Dee-Dee, Cherry and friend.

...ind me to send you an assassin for Christmas': with Spike Milligan in *Kenny Everett's Christmas Carol*, 1985.

'A fine set of udders...': *Top Of The Pops*, 1973.
LFI

Milking the franchise, 1977.
CENTRAL PRESS/GETTY IMAGES

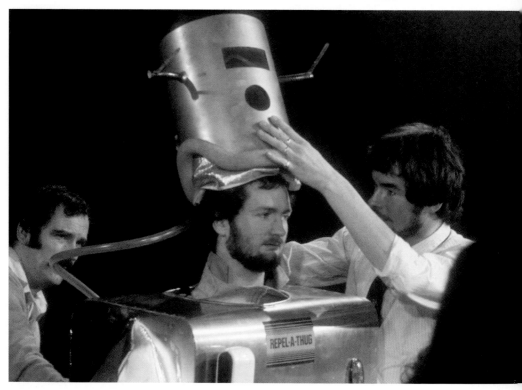

'Who am I in this scene?': 1975.
FREMANTLEMEDIA LTD/REX FEATURES

Snots in *The Kenny Everett New Year's Daze Show*, with David Esssex, Barry Cryer, Ray Cameron and Royston Mayoh, 1980.
ANTLEMEDIA LTD/REX FEATURES

z and Ray reinventing Light Entertainment.
ANTLEMEDIA LTD/REX FEATURES

'Hello, Sid Snot here'.

Hot Gossip brought her bile up. She banged off a letter of complaint describing their antics as "aggressively and deliberately seductive". Thames TV's Publicity Department made sure a copy of the letter found its way into the hands of the tabloids. It made the front page of the *Sun*. The *Express* used a couple of column inches to tell us that Mrs. Whitehouse had described Hot Gossip as "one of the most suggestive groups ever seen on television. Thames say this is the way young people dance. In my view there's a vast difference between young people dancing and the camera picking out these provocative movements."[74] Above the two column inches they published a half-page photograph to demonstrate just how provocative the movements were.

Kenny gave his reply to the *News Of The World*: "It means you've truly made it when Mrs Whitehouse complains. It's like an endorsement that the show is good. She once wrote something nice about me, which was a shock. Quite honestly I'd hate to see my show become the kind of show she likes. Something like *The Cedar Tree* or *Emmerdale Farm* is just about her level. We're not trying to be deliberately outrageous. It was a total accident that in one sketch we had a lady who looked just like her with exploding breasts."[75]

Barry delighted in outraging Mary Whitehouse too. "Once I went to a press do and somebody said, 'Baz, have you ever met Mary Whitehouse?' and there she was. So I went over very politely and I said, 'Hello' and I got hold of her hand far too firmly and I said, 'Thank you.' And she said, 'Sorry, do I know you?' I said, 'I work on the Kenny Everett show. You made us.'"

One of the most immediately popular of Kenny's characters was Sid Snot, the pathologically violent punk who would end his sketches by throwing cigarette after cigarette into the air and trying to catch them in his mouth. Once and only once, Kenny actually caught one of the cigarettes while tape was rolling. He promptly ate it.

Journalist Jenny Rees encountered Sid when she went down to Teddington for a *Daily Mail* feature about the making of the show. "I suppose what we're doing is translating Kenny's radio show on to the telly," Barry tells her. "It's beautifully mad. Kenny's not a comedian, as such, he's just himself."

She finds Kenny/Sid in his leather gear sitting astride a motorcycle with Carol Fletcher, one of the Hot Gossip dancers, on the pillion in matching leathers playing Sid's inamorata, Deirdre. Sid looks down at his shoes.

"'Ere Deirdre, these soles are crepe," says Kenny.

"They're not that bad," says Carol.

"I was down in the park this morning, Deird, feeding the pigeons."

"Really"

"Yeah. To my cat."

Still dressed as Sid, he smashes up a chair. "You know that show *Going For A Song*," he says – referring to the genteel antiques-based quiz show. "Well, we're going to do a rock'n'roll antique show. It's called *What Did That Used To Be Worth?*"

Tape is still rolling, recording every moment. Kenny/Sid gets into a destructive frenzy and smashes a couple of vases, then collapses in giggles.

He goes off to wardrobe, and emerges dressed as a hen, his "tiny face peers out under the great orange beak". Improvising off the costume, he says to David Mallet, "If I pretend to be a bomber, could you use Battle of Britain sound effects?" And rushes around the studio, wings outspread, like a Lancaster.

Barry maintains that the only disagreement that he ever had with Kenny was over the name "Sid Snot". Barry thought they could come up with something better, but Kenny stuck to his guns. He knew his audience.

As Mary Whitehouse had feared, more than a quarter of the show's audience were aged between 12 and 18, an age at which all mucoid emissions are ineluctably funny. Accordingly, Sid remained one of Kenny's most popular characters and 'Snot Rap', Sid's 1983 single, made number nine in the Fab 40.

The relationship between Kenny's characters and gay stereotypes – cousins, perhaps of the Village People – has not gone unnoticed. Sid, in his leather cap, could have sprung straight from the pages of *Jeffrey* or *Zipper* magazine, and although 'Silly Cowboy', the Stetson-clad Western hero, was more Gabby Hayes than *Brokeback Mountain*, he still hung around down at the 'Jessie Boys Ankle Bracelet Saloon'.

The suit target was 'Lord Thames', supposedly the owner of Thames Television who lived behind a cobweb-covered door marked, 'Office Of Saying No'.

Spod from the Planet Thoon [*spelling approx*] arrived as a result of messing about with the new electronic gizmos. Kenny's head floated in a mess of interference patterns and said, "Hello, I'm Spod from the planet Thoon. And this is all I do. Pathetic, isn't it?"

The sexual frenzy that Kenny worked himself into as he announced fresh "naughty bits" and even "extra naughty bits" from Hot Gossip was matched only by that of the 12- to 18-year-old boys at home, watching with their parents and trying hard to feign more interest in their Rubik's Cubes than in the on-screen orgasms.

Hot Gossip cashed in on its instant success with a single, released under the name 'Sarah Brightman and Hot Gossip'. The song 'I Lost My Heart To A Starship Trooper', written by Jeff Calvert and Geraint Hughes, was a catchy little space disco track. Its lyrics, stuffed with references to *Star Wars*, *2001: A Space Odyssey*, *Flash Gordon* and *Close Encounters Of The Third Kind*, ensured that the single was an essential purchase for any 12- to 18-year-old boy with a keen interest both in science fiction *and* in gymnastic young women in skin-tight spangly catsuits showing off the flexibility of their joints while singing "Take me, make me feel the force" and "What my body needs is Close Encounter three."

It made number six in the Fab 40. A subsequent album, *Geisha Girls And Temple Boys,* didn't.

*   *   *

When the TV series started, Kenny gave up his Sunday programme on Capital and just did the Saturday afternoon slot. "Sundays will never be the same…" mourned the London *Evening News* and tried to make a story out of it by suggesting that it left bad blood between Kenny and Capital. The *Evening News* went out of business not long after.

The success of the TV show meant you couldn't open a newspaper without reading some new profile of Kenny or Lee or Kenny and Lee. At the *Daily Mirror,* it seemed, it didn't feel right to put the paper to bed at night without making sure it was tucked up with at least a little picture of Kenny. One day he'd tell them, "I almost became a priest, but the food was awful," and the next, "I'm not particularly proud of it, but I used to take drugs to get my kicks."

"I'm a medium. In the spirit world I'm called Crystal Clear," Lee told them. "My current guide is Chinese, Ling Foo. He's been with me for three years and we have a wonderful spiritual relationship. I believe I am a looked after person.

"I was born with knowledge of reincarnation. I know I've been here three times before, twice as a nun and once as an Indian."

★ ★ ★

The second series of the *Video Show* started on February 19, 1979. At 25 minutes rather than 45, it was shorter, but it was clear now that this was a comedy show with music, rather than a music show with comedy links.

There were new characters ...

Marcel Wave was a French 'airdresser with an outrageous ac*cent* who, to the sounds of a piano accordion, would swan around being vaguely lecherous while waving a cigarette holder. He was the only character Kenny played – including the women – who didn't have a beard.

"I think it was Ev who said, 'I think 'I'll have a false chin on. The Frenchman just has a moustache, so we'll cover his beard with this plastic chin.' And then of course he tore it off at the end – 'You see, it was me all the time.'"

Brother Lee Love was an Evangelist preacher who wore unfeasibly large foam-rubber hands to point out the imperfections and iniquities of his flock. In the first show, the opening shot shows the gnarled hands of a black gospel piano-player weighed down with gaudy rings. The camera pulls out to reveal that the hands are, bafflingly, those of a young, blond, white man.

"I hate pornography," says the good Brother. "I haven't even got a pornograph!"

Fourteen years had gone by since Kenny had been sacked by Radio London. At last he was able to exact proper revenge on Garner Ted Armstrong.

The nerves that were sometimes apparant in series one are gone. Kenny's role as the naughtiest boy in school was confirmed. Barry, Ray Cameron, David Mallet and the crew are his eager accomplices.

"Only Ev could have got away with this," says Barry Cryer. "On one occasion, he got hold of a camera and manhandled it, pulled it round

– and the cameraman let him do it. Obviously you saw people running out of shot and the dusty floor and polystyrene cups and everything and Kenny was going 'Ooh the glamour of it all!'"

"He loved it when we did things while he was costume changing," says Ray Gearing. "On one occasion he had a particularly long costume change into an Orson Welles fat suit. While he was out of the studio we actually took the whole set down including the video wall. The studio was totally empty. We had hidden the camera behind the cyc [*cyclorama – the big white wall at the back of the studio*]. This was all with David Mallet's approval. When Kenny came back he just sat on the floor, called us all bastards and laughed. We actually recorded the second half of the show in an empty studio and he loved it."

"Another time we were using a specially adapted fork-lift truck to hold a camera to get a high shot. Kenny asked me what is was like to be that high, so I said jump on and I'll take you up – this was long before Health and Safety. I took him up to the top from the driver's position and David Mallet said, 'That's a tea break, guys, back in 20 minutes.' Kenny was jokingly screaming at us to get him down and the whole crew just ignored him and went for a 20-minute tea break. When we came back, Kenny was still sat up there, still calling me a bastard. If only Kenny had turned around he would have seen there was a large lever behind him marked in bright red saying 'DOWN'."

During a sketch with the Pretenders, Kenny was called on to appear to plunge a microphone through the camera lens. A plate of glass was put in front of the lens – a trick used before when Angry of Mayfair (who wore pinstripes and bowler from the front view, fishnets and suspenders from the back) smashed the camera with his rolled-up umbrella. This time, when Kenny smacked his microphone on the glass, it exploded, slashing through his hand. Kenny was whisked off to hospital to be stitched up and then had to return to the studio straight away for the afternoon's filming. The next sketch had Kenny playing a violin that explodes at the end of a Paganini violin concerto. Again the stunt backfired, sending him straight back to casualty.

The ratings sometimes peaked at 15 million. Stars were queuing up, not just to churn out their latest hit, but to fool around with Kenny.

"It's been said before that we were the sort of smaller version of Morecambe and Wise," says Barry Cryer, "because everybody wanted to be on Everett's show – Rod Stewart, Cliff Richard – they loved being humiliated and patted about."

Cliff Richard was hung up by his thumbs (a *cliff-hanger*, geddit?). Rod Stewart was first accosted for sexual favours, then assaulted with a cosh. He poured a vodka and coke over Kenny's head. Then they wrestled.

David Bowie was assaulted by Angry of Mayfair. "Look at you, you lily-livered mincer," he says, prodding Bowie with his brolly. "You know, I was in the war – but I didn't see *you* there. I fought for people like you [*woefully*] but I never got one." Then he begs Bowie to beat him up.

"Bryan Ferry, I remember him," says Barry Cryer. "He was in the script for doing some sort of routine with Kenny, but that's as far as it had gone. And Bryan came over to me and said, 'Barry, I had a chat with Ev to find out what I'm supposed to do, but he doesn't know.' So I ad-libbed very quickly and I said, 'Bryan, you do good languid, don't you?' He said, 'What?' I said, 'Light a cigarette and ignore him.' It worked a treat. I told Ev to ask him some questions like, 'Oh, Mr Ferry, you must have had an exciting life, can you tell us about it?' Bryan just ignored him. It worked a treat."

The show kept up with the latest gizmos as they became available.

"We had the only two hand–held cameras in the country then," says Ray Gearing. "They were cumbersome, extremely heavy and you had a bar from the camera down to a leather waistband to try to keep the thing pointing forward, but we were able to do things that a ped [*pedestal camera*] couldn't do for the first time. When Kenny found out that the hand–held cameras could go outside, it was murder."

The show had awards thrown at it. The Royal Television Society gave it a 'Most Original Programme', BAFTA gave it a 'Best Light Entertainment Programme' and the crew was honoured with a 'Best TV Cameraman' for Senior Cameraman John Chapman. It was nominated for a Golden Rose of Montreux. In 1979 Kenny and Penelope Keith, star of the sitcom *To The Manor Born*, were named joint 'TV Personality Of The Year'. In August 1980, a survey conducted by National Opinion Polls, for a "high powered conference on public policy issues", voted Kenny the ninth most powerful (yes, not funny, not 'liable to corrupt and deprave' but powerful) person in the country. The Queen was number one. The Bishop of London and Brian Clough were just ahead

Cupid Stunts

of Kenny. Anna Ford, the newsreader, came in just behind him at number 10.

Kenny was in demand. He was a celeb. His voice-over and sometimes his face was a must for every ad campaign, his presence was required on every game show. He was a regular on Terry Wogan's *Blankety Blank*, a quiz of sorts that awarded TV's tackiest prizes for encouraging the celebs to formulate gross *double entendres* and then choosing the grossest. "The vicar caused a stir at the vegetable show when he showed everybody his giant *blank*," Terry would say. Beryl Reid would answer "cucumber". Liza Goddard would answer "carrot". Lorraine Chase – whose riff was pretending to be dumb – would answer "car". Nobody answered "penis".

Terry Wogan's trademark was the strange microphone he carried on a long wand-like stick made, as Kenny once deflatingly revealed, from an old car aerial. Then he bent it. It made national headlines. "Kenny Everett Bends Terry Wogan's Stick".

The sig tune went, "Blankety Blank, Blankety Blank, Blankety Blank, Blankety Blank, Blankety Blank, Blankety Blank, Blankety Blank, Blankety Blank."

Blankety Blank ran, with different presenters and a short break, for 20 years.

Kenny sat on all the sofas on all the chat shows, too. He made Michael Parkinson twinkle warmly.

"The boy stood on the burning deck," he told Russell Harty, "eating red hot scallops, till one slid down his trouser leg, and didn't half scald his…. ankles." Then, as the laughter faded away, he added, "Missed his bollocks completely." Russell blushed.

The logistics of fitting in the ads, the games and the chat show sofas occasionally defeated him. On his first booking for Mavis Nicholson's *Afternoon Plus* he mixed up the times and failed to turn up until just before the programme's closing credits. For a second booking, the production staff made sure to send a car. Kenny made up for the previous disappointment by having a water fight with Frankie Howerd. Mavis chuckled.

Yet, still…

"Kenny found out that I did hospital radio at St Thomas's on the Embankment," says Ray Gearing, the cameraman. "One day he

175

came in with a 5″ tape-spool full of personalised jingles made for me by him, which I still have to this day. He had such a kind nature to everyone and inspired everyone. My girlfriend (at the time) and I would often go to Capital Radio in the Euston Road and watch him do the show. Not often you get to watch a genius at work in television and radio."

The disparity between the relaxed Kenny in the studio and among colleagues at work, and the uptight Kenny beyond began to grow more glaring; as if the more celebrated he became, the more difficult it was to reconcile Cuddly Ken with awkward, secretive Maurice Cole.

"He said to me once 'people expect me to enter a room turning cartwheels'," says Barry Cryer. "He was quite shy. He was the cliché: he saved it for when he was on. But when you were just sitting having dinner, just me and him and Ray [Cameron], he'd be very funny. He'd relax. He had to be with friends. He had to feel secure. He wasn't funny with a crowd. He wasn't one of those who needs to be the life and soul of the party. He was polite but very quiet."

A similar theme was picked up in an interview Kenny gave to Simon Ludgate for *Cosmopolitan*[76] magazine. Ludgate talks about Kenny's "private personality, well-hidden behind a smokescreen he has carefully created".

"Whenever the conversation strays into a potential knee tremble, like politics, 'boring to anyone but politicians,' and religion, 'it doesn't provide The Answer, just tips,' he becomes very nervous and suddenly his depressive side briefly rears into sight. 'I find humans rather nasty in general and so odd to look at. I think we were dumped from somewhere else to muck it all up.'

"How does he feel about being a recognizable face and a familiar voice? Sotto voce: 'Absolutely terrible. When people creep up on me as I'm buying the cat food and say, 'C'mon, Ken, be wacky,' it's embarrassing for everyone. How do you reply when someone says, 'Oh it's him!' 'Yes, it certainly is?''"

In September 1979, beneath a headline reading, "DJ Kenny is Spirited Away", the *Sunday Mirror*[77] reported that he'd moved out of the marital home in Pembridge Villas and taken a flat across the street. Kenny and Lee were at pains to point out that this implied no alienation of affections. "It is not true we have separated," said Lee. "Kenny sleeps at his flat some nights while he is doing his recording work." The "blood-curdling screams from Captain Kremmen" were making it impossible for Lee to achieve the tranquillity she needed for her own work. "Lee holds a psychic circle at her home two nights a week."

"I think the marriage worked," says Barry Cryer. "I mean everybody went, 'Oh my god, Kenny's married to a woman,' and all that, but she was good for him. He needed – it's fascinating looking back – he sort of needed running and organising. It's a classic pattern. Like Beryl Formby, George Formby's wife – I'm not saying Lee was quite as forceful as that, but you could tell she was running him and getting him organised and everything. They got on well – he would run to her – there was a security there. He had to have his security zone. With work I hope – I think – it was me and Ray. At home he had Lee."

At the end of the year, the *News Of The World* reported that Lee had embarked on a lesbian affair with an American tennis player and had gone through a jokey form of a marriage ceremony with her. This development is perhaps more easily explained by the fact that, as Lee mentions in her memoir *Kinds Of Loving,* in a previous life the tennis player had been her husband.

Lee took the initiative in finding Kenny some happiness too. One night she and Kenny were having dinner with Freddie Mercury at the Joe Allen Restaurant in Covent Garden. Lee noticed that Kenny was eyeing up a young waiter. She grabbed the bull by the horns, called the waiter over and told him that they were all going to a club and would he like to join them? The waiter, an Australian called John (Jay) Pitt, said yes.

Kenny was aghast at the simplicity of it all. After so many years of sly gropings and unhappy crushes, finally his wife had found him a suitable boyfriend.

John moved in with Kenny and their relationship lasted over a year, a warm domestic bubble.

The third series for Thames introduced more new characters including Marvin T. Bombthebastards (later called General Cheeseburger), a US Army 12-star hawk with a Sherman tank and a six-foot shoulder span, the living embodiment of US foreign policy 1952 to the present, whose solution to intellectuals, pinkos and fags was to put them all in a field and, as the name suggests, "bomb the bastards". It was a catchphrase that would eventually come to haunt Kenny.

The show's return was welcomed with open arms. In *The Times*[78], it was TV editor Peter Davalle's number one *Personal Choice*. He even spotted Kenny's primary influence. "In my youth… the radio programme no self-respecting follower of fashion dated to miss was Jack Jackson's record show. … Compared with the innovative Jackson, all other disc jockeys were ordinary, and they remained so until Kenny Everett was unleashed upon an unsuspecting world. Everett's brash, iconoclastic humour made him a star – and also made him too hot for the BBC to handle – but radio never gave him the opportunities he exploits so brilliantly in *The Kenny Everett Video Show*. Perhaps it is not too sweeping to say this is the most original show on television."

Top popsters were still firing agents for failing to get them on the show. Cliff Richard having been bound and gagged on a Christmas special, now sang 'Living Doll' while being showered with life-threatening junk. Freddie Mercury flew halfway across the world to kick the shit out of Sid Snot – their entry for the 'Eurovision Violence Competition'. Billy Connolly was hardly ever off the show, and down the years became practically a resident co-star. He made Kenny laugh a lot. Kenny made Billy laugh a lot. They both made the crew laugh a lot. Production often ground to a damp, hysterical, shuddering halt.

The show, or at least one segment of the show, transferred to the big screen when *Kremmen – The Movie* was released in July 1980. At only 24 minutes long, it failed to qualify for full-feature film status by about an hour and a half, but it was tailored for release as a sort of second feature bundled in with *Can't Stop The Music,* a turkey starring the Village People.

Ray Cameron produced. The budget and schedule were so tight that even Cosgrove Hall, a company well used to shoestrings and heart-attack deadlines, was too upmarket. Instead, Ray turned to John Sunderland, a young animator who has since gone on to great things but was then working out of a back bedroom in Leeds. Under the circumstances,

John and his cohorts performed a miracle, creating in six months and with no money something that looks quite a lot like an animated film. But Barry and Ray's script was lacklustre – the pacing was odd, the story not very good and the jokes ho-hum – and when *Can't Stop The Music* bombed, *Kremmen* bombed with it: although it has to be said that, given the chance, *Kremmen* could have bombed perfectly adequately on its own, without any help at all from the Village People.

Eventually it found its way on to video, augmented by half an hour of Hot Gossip's finest moves, and bombed all over again.

In August, Kenny gave up his Capital Radio show – one of the few times he finished a job without being fired or walking out – but agreed to continue providing episodes of *Kremmen* for the station to slot into the schedule where and when, usually on Mike Smith's *Breakfast Show*. What had once been a labour of love for Kenny had by now turned into a chore. Kremmen was the homework he always left to the last minute.

"The 8 a.m. news would come," says Mike Smith[79], "a three minute bulletin. No sign of Kremmen. Take an early ad break. Still no sign of the spaceman – or even a taxi with a tape. Play a record. During record, cab arrives with tape. Tape gets rewound and transmitted without being checked. This was not a rare occurrence. Daily I chewed my nails waiting for bloody Kremmen to arrive."

But sometimes the metaphorical dog ate the metaphorical homework and all Kenny could offer was, "You remember yesterday's episode? You don't? Well, what's the point in doing this one? Stay tuned for more adventures tomorrow."

Mike Smith was heard on air wondering, "How much are we paying for this?"

In the end, Capital wondered, too, and stopped broadcasting them.

Kenny's attempts still to play, for press and public, the comfortably uxorious breeder, weren't as convincing as they used to be. Nobody, at least nobody in the press, had quite said it out loud – calling somebody 'gay' back then was still considered libellous – but everybody knew. That which, in Wigan playgrounds and Truro care-homes, had once been a matter of speculation, was now a racing certainty, no longer a question of 'if', but of 'when'. Indeed, sometimes it seemed as if the only people in the country still bothering with the pretence of Kenny's heterosexuality were Lee and Kenny.

"We are fed up with gossip column articles written in a snide way which keep suggesting he is gay," Lee complained to the *Daily Mail*.[80] "I've never asked him if he has ever had any physical involvement with men. I think it's all about hero worship. It was the little boy's admiration for the big man."

With Lee, John and Jo Gurnett, Kenny flew out to Australia to promote his show which was being broadcast by ABC (the show routinely had the naughtier bits cut out to suit the – in those days – more delicate sensibilities of the Australians).

On the long flight, Kenny played with his latest gizmo, the state-of-the art Sony Walkman with built-in radio. Fiddling with the dial as the plane flew over the USA, he discovered to his delight that he could pick up fleeting signals from American stations. Three minutes of this one, then it would fade and you'd move within range of another: tunes, ads, DJs, then a more urgent sound. He'd stumbled onto the flight-deck's frequency. The pilot, his pilot, the man up front, was informing ground control at Los Angeles that one of the stewardesses had found a message in the lavatory saying there was a bomb on board.

Kenny's reaction, rather than alerting the other passengers and inciting mass panic, was to down two bottles of champagne quickly and pass out. The plane was landed in Los Angeles and was thoroughly searched. The bomb threat was a hoax. It can give you a bit of perspective on life, a thing like that: make you reassess your options.

When the foursome arrived in Australia, they played musical beds, with John being sneaked into Kenny's room after hours while Lee, the public wife, sneaked down the hall to spend the night (chastely) with Jo Gurnett.

That Christmas, Kenny took a brave and bold step. He introduced John to his family as his new 'wife' and Lee introduced her new boyfriend, and soon-to-be husband, John Alkin.

Thirteen years later, he described the occasion to Sue Lawley on *Desert Island Discs*.

"They didn't know how to handle gayness 'cos in those days it was very odd. You just sort of – if your son was gay you didn't talk about it. Apparently at a party a friend of mine told my father, 'Oh that's

Everett's new boyfriend,' and he just said, 'Oh well, if that's what he wants to be, that's all right.' Wish he'd said that 20 years earlier. I wish I'd asked him earlier, actually."

The fourth series at Thames was blessed with a new title (even Barry Cryer can't remember why) *The Kenny Everett Video Cassette.* It was by now quite definitely a comedy show with music playing a supporting role. Comics and proper actors as well as pop-stars were introduced as Kenny's accomplices and victims. Barry and Ray were beginning to think in terms of sketches rather than one-liners.

"There was an underground gents at Leicester Square," says Barry Cryer, "and this dear man had been working down there for 40 years and he was retiring and a journalist got on to this. He thought he must have some stories and so he went along to interview him. Now the attendant, allegedly, said, 'Oh God, it's changed so much: men coming in together and disappearing into a cubicle and needles on the floor and all that. I tell you, anybody who comes in here for a straightforward shit, it's like a breath of fresh air.' So I told Ev and he laughed and laughed and then I told Billy Connolly and he said, 'We gotta do it.' But then we thought we can't say 'shit' so I said, 'Take one letter out – anybody who comes in here for a straight *sit.*' Billy said, 'Yeah, I'm on.' So Kenny interviewed Billy as the attendant. But what we didn't tell Billy was that behind him a man comes in on a unicycle. Another big butch man goes into a cubicle and comes out almost immediately in full drag and there's all sorts going on while they're doing this joke. But then Billy suddenly spots what's happening behind him on the monitor in front of him and he starts laughing and he can't stop. I think we edited it down but it still ended up about seven minutes."

Cliff Richard took part in one of these longer sketches, too, trying to change his clean-cut, likeable image. Kenny introduces him to a book called *Sarcasm For Rock Stars* which includes full instructions on how to say, 'Oh, that sounds great' with the correct Johnny Rotten inflection. There was a spoof arts and media show, *Fulcrum,* featuring Chas and Dave.

Kremmen was no longer an animation but a live action insert with Kenny as Kremmen and buxom actress Anna Dawson as Carla.

"Captain, can I use your dictaphone?" "No, Carla, use your finger like anybody else."

Old-school Northern club comic Bernard Manning was booked for episode four. "We got him to play a comedian called Billy Banter," says Barry. "He was on a – you couldn't see it at home – a little stage with a backing but it was actually a truck with wheels. He behaved himself, obviously, no filth or any racist stuff or anything, but he kept up this stream of jokes all the time." ("There's this bloke and he's bald and his mate says, 'Why don't you have a transplant then?' And he says, 'What? I'd look even worse with a kidney on my head.'")

"To his credit he did it brilliantly, but all the time he was talking Kenny was shooting him and chucking stuff at him. There were gunshots and bullet holes coming behind him and an assegai spear coming in just behind his head. And he was still talking. Suddenly he was towed out of the studio through the big doors and then we broke for lunch. Bernard sits down with us all and it's like two different worlds. Kenny and Ray and me and some people and then Bernard and his minder. Bernard was doing two more jobs that day somewhere, so his minder keeps saying, 'Bernard, come on.' And he says, 'All right, all right.' And he stood up and said, 'Thank you Barry. Thank you, Ray.' And he walked through this packed restaurant at Thames and he turned at the door and boomed back at Kenny, 'I always thought you were a cunt but you're all right.'" Ev said, 'That's the equivalent of a love letter from him – he loves me.'

By now David Mallet was busy inventing the pop video so *The Kenny Everett Video Cassette* had a new producer-director, Royston Mayoh, who had worked with the likes of comedian/conjuror David Nixon and lot-more-comedian/less-conjuror Tommy Cooper.

The team was the team. Changes, especially at the top, made Kenny nervous. He found other causes for discontent, too.

He objected to the show being scheduled opposite *Top Of The Pops* on BBC1. The *Pops* audience, he rightly argued, was his audience. Apart from the possibility that the aggressive scheduling might damage his own ratings just as easily as the BBC's, it seemed unfair in those pre-video days to deny generally ill-served 12 to 18 year olds the chance of enjoying both treats.

Even more infuriating was the suspicion that censorship was lurking in the bushes.

Barry and Ray had conceived a little soap-opera segment for the series to be called *The Snots* and based around the home life of Sid Snot. It was delightfully violent, aggressive and vulgar. Diana Dors had been approached to play Sid's leather-clad mother and Christopher Biggins to play a camp lodger.

When Kenny arrived for the first day of shooting, the studio was empty. Word went round that the boss, Philip Jones, had seen a script, deemed it unsuitable and cancelled the recording.

On every show they'd made for Thames, what Barry had described as 'the joke' of keeping 'them upstairs' as far as possible in the dark about what 'us downstairs' were doing was never, in fact, so much a joke as diplomatic precaution. What the eye doesn't see, the heart doesn't grieve. Script and shooting schedules were kept deliberately vague. When the ratings were in, that was the time to discuss what kind of content is suitable or unsuitable.

Now somebody had shown Philip Jones an advance copy of the script. Barry Cryer knows who: "Royston Mayoh was being badgered from upstairs by people who wanted to know what we were up to downstairs. He was feeding the scripts such as they were up to Philip Jones."

Kenny was enraged. He would not be bullied. He would not be subjected to <u>very</u> firm production.

"Everett's eyes went steely. I knew that look," says Barry Cryer. "He went straight to Philip Jones' office and asked what was going on. Dear Roy Mayoh apparently had been crying in the gents – this is a charming story, isn't it? – and was sitting in Philip's office, shaking with a white face. Everett said to Philip Jones, without looking at Roy but pointing at him, 'I can't work with this man, Philip.' And Philip Jones said, 'Oh now, calm down. I've booked a table for lunch. Let's talk about this.' Kenny said, 'Ooh, what a shame. Ray and Baz and I are going for lunch in town.' And we left the studio. And then it was all over."

Three years earlier Thames TV had poached top rated Morecambe and Wise from the BBC. Now came the BBC's chance to get their own back.

CHAPTER TEN

For a lapsed Roman Catholic, the BBC makes a fine God substitute. It is all-knowing. It is all-seeing. And its all-forgiving nature even goes so far as to give absolution without demanding any of the Catholic inconveniences of contrition, confession or penance.

Kenny had insulted the BBC, he had broken its commandments, he had bowed down before the false gods of Capital and Thames, but still it forgave him. It welcomed the prodigal back into the fold.

Reconciliation began when Barry Cryer received a tentative phone call from Jim Moir, the BBC's Head of Light Entertainment.

"How are things going on at Thames, Barry?" said Jim.

"I'm only a writer, how would I know?"

"You know what I mean. How are you getting on? I heard not good. Now if you and Ev and Ray Cameron are free on Tuesday and you'd like a bit of bubbly in my office, you'd be very welcome."

"Of course – Thames Television – oh my God!" says Barry. "How they took on. The treachery! Ev had gone to the BBC – just like they'd poached Eric and Ernie from the BBC."

Kenny's frequent appearances on *Blankety Blank* and talk shows had ensured he never became a complete stranger at Television Centre or Broadcasting House, but the renouncement of his Thames citizenship meant he could once again be issued with the Staff Pass, the Club

Membership, the Occasional Parking Rights and the access to the Berol cupboard that are the coveted privileges of the BBC's chosen ones.

Before going on the telly with his own show, at the beginning of October he started a new Saturday morning show on Radio 2, Radio 1's older, kinder brother. Tucked between *Pete Murray's Open House* and *Punchline* — a comedy panel game hosted by the delightfully posh Leslie Randall — it should have been a gentle easing back into the land of fitted carpets. It wasn't. Kenny came off the starting blocks at 500 mph, with all guns firing and didn't ease up for a second. He opens with the wrong station ident:

IDENT: "Isn't it good to know, Capital Radio."
KENNY: Oops.
RADIO 2 IDENT
KENNY: Yes, ladies and gentlemen, I've joined the BBC.
JINGLE: "He's joined the BBC"
KENNY: Yes, folks …
SYNTHESIZER MUSIC
KENNY: (OVER SYNTH) … from this day on we bring you a feast of heavenly delights. All the great tunes of the world, contests with soul-wrenching prizes, classical items that will turn your brain into crème de menthe.
JINGLE: And your liver and onions into a side-street.
SFX: Giggles.
DEEP VOICE: Mostly we'll have records past.
KENNY: It's 10 minutes past 11 and we'll be right back after this …
PAUSE, WHERE AN AD BREAK SHOULD BE
KENNY: (BEMUSED) Oh, no. This is the BBC.

His references to Capital must have mystified listeners outside London, who presumably had assumed that Kenny had abandoned radio when he'd gone on the telly, but he welcomed them, glad to be back on national radio: "Hello, Liverpool, hello the Fens, hello National."

Other than giving free namechecks to a rival station he's on his best behaviour, even managing to play 'Yesterday' without mentioning the word "orgasm".

He plays Chubby Checker's 'Limbo Rock' and Marty Wilde's 'Bad Boy' and Laurie Anderson's 'O Superman'. He plays the high note that

Kiri Te Kanawa sang at Charles and Diana's wedding. He tells us that, "Britain exploded its first atomic bomb on the Montebello Islands on this very day in 1952. It went… " (SOUND EFFECT BANG, CLANG, TINKLE, TINKLE) "… they forgot to wind it up." He says, "It's time to yum-tiddle-um to a famous old classic tune," then plays his three part harmony "yum-tiddle-um" jingle which segues seamlessly (same key, same tempo) into Strauss' 'Radetzky March'. He plays at lot of classical music in his Radio 2 shows just like he had on his Kiddiegram in Hereford Road. "Classical music," he said, "that's the stuff that souls are made of."

He revives his world's worst record slot …

JINGLE: "On Saturday, our show today's, a show that's really great, except for all the records that you hate.

SFX: Extended raspberry.

SFX: Giggles.

KENNY: Yes, the Kenny Everett show, the show that makes you …

SFX: Ha ha ha ha ha hoo.

JINGLE: "When you listen to cuddly Ken's show" (the Beatles sing "Oh, yeah" stolen from 'Happiness Is A Warm Gun') "You get a warm feeling inside your doobries" ("Oh, yeah")

KENNY: Yes folks, contests and rotten records like Jess Conrad and Reggie Bosanquet.

SFX: Ha ha ha ha ha stop it.

SFX: Cymbal tish.

MAJOR DENNIS BLOODKNOCK: (FROM THE GOON SHOW – yes the *Goon Show* that had been his boon companion since Hereford Road) "Somebody open a window, please."

And so it goes on, manic, precision-crafted with no sloppy edits, duff mixes or ragged harmonies, not a beat missed: two hours of the most intricate, most excitingly pointless radio you're ever going to hear and leaving nobody in any doubt that Kenny Everett was back on the BBC and suggesting that this was, on the whole, a good thing.

There was a lot of Kenny about that Christmas. More and more homes were investing in VCRs and finding that buying pre-recorded videos was a damn sight easier than mastering the arcane mysteries of the advance timer. Thames exploited their copyrights by launching a *Best Of The Kenny Everett Video Show.*

The ever-entrepreneurial Ray Cameron, quick to spot the emerging video market, also noticed that, unlike broadcast television, videos could be aimed at the 'adult' market – a word used, in this context, not to mean 'adult' in the sense of 'grown-up' at all, but 'boys between the ages of 12 and 18': in other words, Kenny's primary demographic.

Ray hired the Comedy Store, a recently opened club (more of which later) which Kenny described as a "grotty little Soho shithouse" and booked otherwise respected comics, including Leslie Crowther (that nice man off *Crackerjack),* Willie Rushton, Lennie Bennett, John Junkin and Barry Cryer himself, inviting them to perform their filthiest material. Kenny MCs the show and the audience is dotted with celebs, including, disconcertingly, Robert Powell, the actor who, fresh from playing the lead in the TV mini-series *Jesus Of Nazareth,* wears the same expression of forbearance he used in the crucifixion scenes, as if he's about to leap from his seat at any moment and intone "Forgive them, lord, for they known not what they do."

An episode in which a topless model lounges on a rattan chair, impersonating the poster for the soft-porn movie *Emmanuelle,* and is beholden to remain silent while Kenny does 'funny stuff' around her is perhaps the most worrying, not least because at one point she appears to blush.

Videos were expensive back then. *The Kenny Everett Naughty Joke Box,* as it was called, retailed at £39.99 at a time when the average weekly wage was about £160.

The big one came at 7.45 on Christmas Eve with the debut of Kenny's new BBC show. *The Kenny Everett Television Show* – "amazing happenings with a festive flavour" – was a special, a demonstration of the delights to come when the series proper got going in the New Year.

In opened in black and white. A limo – registration ITV – pulls up at a graveyard. Kenny's lifeless body is taken from the boot and buried. Moments later, a ramshackle Morris Minor Traveller with the plates 'BBC' disgorges two men who dig up the corpse and carry it off. Kenny then appears in studio wearing a T-shirt emblazoned with the Thames TV logo and swizzles round to reveal the BBC logo on the back.

The series proper took off in February. It was different. Gone was the "kick, bollock, scramble" of the Thames days. The BBC didn't do "kick, bollock, scramble".

As Kenny told the *Sunday Telegraph*[81] nearly 10 years later, "It was fine when I started on Thames – we had a jolly time and could misbehave a lot. Then the BBC said, 'Come over to us and we'll turn you into a proper comedian,' and instead of taking two minutes for a 10-second sketch it took three hours, at the end of which they usually used the first take anyway."

Andrew Marshall, with his occasional writing partner David Renwick, provided a lot of material for Kenny's later BBC TV shows. He's one of Britain's most accomplished comedy writers, whose credits include the epic and influential *Whoops, Apocalypse*, *The Two Ronnies*, *Not The Nine O'Clock News* and the long-running *2.4 Children*.

Andrew understands Kenny's nostalgia for the Thames programmes: "They had a sort of rock vibe to the whole editing and feeling of them which I think was very, very good. But when Ken came to the BBC, he had a lot of bigger guests. It was like coming from this small business – Thames in those days was like a little family business – like a small sort of engineering works in Leicester or something, and then entering this huge sort of bureaucratic organization, the BBC. It is like having your programmes made by the Catholic Church or the Church of England. There's this vast array of people saying, 'Well, we've got Everett here and he'll need three studios.' And all this stuff kicks into gear, 'He'll have to have 52 sets per series...' So it all had to be much more regimented into this model of what they had in those days as a 'variety show'. He probably had the same budget and backup staff as Les Dawson or somebody, who was a much more summer season sort of performer. David Mallet didn't come over from Thames and you had to have BBC staff directors, so it was perhaps more up to Barry and Ray to set the tone of the show really. Particularly Ray, who was, I think, quite gifted in deciding what Everett could do and what he couldn't do. I think Ray was quite an important figure in those Thames shows. And of course Barry who provided the – I'm not quite sure how to describe them – more traditional anchoring parts of the comedy so that grandma wasn't too alarmed by what all this strange stuff was."

"We will be having one musical guest per show only," Kenny told the

Radio Times, adding that Kremmen had breathed his last. "I had done all the space jokes and all the tit jokes. In the final episode I had them towing a planet made of crude oil. On the way to earth it caught fire and caused a chain reaction, blowing up the entire universe, including the audience. Let's see someone revive that!"

Hot Gossip were gone, too, although there was never a shortage of underdressed young men and women scattered about to crank up the by now rather lame 'shock value' and try to elicit just one more letter from Mary Whitehouse.

Perhaps most radical of all, the let's-run-the-tape-and-see-what-happens ethos had gone, and with it the in-on-a-private-joke crew laughs. Instead there were – theoretically at least – scripts, rehearsals, the standard working schedule of BBC Light Ents and, most alarming of all, a studio audience.

"As I remember it we worked most days," says Barry Cryer. "We had meetings on the Monday and a read-through. He had to rehearse all week and then the audience came in on Friday. Maybe I'm exaggerating, but I think it was quite a heavy schedule compared to the joyful days at Thames. On Friday, Everett would get in a flap and go, 'They're coming!' and we'd walk into the empty studio and look at the audience seats. 'Ooooh they'll be here tonight.' But the audience loved him and he became very good with a studio audience. He could tap in and do it, but it wasn't his thing really."

It's crucial on your first day at a new school to find a chum. Kenny found his on the first day of shooting for the Christmas special. It was a tough day. General Bombthebastards was having difficulties with his special effects. At a key moment a flag was supposed to ping out of his hat and cannons burst from his epaulettes, spraying the studio with bullets. The cannons malfunctioned, backfiring in a haze of smoke. Through the haze, a by now exhausted and slightly terrified Kenny caught the eye of a pneumatic stunner standing in the shadows out of shot. He rolled his eyes. She smiled encouragingly.

"Have you come to rescue me?" Kenny asked.

They bonded.

She was Cleo Rocos, a Brazilian born, half-Greek, half-English beauty who, to confuse matters further, was later to appear in a Welsh language sitcom. Her impact on that first Christmas show ensured her becoming a regular on the series. By the end of the year, she was sharing the *Blankety Blank* grid with Kenny, too, and for the rest of Kenny's life she remained a source of comfort, understanding and consolation, an invaluable travelling companion and an indispensable ally when it came to turning a humdrum occasion into a memorable evening out. Often their names were linked romantically and they took great sport in confusing the dimwit press.

"I would like to put the record straight right here and now," Kenny would tell the assembled hacks as he emerged from Broadcasting House lasciviously entwined with Cleo, "and state that stories about Cleo and I having a fabulous affair are completely and utterly untrue. We are absolutely not having a glorious and wonderfully immense relationship."

"Sure enough, the headlines the next day went along the lines of 'Kenny and Cleo deny 'Fabulous Affair'," says Cleo in her memoir *Bananas Forever*[82], "which we thought was highly amusing."

"When I was little," she told *Metro* in 2002, "I travelled everywhere and I used to look at TV commercials and always wanted to live in a cereal ad. Everything was perfect and white. And being in Kenny's show felt like that. People don't realise how much of that was totally real. Our life was like that all the time – it was like being in a cartoon."

The BBC version of the cartoon was more along the lines of Disney discipline than Looney Tunes mayhem. At Thames, if Kenny forgot a line, he'd make up another, possibly better one. Here the sketches were longer and the studio audience potentially restless. Autocue helped. Otherwise lines had to be learned or at least writ large and taped to the insides of drawers and the backs of scenery.

Barry, Ray and Kenny did what they could to retain a few vestiges of the old atmosphere. They would insist at the eleventh hour that a sketch they just made up in the car should go in the show. The sight of one of the elaborate sets would inspire a new idea, much better than the one for which it had originally been built. They'd rewrite, busk it, slam it in. They'd stand with the cameraman and, in breach of BBC discipline, laugh their heads off, encouraging the crew to do the same. But it was a losing battle.

It was rumoured that the BBC had hired a man to stand at the back and make sure that words like 'bum' and 'naughty bits' were used rather than 'arse' and 'tits'.

One day, hoping to inject at least a token moment of anarchy, Barry said, "Why don't do that thing with the camera?" The 'thing' being pulling the camera round, like Kenny had done at Thames, to 'show the glamour'. "So he did. Then the producer, Bill Wilson, came down from the gallery and said 'Oh that was very funny, very funny. But can we do it again? There was a bit of a shadow on Ev's face.' You can't do that. It doesn't work."

In revenge, Barry and Ray wrote a boardroom filled with cobwebbed BBC execs discussing the show ("Kenny Everett, who's he? A DJ? A dinner jacket?"), while next door the Director General, swigging from a bottle of Moët, is fondled by underwear models. But the edge was gone. What once might have been construed as criticism of a sacred institution and got him the sack was now barely seen even as taking the piss. The BBC brass indulged him. They were paying him, by his own always dubious testimony, two-and-a-half times more than he'd been getting at Thames and in return he was delivering ratings that made them look like champions.

Cupid Stunt first appeared in the Christmas special. A Hollywood starlet being interviewed by a cardboard cutout of Michael Parkinson, Kenny played her in heavy make-up, mini-skirt, full-beard and an enormous pair of breasts which, at key moments, he would hoik up before exaggeratedly uncrossing and recrossing his legs, half leaping from the sofa as he did so, exposing frilly knickers.

"If you invented a character he'd immediately see what he could do with it," says Barry Cryer. "Like Cupid Stunt crossing her legs – that was Old Mother Riley who he remembered seeing as a kid. She'd cross her legs violently at certain moments. Kenny always remembered things like that."

When Cupid's name caused problems in high places, Barry suggested an alternative spoonerism – Mary Hinge. On balance it was considered safer to stick with Cupid Stunt. The *Radio Times* got round the problem by referring to her merely as 'Cupid'. And by series two her fame had outgrown the spoonerism such that fans had to be reminded.

Kenny's skill at finding and extracting a double-entendre was honed to the extent that in his hands even as innocent a phrase as "look up your ancestors" became unmistakably proctological. Cupid's scripts should be studied by student comedy writers as object lessons in how to cram the maximum amount of innuendo into the minimum number of words.

"I want to stretch myself," she'd say, stretching herself. "I want to lay it on people. The producer was thinking of making some cuts in the series but I told him, 'Hands off my big parts.' I can't wait to get on that studio floor. The things that go on there you wouldn't believe. But I've only had two affairs – one with the director and one with the crew. Oh it's going to be a lovely series and all done [*up go the legs revealing the frilly knickers*] in the best possible taste."

Cupid entered the cultural vocabulary. Even people who had never seen the show knew about Cupid. They knew that she swung her legs high into the air. They knew that her catchphrase was, "And it's all done in the best possible taste." It could be argued that she may have brought about a slight shift in attitudes towards cross dressing, although it would be hard to say whether it was a shift in the right direction or the wrong direction.

Sunmed, the holiday firm, in its 1982 *Go Greek* brochure, advertised Mykonos, as "an up-market holiday spot for gays" featuring, among its attractions a cabaret act by Carlos "a thing of beauty and a boy forever, beautifully coiffured and made up wearing one of his own numbers that looks like it's been fashioned from polythene bin liners," and Angel Jack "eighteen stone of tattooed merchant seaman squeezed into a sequined gown with boobs fashioned from rolled balls of Lurex". Above the text was a Cupid Stunt lookalike, legs in the air, showing off red knickers. According to the *News Of The World*[83], Kenny's lawyers threatened to sue Sunmed for breach of copyright. "It doesn't look a bit like Kenny Everett," the Sunmed spokesman complained, "I know the guy in the picture. It's a chap called Steve." The spokesman suggested that Kenny was prepared to settle out of court for £1,000. The allegation that Sunmed had made the story up to get some free publicity for its *Go Greek* brochure was not made.

Other novelties, added as the series progressed, included Gizzard Puke, a Mohican punk of unsavoury nasal and ocular habits; a running sketch called *The Drains* – clearly a version of *The Snots* that had caused all the unpleasantness at Thames; and the introduction of ultra-violence with Reg Prescott, a DIY expert with pebble glasses – "get a good grip on your tools and you're ready for anything" – who did a good line in smack-on-the-head and cut-off-the-arms spurty-blood gags.

The stars were still queuing to have their dignity and person assaulted. Bob Geldof, Billy Connolly, Joanna Lumley, Terry Wogan, David Frost, Michael Parkinson, Frank Carson and Adam Faith all turned up to be ritually humiliated. Lionel Blair became something of a regular, nearly always hanging from a dungeon wall, being chastised by Miss Whiplash, played by Cleo Rocos.

Rod Stewart was in the first programme of the series, competing, on very unequal terms, with Kenny playing Rod Stewart.

"I honestly think that Kenny's comedy shows were about the funniest things I had seen on TV since *Monty Python*," says Bob Harris. "It was like he would close his eyes and he'd have all these sounds and sound pictures going on that he presented on radio, but with his eyes still shut he could visualise those and put them on TV and they worked in such a brilliant way. The thing of Rod Stewart in his leopard print pants singing, 'Do Ya Think I'm Sexy?' – and there's Kenny taking him off and you think. 'Oh, that a good take off' and then – he's got balloons in the bottoms of his skin-tight leopard print trousers, and of course that was the thing about Rod Stewart at the time, he was all bum and bottom and wiggling his bottom at the audience. So Kenny would turn round he was doing a brilliant impersonation of him. And then you'd get a closer shot. So there's Kenny miming, but the next wide shot, Kenny turns round and his bottom has got bigger and each time you look it gets bigger and bigger and bigger. Till finally you see him begin to float up into the air because his bottom has inflated so much. So simple but brilliant."

In episode three of the first series, Kenny proved he still had his tape-recordist chops, while at the same time the BBC proved that any video wizardry that Thames could do they could do better. In a white jump suit, appropriate wigs and huge gleaming teeth Kenny played all three Bee Gees, and then, in a fourth incarnation as himself, interviewed them. The Bee Gees sang in impeccable three-part harmony. They sang their replies to Kenny's questions, too, with quotes from Bee Gees songs.

"How do you sell so many records?"

"'Cos we're living in a world of fools…"

At home, Kenny had recorded a rough version of the harmonies to use in rehearsal, intending to record a more polished version using posher BBC facilities.

"Ev and I went into the sound place," says Barry Cryer, "and there was an old pro BBC sound man and Ev handed over a – here's a quaint word – a cassette. Ev said, 'Ooh, this may help as a guide,' and gave it to this man. The man said, 'Thanks Kenny', and stuck it into the machine and listened to it. He just said, 'Well, we can't do better than that. That's what we're going to use.' It was superb. He'd recorded three-part harmony for it and my wife, who's a professional singer said 'God, he can really do it.'"

He could too: impeccable pitch, as always, but – rare in an Everett vocal – Bee Gee-accurate melismatic ornamentation, too.

Kenny, whether he liked or not, had become a Much Loved Light Entertainer on a par with Morecambe and Wise, the Two Ronnies and Mike Yarwood. It was only to be expected, then, that he should treat the 1982 Christmas market to an autobiography.

He didn't actually write the autobiography but rather chatted over a series of days to one of his Capital Radio producers, Simon ('Betty') Booker, who wrote up the results of the talks into book form.

The Custard Stops At Hatfield[84] is fluffy and larky, but still deals with his adventures with acid, coke and other substances. The overdose of mandies and subsequent hospitalisation is dismissed with a breezy "oh, silly me". His sexual inclinations are hinted at but so thickly veiled that the casual reader wouldn't notice, and his marriage to Lee discussed mostly in the form of anecdotes – as if they enjoyed a wacky version of the standard sitcom marriage with its ups and downs but rarely if ever sideways bits.

It has to be said that the briefest acquaintance with the facts of Kenny's life reveals the book to be at least 40% and possibly anything up to 80% a work of fiction – a delightful and funny work of fiction (if you like books with the word 'custard' in the title, otherwise you might be better suited to the works of, say, Hilary Mantel) but fiction nonetheless. Even the title is based on the erroneous and frankly weird assumption that custard is available only in the north of England.

Kenny's particularly cavalier with the truth when describing his childhood, painting an 'eee it's grim up north' picture of back-to-back privation, a far cry from the genteel working-class seaside suburbia that had provided him with not one but two tape recorders.

His family was not thrilled. His mother was furious. But Kenny claimed that the book, like everything he did, was an entertainment. Fluff. Not to be taken seriously.

The book enjoyed healthy sales and that year his TV Christmas special was just pipped to the number one spot in the BBC1 ratings by *Hi-De-Hi*. More significantly, it thrashed Morecambe and Wise's Christmas special on Thames by half a million viewers. The BBC loved Cuddly Ken. The press loved Cuddly Ken. The public loved Cuddly Ken.

Obviously it all had to go ever so badly wrong.

CHAPTER ELEVEN

It was Margaret Thatcher's fault. Or Michael Foot's. Or Lynsey de Paul's. Or Michael Winner's. One of them. Or more likely still it was Kenny's fault.

Margaret Thatcher had been swept into power in the 1979 general election with a Conservative majority of 44 to become Britain's first woman Prime Minister. A hard-line right-wing monetarist Tory, her first term of office saw manufacturing output cut by 30% with closure of factories, mines and shipyards. Unemployment rose to its highest level since the Great Depression of the thirties and there were riots in Liverpool, London, Birmingham and Leeds.

Michael Foot was the Labour leader of the opposition; a left-wing intellectual and chronic asthmatic who often used a walking stick to support a tricky leg he'd acquired in a car accident some years earlier.

Lynsey de Paul was a pioneering female singer-songwriter, whose hits like 'Sugar Me', 'No Honestly' and 'Rock Bottom' brought a rueful moment to those who had nurtured a fond belief in pop as a great liberator that would free the human spirit and let it soar. She has been 'romantically linked' with Ringo Starr, George Best and Sean Connery, among many others.

Michael Winner was a well-respected film director, producer and restaurant critic responsible for such notable works as *Death Wish, I'll*

Never Forget What's'isname and the lesser known *Won Ton Ton: The Dog Who Saved Hollywood.*

In May 1983, Kenny and Cleo Rocos went to a party at Lynsey de Paul's house. Michael Winner gave them a lift home. On the way Michael, a Tory in those days, asked Kenny whether he'd mind getting up on stage at a Young Conservatives' Pre-General Election Rally at Wembley. Bob Monkhouse and Jimmy Tarbuck would be acting as Masters of Ceremony, Lynsey would be singing a song, wrestler Mick McManus, swimmer Sharron Davies, cricketer Freddie Trueman and a bunch of other celebs would be up on stage, too – so no pressure. Although he was never keen appearing in front of a live audience, Kenny agreed and didn't give it much further thought.

He turned up at Wembley Conference Centre on June 5 with a borrowed costume and the big pair of foam hands that he used for the evangelist preacher, Brother Lee Love. Everything was last minute. His agent, Jo Gurnett, had been asked to fetch the hands from his flat. "He lived on the top floor and it was a long way, carrying two bloody big hands for him."

In Evelyn Waugh's novel *Decline And Fall,* the hero sits in his rooms at Oxford while outside the aristocratic vandals of some dining club, drunk, roam in search of havoc to wreak. All at once the shouts acquire a "shriller note": "any who have heard that sound will shrink from the recollection of it; it is the sound of the English country families baying for broken glass."

That night, in the Wembley Conference Centre, although representatives of the English country families would have been far outnumbered by rat-faced trainee estate agents and blubbery business-studies graduates, that same, unmistakable, "shrill note" could be heard.

Lynsey de Paul sang the song she'd specially composed for the occasion.

"Vote Tory, Tory, Tory
For election glory
We don't want U turns
So we'll vote for Maggie T"

Kenny took the stage wearing his giant foam hands, no script, nothing planned, but an audience to please. He had their measure. He gave satisfaction.

"Let's bomb Russia!" he shouted.

There were wild cheers.

"Let's kick Michael Foot's stick away!"

The crowd went crazy.

Seeing he was on a roll, he leaned into the microphone and confided: "Do you know, I was talking to Maggie the other day – we were having one of our little teas together and I said to her, I said 'Maggie', I said 'you're rolling that joint all wrong...'"

The audience laughed and snorted and bayed themselves hoarse. They were in the palm of his huge foam hand.

If he had taken a dollop of actual shit and thrown it at an actual fan the effect could not have been more dramatic. Obviously Kenny was 'joking' but what, in this context, does 'joking' actually mean? Was bombing Russia and kicking Michael Foot's stick away official Conservative Party policy, people wondered, and if not why were Kenny's proposals so enthusiastically cheered? Did *Kenny* want to bomb Russia and kick Michael Foot's stick away? Did Margaret Thatcher smoke dope?

The Prime Minister found it necessary to issue a statement insisting that, "no one is talking politically about bombing the Russians. Every single thing I do is to deter any hostilities of any kind of breaking out. No one was seriously suggesting anything to the contrary at the time."

Representations were made to the Russian Embassy to explain that Kenny Everett had no control over Britain's nuclear arsenal, and neither were his views representative of Britain's foreign policy.

Barry Cryer has no doubts about what Kenny was up to. "He was taking the piss out of the whole audience," he says. "He thought it was like a Nuremberg rally."

The Nuremberg theme was picked up by the press, too. But Kenny, rather than being applauded for exposing some great horror about Young Conservatives, was cast as something closer to the Hitler role.

The News Of The World went with "Not funny, Kenny."

The People voted him "Wally of the Week."

"When Mr Kenny Everett bounced onto the stage at a Conservative youth rally and shrieked 'Let's bomb Russia, Let's kick Michael Foot's stick away,'" said the *Daily Mirror,* "he was being himself. He is a fool by profession. Mr Everett may be the foolish face of Toryism.

But his audience was an ugly one. Mr David Steele described their type yesterday, 'I find there is a breed of Conservative candidate,' he said, 'which is frankly unpleasant. There is an abrasive quality, an uncaring quality, a very right-wing quality about many of the Tory candidates.'"

Billy Connolly, who had turned out in support of a Labour candidate, rushed to his friend's defence, "I know Kenny and there's not an ounce of bigotry in him. It is the donkeys at the back of the hall who were bawling support that I worry about. I abhor what he said but I didn't take it seriously."

Barry Cryer had a possible solution. "I said to him, 'You must go to every party meeting – Tory, Labour, SDP to confuse them. Just turn up everywhere!' That would have been perfect." Kenny didn't take the advice.

"That was then that the press turned," says Barry. "It's the old story. It's a cliché – you can praise people and build them up and knock them down. They had something to beat Ev up with now and that hurt him. I was with him a lot through the years subsequently when he was being interviewed and every single journalist brought it up. And he'd look at me and go 'Oh here we go.'"

As if to atone for his gaffe, subsequently Kenny never missed an opportunity to have a go at Thatcher.

One of his great treats for a while was to be taken by his friend Francis Butler, a restaurateur, to Francis' parents' house in Gerrards Cross for Sunday lunch. He adored Mr and Mrs Butler and embroidered them a little sampler, intertwining their names, framed in a pink frame. They hung it in their downstairs toilet. Their daughter, Francis' sister, had married Ben Cross, the actor. And thereby hangs a tale.

"Margaret Thatcher, in the early eighties, threw a party at 10 Downing Street for television celebrities and stars," says Francis. "My brother-in-law, Ben Cross, was invited. My sister went along and she bumped into Kenny there and Kenny clung on to my sister because he was feeling a bit inadequate. Anyway, he was sitting on a sofa with my sister and Margaret Thatcher stalked by with this white gaunt face with the dash of purple lipstick. And as she strode past Kenny said, 'Oh waitress, could we have two cups of tea, please?'"

Later, in his TV show, he did a sketch in which Sid Snot spots a picture of Margaret Thatcher in the pub and remarks that she looks like a pig. A fellow drinker takes offence and lays into Kenny with a starting-handle. They roll about fighting until Sid manages to blurt out an apology, saying he didn't realise his assailant was a Conservative. "I'm not," says the thug, "I'm a pig farmer."

The best came in November 1983 when – this is the way he told the story anyway – at the end of his Radio 2 programme his producer handed him a joke on a bit of paper. Without scanning the contents first, Kenny read it out on air. "When Britain was an empire," he said, "it was ruled by an emperor. When we were a kingdom, we had a king. Now we are a country, we're ruled by Margaret Thatcher."

The following March the BBC did not exercise its option to renew his Radio 2 contract. "His programme is not scheduled for this quarter," they said. "Kenny does a short term series. And it hasn't been decided what the next schedule is to be."

Kenny was convinced he'd been sacked for the Thatcher crack. "The whole affair is over one joke. But talk to the BBC and they'll tell you we had artistic differences."

Kenny never did another regular show for BBC Radio. He should worry. Capital welcomed him back with open arms and he took over a Saturday morning slot.

There's no doubt that Kenny, inasmuch as he had any awareness of politics at all, leaned to the right: mostly, it has to be said, because of the Tories' attitude towards the wireless. Kenny's experience with the pirates had convinced him that commercial radio was funkier and freer than the BBC. The Conservatives had supported commercial radio. Labour had opposed it. Therefore Conservatives must be better.

"The only political feelings I have," he told *The News Of The World*[85], "are that I'm doing quite well now, and I'd like to keep it that way, so I suppose I am a Conservative. The Labour party keeps saying offensive things like 'we're going to squeeze the rich.' And they dress so badly. I'm not the best dressed person in the world but, if I was after votes, I would really wear a decent frock."

The General Election, four days after the 'Let's Bomb Russia' incident, swept the Conservatives back into office with a massively increased majority. The swing even further to the right opened up a political divide deeper and angrier than anything Britain had known since before the war.

At around the same time as the first Thatcher victory, in 1979, two entrepreneurs, Peter Rosengard and Don Ward, had opened a club – modelled on and named after the Comedy Store in Los Angeles – that quickly became a focus for a new wave of comedians whose origins could vaguely be located somewhere between punk rock and the Fringe Theatre movement. They performed mostly in the Fringe Theatre venues because in 1979 there was no 'comedy circuit'. Back then, all you'd have seen in the thousands of upstairs rooms in local pubs that later hosted 'Gagsters', 'The Ha-Ha' and 'Larfer Daily's' was a meeting of the darts club or the mirthless passing of balloons by Jack's 60th birthday celebrants.

The Comedy Store ran on the Gong system. The acts would come out. If they were funny they were allowed their moment in the spotlight. Otherwise they were Gonged. The acts were ragged, raw and energised by the ever-present threat, never quite fulfilled, of violence. Alexei Sayle was master of ceremonies.

"The opening of the club coincided with that first wave of Thatcherism," says Alexei. "Politics was central to everything. It was a time when the world seemed it was on fire. It was the two great ideologies – Thatcherism and the liberal consensus. Heath had subscribed to essentially the same philosophy as Callaghan. Both were operating within the terms of – to use a Hobbesian term – the social contract, the liberal consensus. But Thatcher was really a radical. She clearly had a project to throw the social contract out of the window. There were riots, mass unemployment. In the Comedy Store, there was – in the best performers – an awareness of all that. It informed everything we did."

Other regulars at the Comedy Store included Tony Allen, Rik Mayall, Adrian Edmondson, Arnold Brown, Nigel Planer, Peter Richardson, Keith Allen, Jim Barclay.

They all signed up to another, related, liberationist agenda, too. The term 'politically correct', bandied for years by front-line activists and used to judge anything from a policy on world hunger to a pair of trousers, was becoming common currency. Attitudes to race, gender and sexual orientation were being questioned. Use, even casual 'jokey' use, of words like 'Paki', 'poof' and 'bint' were increasingly regarded with distaste.

Sexism and racism were not tolerated at the Comedy Store. Innuendo was considered weasly. Why say, "at it" or "rumpy-pumpy" when the word "fucking" is available? Why make sly references to ocular disorders when you can talk about wanking? They used what Kenny would coyly have referred to as 'naughty words' without a second thought. As did most people. Or at least most people who'd make the effort to go to a comedy club.

The new wave got called alternative comedy and it got noticed. Some of the Comedy Store acts set up their own club which they called the Comic Strip. They were commissioned to make a film, *Five Go Mad In Dorset,* which was broadcast to great acclaim on the opening night of Channel 4 in November 1982.

BBC producer Paul Jackson, who had meanwhile put on a couple of Comedy Store specials, commissioned a sitcom, *The Young Ones,* starring some of the best of the alternatives. The first episode went out in the same month as the Channel 4 film. This new lot were suddenly all over everything.

Superficially Kenny seemed to have much in common with the alternatives. He had come up through pop music rather than the Working Men's Clubs (training ground for a whole generation of post-variety, pre-alternative comics), and he was, in the broadest sense, anti-establishment, iconoclastic, and Mary Whitehouse hated him.

Back in the days when his show was still on Thames, he had made an appearance on *Not The Nine O'Clock News,* the sort of Oxbridge wing of alternative comedy. After the opening titles, the voice-over announces, "And here is your host for tonight, Kenny Everett."

Kenny, in full dinner jacket and bow tie, comes down a sweeping staircase to great applause and cheers.

"Well, good evening fans and welcome to *Not The Nine O'Clock News.* Yes, the BBC and I have settled our old differences and they have agreed to give me my own show as long as I don't say the word 'pubes'."

The floor manager appears. "All right, that's it, clear out."

Kenny tries to protest.

"We have warned you."

He begins to move off.

"Go on, keep going."

On paper Kenny had much in common with Alexei Sayle. Both were from Liverpool. Kenny's dad worked on the tugboats, Alexei's dad was a goods-guard, working on the railways. But whereas Kenny's parents were devout Roman Catholics, Alexei's were devout Communists. It resulted in irreconcilable differences.

The energy, aggression and agenda of the alternatives posed an immediate threat to Kenny's hold over the 12 to 18 year olds who had been his most devoted fans. In just five years, it seemed, he had gone from being the edgy, anti-establishment, new big thing, to being un-PC old hat. And Thatcherite un-PC old hat at that.

"I was at the BBC Christmas party chatting with Ev," says Barry Cryer, "and Alexei Sayle was there. Ev went, 'Ooh, Alexei Sayle' – he admired stand-up comedians – and I said, 'Do you want to meet him?'" Barry knew and knows everybody in comedy. It is his business to do so. "And Ev said, 'Yeah.' I took him over and said, 'Alexei, this is Kenny Everett.' And Alexei said, 'Fuck off.' Very forcefully. Ev was shattered. He went home early."

Alexei remembers it differently.

"You see, I never did say '"fuck off,"'" he says. "Barry Cryer was at the party but he didn't introduce us. It was the Christmas Party in 1983, after Kenny had done the 'Let's Bomb Russia' thing. That's why I was shirty to him. But I never did say, 'fuck off'. What happened was, Jimmy Moir brought Kenny over to me and he said – actually it's much wittier than the story Barry told – he said, 'You know who this is, don't you?' And I said, 'Yes' and walked off. But I didn't say 'fuck off.' I wasn't that rude. It was a bit inflammatory of me doing that because the Light Ent Christmas Party was a big deal. It was quite stuffy. The big scandal was that in the sixties, which was the last time that they invited the younger types, the Pythons had come in jeans and I think that Graham Chapman had created a scene, crawling around on the floor, very drunk. So after that they never invited anybody controversial. So inviting the alternatives was a big deal because it meant you were part of the Comedy Family. And we all behaved very well. I wore a suit – but not black tie. I swore never to wear a dickey-bow until Palestine was free. The stars of *It Ain't Half Hot, Mum* were there, Ronnie Barker was there, Ronnie Corbett was there. They were bigger names than Kenny in strictly Light Ent terms. Kenny didn't have a history in Light Ent. He was a disc jockey. He was less at home there than I was. I feel guilty about it, now. I was being a prick. Jim Moir assumed it was just some kind of show business spat. He probably thought it was a row about dressing rooms or something,"

In 1982, Mrs Mary Whitehouse was too distracted by anal rape to have much time for Kenny. She was pursuing a private prosecution against Michael Bogdanov, the director of Howard Brenton's *The Romans In Britain,* a play which featured simulated sex acts between naked actors besides which Kenny's half-hours of underwear and innuendo seemed like weekly Quaker Meetings in Guildford.

The new, strident Channel 4 and its insistence on showing tasty extracts from films like *SS Experiment Camp* and *I Spit On Your Grave* was taking up a lot of her time, too, as was the arrest of her son in a drugs raid.

The Department of Education stepped into the breach. Just a couple of weeks after the 'Let's Bomb Russia' incident, a report, *Popular TV And Schoolchildren,* drawn up by a committee of 15 teachers, examined the image of adult life that TV presented to kids. *Minder, Crossroads* and *Dallas* all came in for criticism but Kenny's show was singled out: "As far as TV personalities are concerned," the report said, "by far the most popular is Kenny Everett. It is clear from what young people say that his appeal is based on his versatility and his irreverence: he is naughty and does rude things. Such qualities are hardly new (or reprehensible) in children's entertainment and playground culture, but what is disconcerting is the delivery of cheap smut into the living room at a time when people of all ages are watching, often in a family group. The presentation of physical violence was unacceptable... and the casual linking of violence with sex in some scenes." It also found the programme's attitude towards women, "degrading and offensive".

The Times[86] editorial thundered, "Cultural criticism of this kind often is left to Mrs Mary Whitehouse and her viewers' association and is derided as a result." It went on to say that BBC executives would be fulfilling their duties more adequately if they "sat down and registered how many times they winced during a Kenny Everett half hour at the paltriness of it all."

What five years ago had been hailed as "refreshing", "honest" and "steamy" was now "paltry", "cheap smut", "degrading and offensive". Kenny came up with the standard defence, "These teachers just don't credit these children with the ability to recognize what's real on TV and what isn't. To say I could be responsible for encouraging sex and violence among schoolchildren is like saying Vincent Price is encouraging people to go round sucking each other's blood."

With Let's-Bomb-Russia on the 5th and the teacher's report on the 21st, June 1983 was turning into a rough month. To compound matters still further, on the 26th *The People* announced, "The private life of Kenny Everett has even his friends a little puzzled." Then it spilled the beans, or at least some of the beans about the domestic arrangements Kenny and Lee had been enjoying for some time: the state of play being that both had new (as far as the press was concerned) boyfriends; Lee had John Alkin; Kenny had a Russian, a former Red Army soldier called Nikolai (*The People* identifies him as "Vladimir"). The exact nature of the relationship between Kenny and "Vladimir" is not specified.

Lee had a busy life. As well as regressions and healings, she'd opened a shop/clinic/school called 'The House Of Spirit' and she'd published a book, *The Happy Medium*. Kenny, she told *The People,* was "un-liveable with".

At the beginning of September Kenny and Lee announced their impending divorce. Back in 1981, she'd said, "His mother thinks that when Ev left home he had a mental age of around seven. Now he is 36, I reckon he is getting into his teens. He is a happy 18."[87] Two years later she was describing her life as "rather like rearing a difficult baby", adding, "We grew apart when my mission was over. He had no need for me – only as a friend." Nearly every account makes mention of the mysterious 'Vladimir', leaving readers to draw their own conclusions.

It was to be an amicable split, said Kenny and Lee, to be celebrated with a party: "We are friends – and we needed an excuse for a good party anyway." In December it was announced that Kenny, Lee and John Alkin would be spending Christmas together and, in February, Kenny would be Best Man at Lee and John's wedding.

So who was Kenny being seen about town with? The tabloids, failing to get a photo of Kenny with Nikolai, instead cobbled together a story around whatever photo they could get. Usually it was Kenny with Cleo – "Kenny in breakfast date with Miss Whiplash. Is he carrying on with the sultry siren or was their dawn get-together really in the best possible taste?"

At other times it was Kenny and "a mystery blonde who answers to the name of Melanie Bubbles." This was Kenny's favourite new fun buddy, Ray Cameron's wife, Kati.

Ray was in his late thirties and Kati was 19 when they married. They had two children in quick succession. With the oldest, Michael (who later found fame and fortune as the stadium stand-up Michael McIntyre) in school, Kati decided to spread her wings and enjoy some me time with her new best girlfriend, Kenny Everett.

They were regularly snapped by the paps falling out of clubs in the small hours. She wasn't always Melanie Bubbles, sometimes it was Melody, sometimes Marianne.

They'd go shopping together, cruise into Waitrose, snatch a bottle of Krug from the shelf, pop the cork and scandalise the staff by necking it while throwing groceries into their trolleys. The other shoppers loved it. Here he was, the wackiest man in the country being wacky just like he was supposed to.

Sometimes Kenny and Kati picked up little Michael McIntyre from school. "Is Kenny Everett your dad?" the other kids asked.

"I paused," Michael wrote in his autobiography[88], "thinking of my real dad, who I loved and was my hero.

"'Yes, Kenny Everett is my dad,' I said. It made me the most popular kid in school – until the next school sports day fathers' race."

Ray Cameron was by this time all but directing Kenny's show as well as co-writing it. Cleo Rocos maintains that he was the heartbeat of the show: a driving force. Unbowed by the less than spectacular success of *Kremmen – The Movie* he decided to have another shot at transferring the Everett brand to the big screen.

Comedy horror was doing well. John Landis' *An American Werewolf In London*, *The Rocky Horror Picture Show* and *Love At First Bite* had all taken mouthwatering sums of money at the box office, still played to packed houses whenever they were screened and looked as if they were going to do so until somebody did the thing with the wooden stake.

Accordingly, Ray and Barry set to work on *Bloodbath At The House Of Death*, a suck-fest fit to give even the most stout hearted the willies while simultaneously bending them backward with chuckles. Ray would direct. Producers were schmoozed, funds were raised, top stars were booked.

Kenny would play Dr Lukas Mandeville, a scientist who, at moments of stress, would forget himself, lapse into a German accent (a cross between Dr Gitfinger from *Kremmen* and Peter Sellers in *Dr Strangelove)* and let slip his cover to reveal his true identity as a disgraced surgeon, Ludwig Mannheim of Frankfurt.

Pamela Stephenson, star of BBC's award-winning *Not The Nine O'Clock News* and inamorata of Kenny's pal Billy Connolly, is Dr Lukas' sidekick, the very prim Dr Barbara Coyle.

Gareth Hunt of *The New Avengers* and Don Warrington of *Rising Damp* would play two closet gay scientists. There were a lot of other scientists too – played by Sheila Steafel, John Fortune, John Stephen Hill and, of course, Cleo Rocos (who was also given the task of getting Kenny up in the morning and to the set on time).

The scientists had all come to investigate "strange radioactive readings" at Headstone Manor, a country house that had been the scene of many unusual deaths. "There's something here that doesn't quite smell right," says Gareth Hunt. "Yes, I'm terribly sorry,' says Don Warrington, "I'll open a window."

The source of all Headstone Manor's problems turns out to be a character known simply as The Sinister Man and played by the master of horror, Vincent Price, booked, to cut costs, for just four days shooting. They got their money's worth.

"I'd worked with Vincent on television shows before so I knew him," says Barry Cryer. "But it had been a long time and during the intervening years I'd gone grey. The great man came into the room where me and Ev were, and he saw me and he said, 'The child has gone white in the service of comedy.' He was great. Ev felt in awe of Vincent but they hit it off immediately. We gave Vincent a trailer because he was a big star, but he was never in it. He queued with the crew for the bacon sandwiches and the cup of tea. Of course, he was bisexual. There was a rapport with him and Everett. Kenny thought, 'Oh my god, this big star and me are mates.' They just laughed all the time. It was lovely."

Vincent, in the short time he was there, did his best to boost Kenny's confidence, but on the set Kenny was nervous. Even straightforward scenes would sometimes have to go to 20-plus takes as he fluffed or forgot his lines over and over again. The whole process of filming – the waiting, the retakes and worst of all the absence of even crew laughs – was to him a straightjacket more constricting than anything even the BBC could devise.

As a result, far from dominating a film that was supposed to be a vehicle for his talents, he seems to lurk in the shadows, at best a rather weak component of an ensemble piece. His difficulties weren't helped by an inability to bond with his co-star.

"Pamela Stephenson is very serious about acting," he says in one of the 'extras' on the video release of *Bloodbath*. "She goes into corners with her head in her hands and makes lots and lots of serious learning noises. I learn the plot for the film tucked up in bed at night, then I dream about it, then I think about it again at breakfast – and as soon as the red light goes on for the scene, I just do it." And then, after 20 more takes, he's got it.

Kenny and others described Pamela as "snooty". Later it transpired that she had good reason for being perhaps a little withdrawn and distracted. She was pregnant. She and Billy were going to have their first baby. "But she didn't tell us," says Barry. "She even had a nude scene."

Pregnant or not, any actor would have had to exercise extreme professionalism not to let their misgivings about the project show.

Year later, cast members still shudder at the memory. "Oh, God," says Sheila Steafel. "... that."

The film has two redeeming features. The lighting in one or two scenes is quite good and some of the props are reasonably well made. It contains some inept parodies of other horror and sci-fi films – there are nods to *Carrie, Star Wars, E.T.* (with the young Michael McIntyre doing his voice) and several others – but for two writers as prolific as Barry and Ray, the gags are few and far between and when they eventually arrive they're not of the finest quality.

"We must grab all the faggots and burn them," says Vincent Price.

"Don't worry, Brother Theresa," says an acolyte. "He means wood."

"Look out! A bat!" says Pamela Stephenson as she and Kenny walk through the cellars. Something hard hits Kenny on the head. "Oh, no," he says, "a cricket bat." A door opens. "Obviously an opening bat."

"I hope," says Pamela, "it doesn't lead to a sticky wicket."

More tellingly, "Are you laughing at me?" says Kenny, lapsing into his Ludwig Mannheim accent, "I can't stand it when people laugh at me."

"Nobody's laughing at you," says John Stephen Hill. And if ever a line was a hostage to fortune...

Vincent Price went on to do some sterling work in the 10 years until his death, but this was the last time he would wear cardinal's robes or stride with torch-bearing cohorts through moonlit woods or mutter the incantations required to summon Satan. It was a shabby swan song.

"I don't believe it," he declaims at one point. "Seven hundred years undead. And now this."

It was released in the same week as *Yentl,* Barbra Streisand's folk-tale of cross-dressing Jews ("Mentl!" *Time Out*). The critics dug deep to find fitting calumnies, but came back empty handed. "Words cannot adequately describe how bad *Bloodbath At The House Of Death* is," said one. The *Express* called it a "feeble send up".

"It's a fairly terrible film," says Laurence Myers, one of the executive producers. "I recall showing it to [censor] James Ferman who thought it was fine and funny enough, but thought we were showing him the reels in the wrong order. We weren't – the film just doesn't make sense."[89]

"Oh, we had a lot of fun making it but it sank without trace," says Barry Cryer. "Afterwards it became a bit of a cult film. A man emailed me recently and said, 'Oh I've got it at home – I watch it all the time because it's full of in-jokes and references to other films – there's *Alien* in there and all sorts of stuff. This man said – oh I love it – there are 18 references to films I spotted. I just said 'You should get out more.'"

Bloodbath At The House Of Death contains one genuinely chilling moment. Gareth Hunt and Don Warrington, the two closet gays, are lounging. Gareth idly flicks through a gay magazine called *HIM.*

Presumably nobody on the set had paid much attention to the magazine, beyond the fact that it contained appropriate images of fit young men. Even if they had paid attention, the magazine's cover line wouldn't have meant anything. In 1983, it didn't mean much to anybody. In consisted of just four letters – with a full stop after each. A.I.D.S.

CHAPTER TWELVE

There always had been a sort of parallel universe into which, in the dark days before decriminalisation, gay people could disappear and live their lives without fear of disturbing the horses or inviting the law. London had a network of pubs, clubs, steam baths, cinemas and hotels — some had been around since Victorian times, others came and went in a matter of weeks or days.

The Coleherne, a pub in Earls Court, had been a gay hangout since not long after the end of World War II. By the seventies, it was attracting a celebrity clientele: you might bump into Rudolph Nureyev, chiselled prince of the Royal Ballet; American visitors like Anthony Perkins, star of Hitchcock's *Psycho*, or Armistead Maupin, author of the *Tales Of The City* books (the Coleherne even gets a namecheck in his *Babycakes*) who would pop by, check out the action and maybe share a joke with say, Freddie Mercury, or even Kenny Everett. And if nothing was doing at the Coleherne, they could move on to the Boltons, the Chepstow, the Laurel Tree, or a score of other pubs, or maybe the Tricky Dicky Disco on Bishopsgate or Mandy's or the Pink Elephant or the Masquerade. Places were good for a while and then fell out of fashion. But none of them were as good as Heaven.

Heaven opened in 1979 in what used to be the wine cellars of the Adelphi Hotel, beneath Charing Cross railway station in central London.

There was never anything hole-in-the-wall or basementy about Heaven, though. It was 21,000 square feet of Hi-NRG celebration where the best-dressed, most beautiful people in the world came to find pleasure. Madonna, Kylie, Divine, Grace Jones, Eartha Kitt, the Eurythmics – they all played Heaven. It was the location for Frankie Goes To Hollywood's 'Relax' video. On New Year's Eve, 1981, a 20 foot penis emerged from the stage and, as the countdown to midnight began, second by second throbbed into full erection. On the stroke of 12 it ejaculated party glitter all over the dance floor.

Kenny loved it. At Heaven, the Fairlight fanfare opening of Donna Summer's 'She Works Hard For The Money' would dispel every last memory of caution, guilt, denial and self-loathing. He could relax, surrounded by the mass of leaping, laughing bodies. He felt safe. He had found another comfort zone.

Heaven the club, like heaven in the sky, was never exclusive. Though the population was predominantly gay and male, on the dance floor you could rub shoulders with every nuance of orientation.

Even Barry Cryer gave it a go. Anywhere that sells lager is OK by Barry. Kenny used to take him to Heaven after a hard day's filming. "Come on, let's dance," Kenny would say. So Barry would dance with Kenny. "Everybody's saying, 'Who's that old man dancing with Ev?'" Kenny would say. And Barry would reply, "No they're not. They're saying, 'Who's that dwarf dancing with Baz?'"

Lager was not the most highly favoured stimulant. On a trip to America, Kenny had discovered methylenedioxyamphetamine (MDA, Mary Don't Ask, 'the love drug'). "I boogied for 12 hours," he told the *Daily Express* (he was never coy about drugs), "but a week later I was on my back for a week." MDA, sometimes mixed with a little acid, became his pharmaceutical of choice and endless boogying his favourite recreation.

One night, on the dance floor of Heaven, sometime in 1980, Nikolai Grishanovich, a Russian with an Olympic gymnast's body and the face of a poet, approached. He told Kenny he was the sexiest man in the club. He told him he wanted to spend the rest of his life with him. Kenny was understandably bowled over. His relationship with John, the waiter that Lee had picked out for him in Joe Allen's, was reaching its end anyway.

A few nights later, Kenny met the Russian again and the two of them went back to Nikolai's place.

Francis Butler, the restaurateur, was later picked up by Nikolai himself on the King's Road ("we had tea in Habitat which was what was done in those days"). Soon after they met, Nikolai introduced him to Kenny. He knows the whole story.

"Nikolai rented a room off an ageing actress in Maida Vale," he says, "actually she might have been a ballerina – anyway, she would have been in her mid-seventies and old school. In the morning she opened Nikolai's door and found Kenny and Nikolai in bed together. So Nikolai was thrown out on the spot. That's how it all happened. Kenny asked him to move in, so he did."

"Nikolai was a man who had no depth at all – totally shallow. He was brought up in Moscow by his mother, I think his father had been – I mean, this is what Nikolai told me anyway – his father had been a German soldier who probably didn't even survive the siege of Stalingrad. He had had a younger brother, who had a different father, but his younger brother died during the Russian/Afghan conflict. The mother sent Nikolai a photograph of his brother's corpse, I remember. It was all very odd.

"The hold that Nikolai had over Kenny was purely sexual," continues Butler. "His English was good, but he had nothing to say for himself. He was totally, totally hedonistic. That's not to say he wasn't intelligent. I'm sure he was highly intelligent, but he was just interested in one thing and one thing alone and that was sex and having a party."

No conversation about Nikolai seems complete without, at some point, the words 'vacuum cleaner' cropping up. Either in the context that if nothing with a pulse and/or warmish blood was knocking around Nikolai would have sex with a vacuum cleaner, or that Nikolai was a vacuum cleaner, physically and spiritually sucking body fluids, emotions and souls.

"Oh, he gave me the creeps," says Barry Cryer. "He put his tongue down my throat once in McDonald's and said, [Greta Garbo *Ninotchka* Russian accent] 'Bar-r-r-y, I love you!' Ev came home one night and found Nikolai at it with a woman. He said, 'I've heard of being unfaithful, but this is ridiculous!' We always said Nikolai was like a vacuum cleaner, if you get my meaning. My wife, with her female instinct, immediately the moment she met him said he was trouble. A charming, gregarious and extrovert man – if he came in this pub now everybody'd be going, 'Oh, he's a laugh. He's all right.' He was everything that Ev wanted at that time. He overpowered Ev. And he was trouble."

For good or ill – mostly for ill – Nikolai became Kenny's mentor, his advisor, his enabler and his counsellor.

"Kenny found release in Nikolai," says Francis. "Nikolai almost took on the role of sex therapist for Kenny. Sorted him out in that department."

It became clear early on in the relationship that a repressed Roman Catholic tape-recording nerd from Crosby, Liverpool, with a well-developed sense of self-effacement and the body of an underfed skunk (Clive James once described him as a 'rat looking though a lavatory brush') was never going to adapt easily to a life of international gay playboy hedonism.

"I remember him saying he'd gone with Nikolai to some place in America," says Andrew Marshall, "some sort of nocturnal cruising venue – Fire Island or somewhere. They'd gone into these woods and gone down this path and then in a clearing by the light of the moon they found all these extraordinarily handsome men having all the different sex you could ever dream of in your life. Kenny said, 'I waddled after Nikolai like Hilda Baker.' And he saw all this pulchritude in front of him and he just said, 'I'm terribly sorry, I'm English' and went home. He really didn't have a good self image."

"Kenny was never promiscuous," says Francis Butler. "He was indulging Nikolai's promiscuity but it was all fantasy. He was tantalising himself with fantasy. Kenny and I would do a few gay bars but neither of us was interested really. Nikolai would be rushing around, almost like a recruiting officer. Kenny was a terribly nervous, inhibited man – the most inhibited person I think I've ever met. Nikolai was his agent provocateur who would take him out and organise him. He'd say, 'Come on, we will take this man home and I will fuck him.'"

Nikolai might have been infinitely less inhibited, more experienced and more daring than Kenny, but when it came to devising sexual fantasies the years of writing Kremmen gave Kenny a distinct edge.

"His biggest fantasy," says Francis Butler, "was that he was in a

German wartime submarine and the submarine would sort of sink to the bottom of the ocean floor and everyone would escape except for him and this sadistic Kommandant. The Kommandant would then give him a good seeing to. They'd play out this fantasy, then Nikolai would leave him tied up and go out. He used to come and visit me."

Thankfully, Kenny was an early adopter of the push-button tone-dial phone with speed-dial facility. Even if he was tied up and hanging from the ceiling, as long as the phone was in reach, he could get through to Francis with one toe.

"Three separate times," says Francis. "I remember the phone ringing and there was this 'uuuggh urrgh.' It was Kenny, bound and gagged. I'd say, 'Nikolai, you've gone too far.'

"There was one time I was having a very interesting tea-party and Nikolai was there, and Kenny rang in the middle of it to say, 'Uurgh urrgh' and Nikolai was very cross because he had to leave and go home to see what was wrong with Kenny. He came back half an hour later and we were all agog. Nikolai was never known for his discretion, so everyone at the tea-party knew what had happened and wanted to know what was going on. 'Oh don't worry,' he said. 'I had just left an open bottle of Amyl Nitrate on top of the gas heater. Kenny had seen it there and was worried that it might burst into flames. So he tried to get the telephone. But the telephone was in another room and, because he was tied up, he fell down the stairs."

Kenny had made it to the kitchen and freed his fingers enough to get hold of a knife and try to cut through his bonds. He missed and cut himself instead. Nikolai had gone round, bandaged up the cuts, and put Kenny to bed. Then he had returned to Francis' house to finish his tea.

Tessa Ditner is a novelist and journalist who writes regularly for the BDSM (bondage, discipline, sadism and masochism) magazine, *Skin Two*. Her analysis of Kenny's submarine fantasy – the details of which were given to her without names, circumstances or even genders attached – is perceptive and heartwarming. "The idea behind it could be that the tied-up person is helpless and therefore freed of any guilt: 'Oh I'm stuck in this submarine and it's not my fault that I'm getting turned on by this Kommandant in a sexy uniform. It's just because I am in such an unusual circumstance. If I were in Sainsbury's, I'd definitely just be getting turned on by Delia Smith, but I'm not, so my behaviour is a matter of survival.'

"It sounds like quite a sexy role-play scenario, particularly if his partner is leaving the house after he's tied him up. That way the tied-up person can spend ages wondering what the Kommandant is going to do with him when he gets home/back to the submarine.

"In terms of their relationship, obviously, it means his partner was the dominator and he was the submissive partner in that game. It might have been that in the real world he earned more money and looked after his partner, which is why the fantasy is reversing that daytime role. They sound quite in love really. Sweet!"

The public coming-out was at first a gradual thing, a testing of the water, dropping more obvious hints, giving the press confidence that instead of just printing his name as Madcap Kenny Everett (39), he could, without risk of prosecution, be dubbed, 'Madcap *Gay* Kenny Everett (39).

In May 1984, the *Daily Express*[90] interviewed Nikolai, indentifying him as the mysterious 'Vladimir' previously reported to be Kenny's 'flatmate'. Nikolai told them that he had fled Russia three years before and was now working as a freelance computer analyst. He claimed that his wife, Shelia, was living with them too. "She doesn't mind what I do, so long as I keep her happy too. Kenny needs me to look after him. He is very sweet. But there are times when he gets bad tempered and moody."

"I'm not a homosexual," said Kenny, planting a kiss on Nikolai, "just helping out."

It quickly became clear that Nikolai didn't have a wife called 'Sheila' but he did have a boyfriend called Pepe – a Spanish waiter who was also living with them.

"Kenny jealous?" says Francis. "Yes, he was jealous when Pepe was on the scene. Kenny's way of dealing with it was to announce that he had fallen in love with Pepe as well. He would then try to get into bed with Pepe – who basically wasn't very interested in him, but Nikolai would say, 'You've got to do it because Kenny's paying our bills.' Pepe, being from Spain, got terribly proud but not so proud he'd turn down the money. I mean, it wasn't big time, it was just money to pay the bills and eat."

The full and frank disclosure finally came on October 6, 1985. Kenny told the *Sunday Mirror*[91], "In the past I have hinted in interviews that I am bisexual. I'm gay, but it's boring to make a big deal about it."

A couple of weeks later, he did make a big deal out of it when Pepe went home to Spain for a few days and, on his return to Britain, was refused entry.

Kenny made a campaign of his outrage. His fight to keep his "gay pals act" together appeared in the *Daily Mirror*[92] with a smiling picture of Kenny, Nikolai and Pepe and a headline "My Husbands And I."

"There's nothing worse than having only one husband," Kenny announced.

A few days later, in a "Kenny Quits Britain" shock, he'd decided that if Pepe couldn't live here, he and Nikolai would move to Marbella. He was, the *Mirror* reported, "fed up with cruel jokes about his gay love life". "I'm fed up to the teeth with being called a pervert," he said. He told the press that he'd put his flat on the market and was planning to move in with Lee for a few days. "I think I'll seek solace from her," he said. "She's a woman, you know."

He did in fact go to Spain. He stayed four days and returned without Pepe. "I love England," he said. "It's the only place I really want to live. I never intended to leave England. My friends are here. My work is here."

"I've got a science quiz and another radio show lined up," he told the *Express,* "so I'll stay."

In March 1986, he was denying that there had ever been a threesome and admitting he was essentially monogamous. "I want to find someone to live the rest of my life with. Someone totally committed. Someone who adores me as much as I adore him. It is not an easy situation for a gay man to find. Gays are inclined to be very promiscuous. I don't like that. I have never been into one-night stands. I want companionship and love."[93]

"I think he was aware that Nikolai was a totally unsuitable long term partner," says Andrew Marshall. "He was looking for someone more suitable but how do you find such a person? It's very difficult. One of his solutions was to have parties where he'd go out to various bars in Earls Court or the Bromptons and go around and look at people who looked quite good and then invite them to his parties. It's a bit like

Cinderella, really, this idea that one of them somehow would be the one for Kenny. So you'd go round to his flat and there'd be this party and there'd be all these extraordinary people there and you'd think 'this is not the way'. There would be lots of booze and everybody would be very drunk and so forth and you'd think, 'this is not the way to meet partners.' Really, it's not a good starting point. But he wanted to settle down and live happily ever after. I expect he probably wanted to have a little house in the Cotswolds with slippers and things. I think he just wanted to be happy. I think that's how you see happiness, isn't it, when you're, say, 15?"

Francis Butler is not so much concerned with the Cinderella-strategy that Kenny was deploying in his quest to find a life-partner as the kind of person he was auditioning for the role. "He was a little man. He wasn't an attractive man. He was mousy. And he was shy. I didn't find him attractive socially and, of course, when he went up to the gay clubs he surrounded himself with other sort of strangely suburban little men."

The drink, drugs and partying were causing concern, not least to Kenny himself. "Alcohol does terrible things to my memory," he said. 'Didn't we have fun last night?' someone will say to me and I reply, 'Did we? What did we do?' Apparently I had all this fun and I'd been too drunk to realise it. I've asked my doctor for some pills which will make me sick, if I drink. The trouble is I'll have to wait for two days before I can take one, until all the alcohol is out of my system. Oh Betty Ford, where are you when I need you?"[94]

On Valentine's Day, 1985, Lee married John Alkin at the Pembridge Spiritualist Church in Notting Hill. This time, instead of a tablecloth, Lee wore a demure two-piece and carried a chihuahua nestling in her bouquet. Elton John was present with his wife, Renata, whom he'd married exactly one year earlier. He wore a straw hat, just like he had in the 'I'm Still Standing' video. Kenny, in dapper dickey-bow, was best man.

The reception was at Geale's Fish and Chip restaurant at Notting Hill Gate. Ev stood up, fixed John Alkin with a beady stare and said, "For God's sake, don't tell her about us, will you?"

Coming out to your family and delighting in the discovery that far from disowning you they provide a bottomless resource of love and support is one thing; coming out to the general public, when that public is as huge as Kenny's, is another. In 1986, Kenny's mum and dad emigrated to Australia to join his sister who was already living out there. "I am heartbroken that my mother is so far away," he told the *Daily Mail*.[95] "She is the most important woman in my life. When it went public my mother felt a degree of shame. She was close to suicide – it was frightening – and in the end she had to go and live in Perth with my sister. I am desperately unhappy about the situation."

Later the same year he had a huge bust up with Freddie Mercury ostensibly about cocaine. Kenny thought that Freddie was helping himself too freely to his stash. People with coke up their noses tend to scrap anyway, but this fight, almost certainly heated by years of simmering resentment – fuelled possibly by jealousy about Freddie's occasional dalliances with Nikolai – was remembered the following day and the day after that. They never made it up. If they found themselves accidentally in the same club, they would compete to see which could devise the more insulting snub.

At the end of the third BBC series, in 1985, Ray Cameron left the team on a sour note.

Ray's wife, Kati, was still frequently seen out and about on the town, squired by her best friend Kenny. She and Ray were having some work done at their house. One night Kati confided in Kenny. She told him that she was having an affair with Steve, their builder and it was turning serious. Kenny, foolishly, sent the two of them a card. Ray found it. Kenny knew about the affair and hadn't told him. As a co-conspirator he was part of the infidelity.

The atmosphere in the studio was chilly. When the series ended, Ray left.

Which was when Andrew Marshall and his writing partner David Renwick joined the team. They approached Kenny with a certain degree of caution. "He was, I suppose," says Andrew, "the sort of naughty imp who was the spirit of disorder – almost Dionysian – the Lord of Misrule. He was Puck – a sort of pop era Puck. He was really a sort of strange sprite who entertains and says things other people can't say and is sort of somehow slightly otherworldly. The eternal child.

"Kenny had access to this extraordinary talent which was perfectly suited to radio but on TV it was a difficult talent to corral. It was difficult to know what it is you're actually showcasing. I'm not sure whether even the successful TV shows worked. They were a sort of shadow of Everett. They never really quite captured the radio quality, which was far more spontaneous. Nothing scripted can ever replicate that spontaneity; and of course in sound Ev could make these extraordinary pictures and jingles and things which don't translate to TV at all.

"My abiding memory of the TV studio is Kenny being dressed up as a crab or something and saying to me, 'Who am I in this sketch, Andrew?'"

The gilt on the gingerbread had begun to tarnish. William Marshall of the *Daily Mirror*[96] wrote off series three with: "We hereby mourn the passing of one of the most vaunted funnymen in the business. I speak of one Kenny Everett of the *Kenny Everett Television Show*. We mourn for the abominable lack of anything resembling the Kenny Everett of yesteryear. This Kenny Everett is as tame as a neutered pussy, fangs removed, tail snipped, whiskers demolished. No longer the lunatic gleam in the eye or the trembling moment when Kenny seemed to be on the verge of delivering the most insufferable and outrageous lampoon of all that's holy and respected."

An albeit half-hearted attempt to do something new came up in March 1985 when *QED*, a long running BBC1 popular science series that covered everything from autism to spontaneous combustion, asked Kenny to present a programme – right up his street – about Quantel, CSO and all the other still relatively novel digital video devices, or "computerised doo-dahs that send your picture potty", as he called them. The *Radio Times* billed it as "his first semi-sensible television role".

He shrieked his bafflement, fought a video duel with an Apache warrior and made some politicians' heads explode. *QED* did ask him back, just the once, two years later, to present a "light-hearted look" at the entire history of the Universe from big bang to the moment of his birth, but even "semi-sensible" he never gave Raymond Baxter or Michael Burke a moment's anxiety.

For the Christmas special that year, Barry and Neil Shand had written a version of Dickens' *A Christmas Carol*. Spike Milligan, Willie Rushton and Peter Cook were booked to play the three ghosts. Kenny was playing Scrooge, Tiny Tim and Queen Victoria.

As usual, his lines were on Autocue – the prompting device which puts the script on the camera lens. Spike Milligan arrived on set and spotted the Autocue.

"What's this?"

"Ev always has Autocue."

"I've been up all night learning my lines," he complained.

When Kenny arrived on set he was greeted as, "Mr Autocue Everett. Remind me to send you an assassin for Christmas."

There were two more TV series. The law of diminishing returns is inexorable. The shows had lost their edge, either because the world had grown crueller or because Kenny had mellowed. Possibly a bit of each.

"You don't have to be vile to make people laugh," Kenny told *Woman's Own*[97]. "I was watching *Terry And June* [a mild-mannered mainstream sitcom starring Terry Scott and June Whitfield] the other night and years ago I would have thought, 'what a load of rubbish,' but now I think, 'how civilised, how pleasant, charming situations with witty turns.'"

Hot Gossip were bought back for series four to "bring back some of the old spirit' according to their manager Michael Summerton. Only one of the original line-up remained in the group of three boys and six girls but Arlene Phillips promised they would be as raunchy as ever.

They were as raunchy as ever, but 'the old spirit' proved to be a hopeless case even when treated with industrial doses of inadequate wet-look PVC straps, studs, wild hair and 'Purple Rain'.

And besides, by 1986, "raunch" or anything to do with casual sex was looking fiercely inappropriate.

CHAPTER THIRTEEN

"There is now a danger that has become a threat to us all," said John Hurt over images of a 2001-style monolith/tombstone carved with the single word 'AIDS'. "It is a killer disease and there is no known cure."

The 'Tombstone' ads hit British TV screens in January 1987. They were backed up by leaflets shoved through everybody's door bearing the same apocalyptic images, but with some practical advice about wearing condoms and watching out for blood.

It came – possibly – from monkeys in Cameroon, Equatorial Guinea. Doctors first began to realise that they were dealing with something new, possibly an epidemic, in 1979, when multiple cases emerged simultaneously in New York, San Francisco and Los Angeles. They initially called it 'the 4H disease' after the four social groups it seemed mostly to affect – homosexuals, Haitians, heroin users and haemophiliacs; or 'GRID' – Gay Related Immune Deficiency. Eventually doctors and researchers settled on the name Acquired Immune Deficiency Syndrome – AIDS.

By the end of 1982, 1,300 cases had been identified in the US and AIDS had spread to Britain. Terry Higgins, among the first in the UK to die of the disease, was a reporter who worked in the evenings as a barman at Heaven.

It was of course, a gift for the American Bible Belt. "The Gay Plague" was clearly God's retribution visited on those who failed to obey His strictures. And when cases in Zaire first began to link AIDS to Africa, it was clear that His Great Purpose was to wipe out the entire population of the world except for White Heterosexuals who drove Chevy Silverados and smoked Winstons, thereby utterly vindicating everything they'd been saying for years. Even liberal doctors, nurses, politicians and social workers, who really should have known better, found it hard entirely to escape the idea that AIDS was some sort of just deserts. Ideas like karma and "what goes around comes around" and "whatsoever a man soweth, that shall he also reap", had many adherents – including Kenny.

"That's the thing about life," he once said, referring at the time to drugs and to fun in general rather than to AIDS, but the thought was there all the same, "you pay for every thrill."

The apocalyptic nature of the 'plague' prompted some extravagant claims about its origins. Some suggested it was a by-product of Haitian voodoo or that a single, possibly Haitian, individual had had sex with a pig that was carrying African Swine Fever. Meteorites from the outer reaches of the galaxy or astronauts inadvertently bringing home alien viruses on their space suits were strongly suspected by sci-fi fans, while conspiracy and cock-up theorists devised various scenarios involving the medical establishment, the drug companies, the White House and the military, most of which sounded a damn sight more plausible than the generally accepted explanation about having sex with and/or eating Cameroon monkeys.

Nobody knew. And nobody knew enough about the disease to offer sound advice. How could you tell if somebody had "the AIDS"? Was it safe to shake their hand, be in the same room, kiss them, give them a blow-job? Would we all eventually succumb? Did "gayness" cause AIDS or was it a symptom?

When it was realised that the disease could be passed on by infected blood, a request was put out asking homosexuals not to volunteer their services as blood donors. Thus, when the transfusion van came to the car park, anybody who didn't roll up his sleeve was obviously "a queer". So, counterproductively, many gay men who wouldn't normally have given blood now did so rather than face the taunts.

In learned papers, usually temperate scientists described the 'mystery disease' as 'frightening', 'scary', 'terrifying'. "There is no precedent for this complete collapse of the immune system." "Something unknown is killing people."

Headlines went Hammer Horror and competed to condense maximum fear and bigotry into the minimum number of words: "Kiss Of Death", "March Of The Gay Plague", "AIDS – Wrath Of God Says Vicar", "Tide Of Fear".

Because six months or more might pass between infection and the first development of symptoms, in the early days, AIDS was impossible to diagnose. By 1984, it had been linked with a virus, eventually called HIV, and a test devised. The first batch of tests to be conducted in Britain revealed that one in three homosexuals was already HIV positive. Several more years were to pass before the range of drugs used to manage the HIV infection became available.

By the late eighties, the appointments pages of many Filofaxes and Datadays were scribbles of hospital visits and funerals. Conversation in the pub went, "Has anybody seen so-and-so lately?" "Oh, didn't you know?"

"It was a bit like being an old person and all your friends are dying," says Andrew Marshall. "Except you're all in your thirties. Like going through a war, I suppose. You're walking along the front line with a lot of people and snipers are just taking them out."

It could never be proved, but one story has it that AIDS was brought to the UK by an unnamed American who went to the Coleherne and picked up a likely stranger. The stranger was Nikolai Grishanovich, "that careless twat Nikolai", who thus became, the story goes, the source of all AIDS in the UK.

But it is no more than a story.

"I knew many, many people like Nikolai," says Francis Butler. "Heaven had a big dark room. You'd get 100 guys in that room and each one would have sex with 20 people in any given night. Now you multiply that out and that's probably 500 contacts per night or maybe more. They were all infecting one another, no two ways about it."

Nobody knew they were infecting each other. Back then gay sex *was* safe sex. Crabs were dealt with by the man at the hospital who'd paint your pubes with his big brush. Clap and pox could be treated with a shot. The increased risk of hepatitis was still a matter for research papers. Nobody got pregnant or had abortions or had unwanted kids who were neglected, abused or starved. Where's the problem?

It took time for the message to get through. In May 1983, Mel Rosen, director of the Gay Men's Health Crisis in New York, addressing a conference on AIDS announced, "An express train is coming down the track and it's heading straight for you."

In London, the warning was even more blunt. "I remember going to a Terrence Higgins Trust thing at a big house in Holland Park," says Francis Butler. "They told us that in five years time there's every chance that 80% of the people in this room are going to be dead. And I reckon they were right."

Hollywood heartthrob Rock Hudson was one of the first big stars to go. Tabloid journalists found their pulses quickening. Celeb+sex+disease had long been established as the recipe for a perfect story. The spread of the disease and the prevalence of gay celebs could potentially deliver at least one 'Gay Soap Star In AIDS Tragedy' story a day. Would the public ever tire of them? Not if it was played right. Think of the variations. Think of the pictures. Some of them would have wives and children. They might have infected them, too. Think of the shock. Think of the horror. The wives might stand by their spouses. They might leave in disgust. Either way the kiddies on the hospital steps would weep.

Overnight, doorstepping gay and potentially gay celebrities to find out whether they'd be next became a top tabloid sport.

Kenny with his 'two husbands' was an obvious mark. His agent's phone never stopped ringing. "Does Kenny have AIDS?" Eventually Kenny got the filth off her and his back by putting out a statement. "No, I don't have AIDS – as far as I'm aware. If people thought I did I would be heartbroken. I don't want people to stop kissing me, hugging me, inviting me to parties… and I'd never be able to sell my flat."

"Two years ago when this whole AIDS scare began I came to an agreement with my constant companions Nikolai and Pepe. We decided if any one of us got AIDS then we would have to assume that all three us would have it. If that happens, and God forbid that it ever does, we would look after and care for each other. We have talked about it – and know exactly what to do. It would mean abandoning everything – selling our homes and everything we own, leaving our jobs and taking off around the world until we drop dead. We wouldn't give in to AIDS but go out in style, in one last wild fling."[98]

The note of resignation is understandable. It was 1985. Kenny had known about AIDS for two years at least. He'd known Nikolai for five years.

"Kenny was very fatalistic about AIDS," says Andrew Marshall. "He was convinced that all gays were just going to die. He thought it was bad luck but he reckoned that was it. We would all die off. A whole generation. So, his attitude was, 'I may as well just go and enjoy myself.' That's one attitude. I was convinced myself that if you practised safe sex and if you hadn't slept around a lot, you'd probably be OK and indeed I was."

Kenny could perhaps have been OK, too. He was not, after all, promiscuous by nature. He was the man who, faced with an orgy, made his excuses and waddled away like Hilda Baker; who wanted a life partner far more than he ever wanted sex. The partner he had, though, was death on legs.

"Had it not been for Nikolai, Kenny would be alive today," says Francis Butler. "There's no two ways about it."

A year later, in 1986, Nikolai was diagnosed as HIV positive. He did nothing to change his behaviour.

"Kenny arranged for Nikolai to stay with me when they fell out for a while," says Francis, "because Kenny trusted me to keep an eye on Nikolai – which was very hard to do. I mean – male, female, animal, fish, mammal – he'd take it into his bedroom and shut the door. I had an old man of 80 called John who I was employing to paint all the doors in my house while Nikolai was staying and I said, 'You've been painting that door for over an hour.' He was just standing there going up and down with his brush. Turned out that Nikolai had bought a girl back and they were in his room. 'Yeah,' he said. 'They're at it in there, aren't they?'"

Kenny's world was turning into a hostile place. More dangers of being a cruising homosexual were underlined when Michael Lupo, a successful hairdresser, was arrested and charged with four murders. Lupo is Italian for 'wolf'. 'The Wolf Man' was a face on the scene whose promiscuity outdid even Nikolai's. He boasted of having had 4,000 lovers. Early in 1986, he was diagnosed as being HIV positive. What followed has been described as "revenge on the gay community". His first victim, James Burns, was found in a basement, strangled, mutilated with a razor and smeared with excrement. His second, Anthony Connolly, was found in a railway shed in a similar condition. There were two other murders and two attempted murders. Lupo was a great record keeper. His journals contained detailed accounts of his conquests. His address book contained thousands of names, "including those of a leading television comedian, a top fashion designer and other professional figures." The 'leading television comedian' was Kenny. The police called round and asked a few questions. Kenny could not remember ever having met Lupo.

The press were turning against him, too. They used to love Kenny. As the BBC's senior whistle-blower and dirt-disher he could be relied on for terrific copy. He had the knack of keeping them away from the stories he didn't want told by always making sure they scurried back to their editors with something juicy. For years the complaints about the BBC, the 'The Maurice And Audrey Show', the candid confessions about his drug-taking and the loveless horrors of his pretend childhood had kept them so busy they never had time to ask, never needed to ask anything difficult like, 'Are you gay?'

They turned on him a bit after the 'Let's Bomb Russia' caper and the awful movie, but they quite enjoyed the divorce, and when, finally, he was prepared to come out and gag about his threesome ménage, they quite enjoyed 'Gay Kenny' too – as if his sexuality was just another aspect of his 'wackiness'.

AIDS changed things. 'Gays' could not be wacky. They were diseased. They were infectious. They were pariahs. And we'll only find out how diseased they are, the press argued, if we hang around like jackals, waiting for them to die.

Whatever the rest of the press were doing – and in retrospect, even the politically correct *Guardian* had its iffy moments reporting AIDS – the 'Soaraway' *Sun* did bigger and better. In the late seventies, the *Sun*, after a bitter circulation war, had finally triumphed over its closest rival the *Daily Mirror*. It spent the next 10 years waving its all-conquering willy at politicians, the Press Council, journalistic standards and taste. Anybody who didn't like its daily diet of nipples, bingo and gossip was a poof loony lefty snob lezzer who should go and try living in East Germany for a bit to see how that suits you, eh?

The British press had never exactly been in thrall to ethics, but throughout the eighties and nineties the red-tops, led by the *Sun,* dug holes in the ground so that the bar could be set lower still.

When the *Sun* celebrated the sinking of the Argentine light cruiser the *General Belgrano* during the Falklands War with the headline "GOTCHA", British sailors, disgusted by the triumphalism, mindful of the death and suffering the action had brought and the widows and orphans it had made, ritually chucked their copies of the paper overboard.

When it printed cruel lies about the Hillsborough disaster, people in Liverpool and elsewhere burned their copies and forever boycotted shops that sold it.

Elton John sued successfully and was awarded £1m damages when the *Sun* made allegations about his sexual habits and animal cruelty.

Kelvin MacKenzie, the *Sun's* editor between 1981 and 1984, was intractably unrepentant: "When I published those stories, they were not lies. They were great stories that later turned out to be untrue – and that is different. What am I supposed to feel ashamed about?"

To the red-tops, then as now, the lost weekends of soccer heroes and the adulterous shenanigans of soap stars were meat and drink. MacKenzie made a bold claim that the celebrity exposé was in the great tradition of campaigning journalism.

"Living a lie and hypocrisy on high can have no place in our society," went a 1988 *Sun* editorial. "If a star who profits enormously from being idolised takes drugs we shall say so. Such an act is a breach of public trust. If a TV performer who sets himself up as a paragon of domestic decencies is a lying sham, we shall say so."

And if Tony Benn, 'Loony Leftie' Labour politician, 'set himself up' as being as sane as the next man, the paper would produce a fake psychiatric report to 'prove' that in fact he was indeed what top shrinks would describe as 'loony'. And if Michael Foot, the Leader of the Labour Party (1980–83) 'set himself up' as being a fit person to become Prime Minister, the paper would prove him a 'lying sham' by establishing that he was far too old and far too badly dressed for such a post.

Benn and Foot were exceptions. Most of the red-top 'campaigns' dealt not with the pretensions of those in power, but the harmless debauchery of personality-deficient celebs who never for a moment pretended to be righteous or responsible, never pretended to be 'paragons of domestic decency', just drunk.

The paper's obsession with gay celebrities was often downright creepy. In their excellent history of the *Sun, Stick It Up Your Punter*[99], Peter Chippindale and Chris Horrie explore the quirks of Kelvin.

"'Oh Christ, not another one!' he would say as a group or a singer 'came out', genuinely perplexed by successes like Boy George, Freddie Mercury and Frankie Goes to Hollywood. MacKenzie could not understand the popularity of 'musical poofters'. Eventually he made sense of it all by putting it down to some sort of conspiracy, whereby gays worked together to promote each other's records.

"At one editorial conference, MacKenzie had even proposed a special feature to bring readers up to date with the current state of play. 'What we need is a fucking table to sort them all out,' he announced. 'We'll have three columns with little symbols, eh? – those who are gay, those who are straight and those who haven't said.'"

Another feature was actually headlined, "The Poofs of Pop".

The Leveson inquiry eventually showed the world something of the absurd and illegal lengths journalists would go to in search usually of tittle-tattle. Technology, phones and emails have made intrusion sneakier, easier and more sinister, but the underlying ethics – or lack of them – have never changed.

When AIDS came, outing the 'poofs' – not just of pop, any sort of famous 'poof' would do – and exposing their disease in all its horror, with shock photos, became more than just a campaign. It was a mission of moral righteousness in which the means, they reckoned, would always justify the end.

Russell Harty was a TV presenter and chat-show host with a lovely line in self-deprecating humour. In 1988 he died of Hepatitis-B. He had, up until the moment of his death, been hounded by journalists desperate to 'out' him as a gay man dying of AIDS. A working-class upbringing in Blackburn, Lancashire, had left him, like Kenny, reticent, in public at least, about his sex life. He was not, and had never pretended to be, a 'paragon of domestic virtue'.

nd Baz, December 1991.

Marcel Wave, the only beardless character he ever played.
FREMANTLEMEDIA LTD/REX FEATURES

'When I grow up I'm going to be Kenny Everett ...'
FREMANTLEMEDIA LTD/REX FEATURES

'I'm just dying to take the weight off my chest': Cupid Stunt, 1982.
STEN ROSELUND/REX FEATURES

bomb them!'

an in the realms of glory: *Blankety Blank Christmas*
l, 1979.

Kenny—not knowing which way to turn—with Cleo Rocos and
Nikolai Grisanovich.

Kenny and Lulu on the town in 1983.
JEROME YEATS/ALAMY

Kenny with PM, 1983: 'Maggie, you're rolling that joint all wrong...'
GRAHAM WOOD/DAILY MAIL/REX FEATURES

Kenny with 'that careless twat' Nikolai.
PA ARCHIVE/PRESS ASSOCIATION IMAGES

'There's nothing worse than having only one husband': Nikolai, Kenny and Pepe, 1985.
BILL ROWNTREE/MIRRORPIX

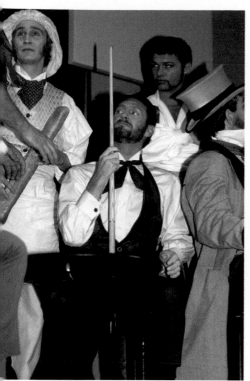

'unctuous' billiard marker 'Dancing Towards Disaster',
ing Of The Snark. EMPICS ENTERTAINMENT

Checking Cleo's still breathing, 1988.
REX FEATURES

g to avoid the press, disguised as Kenny Everett after the
5 revelation.
CHIVE/PRESS ASSOCIATION IMAGES

Receiving The Sony Gold Award for Outstanding Contribution to
Radio from Sir George Martin, 1994.
CLIVE LIMPKIN/ASSOCIATED NEWSPAPERS/REX FEATURES

Immaculate on Des O'Connor's show: shame about the shoes, 1991.
FREMANTLEMEDIA LTD/REX FEATURES

At his memorial service, his friend, the playwright Alan Bennett, spoke of how the *News Of The World* had set up Harty; how reporters had bribed children in the village where he lived and even tried to bribe the vicar; and how, when he was in hospital fighting for his life, a reporter, posing as a junior doctor, went into the ward and demanded to see Harty's medical notes. "One newspaper took a flat opposite," said Bennett "and had a camera with a long lens trained on the window of his ward. The gutter press finished him."

The *Sun* replied in print the next day (readers with a shred of decency should look away now): "Stress did not kill Russell Harty. The truth is that he died from a sexually transmitted disease. The press didn't give it to him. He caught it from his own choice. And by paying young rent boys he broke the law. Some – like ageing bachelor Mr Bennett – can see no harm in that. He has no family. But what if it had been *your* son Harty had bedded?"

When Boy George was sick with heroin addiction, a *Sun* photographer stuck a lens in his face and ran the picture: "Junkie George Has Only Eight Weeks To Live". George is still with us. The *Sun's* sister paper, the *News Of The World*, is dead.

Unless living with two husbands counts, Kenny hadn't set himself up as a 'paragon of domestic decency' for years, and from the start he'd rather overdone the confessions of a pothead acidhead pill popper, so no public trust was being betrayed there.

In November 1986, the press got a tip-off from a 'friend' that Nikolai had been diagnosed HIV positive. "Poor Kenny must be terribly worried," the 'friend' was reported as saying. "All his friends are concerned for his health because of this man's illness. This man was the worst thing that ever happened to Kenny. But women aren't the only ones who fall for the person that treats them the worst."[100]

The *News Of The World* hack was persistent. He turned up at Kenny's flat in Kensington and leaned on the bell. Eventually Kenny spoke on the doorphone.

"I am sorry. I am not being impolite but I do not wish to discuss this."

Another – or maybe the same – reporter waited to nab Kenny outside Capital Radio. Kenny sneaked out the back door.

But the news was out. As well as the *News Of The World's* "TV Kenny AIDS Peril", the *Mirror* had "Kenny In AIDS Agony" and the *Sun,* "I Fear AIDS says comic Kenny".

It was a while before Kenny plucked up the courage to be tested. Lee nagged him. In order to protect others, he should get tested.

He kept the results to himself, telling only one or two close friends who were possibly in the same boat. There was nothing you could do back then. No drugs you could take. Stay healthy. Stay clean. Don't infect others. Wait. Try to keep a glimmer of hope burning and for God's sake don't tell the press. They'll tear you to pieces.

Francis Butler was running an avocado farm/restaurant in Spain: "At one point the *Sun* sent a team of people down to corner me. They offered me £12,000. They wanted specifically for me to tell them whether or not Kenny was HIV positive. I knew I was the first person he'd told and I refused to play ball. But they came back the next day and upped it to £18,000 – this was back in – what – '87 and my God, I could have done with £18,000. I got them to take me out to Marbella's number one restaurant for lunch and they turned up with tape recorders, cameras – the lot. I twittered away and ordered foie gras, champagne, caviar everything, but I didn't give them what they wanted. It was a female journalist and she said to me that the editor of the *Sun* would pay anything to screw Kenny."

Lee wrote a memoir, *A Kind Of Loving*, published in April 1987, a generous but frank account of her marriage to Kenny. Initially, Kenny had encouraged her, suggesting that he should join her on a book tour. He even wrote a foreword:"In between the disasters, Lee and I had loads of good times and the rafters rang with merry sounds of laughter. One's memory has a wonderful capacity for erasing the bad bits and enhancing the good moments, so when I eventually become a creaking OAP in my electric wheelchair with compact disc and built in colour TV, I'll have nothing but wonderful memories of our times together."

The *Daily Star* serialised extracts from the book, concentrating, as newspapers have a tendency to do with any biography, on the more lurid, sensational episodes, painting a not very pleasant picture of Kenny in his twenties and thirties as a whining, drug-addled, out-of-control depressive, all of which was, of course, true if you caught him on an off day, but had nothing to do with the sunny, likeable, talented chap he was most of the time.

Kenny was not pleased. In a *Mail On Sunday*[101] interview, he made it clear that his attitude towards Lee writing the book was now, "I wish she hadn't."

At Elton John's 40th birthday party, Kenny and Lee had a blazing and very public row. Other rows followed. Eventually Kenny stopped speaking to Lee entirely. Most of the friends, including Elton, took Lee's side.

"I think Lee was probably very good for Kenny," says Andrew Marshall, "and perhaps in some ways it would have been better if they just stayed together and had an arrangement. But that would have been unfair to her. It's so difficult. I think she continued to worry about him."

"You see," Kenny said, "through a lot of the years described in the book I thought it was the world that wanted fixing, not me. Of course, you can't fix everything about yourself. Just when you think you've got it all sorted – Oh, so that's how it works – God bungs you another one you're not prepared for. But I'm learning. Right now I'm gently cutting away those people who want to be around 'Kenny Everett' as opposed to me."

Kenny no longer wanted to be the Kenny Everett that Lee had known. He'd reinvented himself.

Over the course of his life there were, to grossly oversimplify, four versions of 'Kenny Everett'; four identities adapted to suit changing circumstances.

The first, Maurice Cole, was too changeable a thing to be described as an identity. Little Maurice, like most children and adolescents, was in the process of becoming, with few fixed points. But unlike other kids who make a reasonable fist at being 'child' and 'adolescent' – fulfilling the social norms, the psychological profiles, expressing the right urges at the right times and so on – the 'Maurice' identity was unfit for purpose. He never quite got the knack of education, he was useless at rough and tumble in the playground and failed even to see the point of fancying girls. He was permanently out of sorts, out of place, out of time, as uncomfortable in his own skin as he was in a woolly vest.

Kenny Everett *Mark I* was more satisfactory. This was the version that started life on a pirate ship, that had a girlfriend, got married, bought a house, talked about 'the missus' on the radio. It was an identity that served him well for 15 years or so. Of course it had to accommodate howling contradictions which often brought pain to himself and to others, but it also brought him good times, frequent contentment, intense and loving relationships and immense success in a creatively fulfilling career.

Kenny Everett *Mark II* lived with two men, went out 'boogying' every night and got to pretend he was trapped in a wrecked submarine. For a time, the emergence from *Mark I* to *Mark II* must have felt like a jailbreak. Long repressed needs could at last be satisfied. Pretences could be dropped. He was able at last to express that most dubious of all constructs, 'his true self'.

Selves are annoyingly complicated things. Kenny Everett *Mark II* discovered that in the constant round of drugs, disco and the emotional clamour of Nikolai and Pepe there was little room for the contented stillness of the breakfast table, the thrum of the washing machine, for quiet companionship, walks in the country, proper Sunday dinners with a gravy boat and a hot pudding.

And so, to continue the shameful oversimplification, Kenny Everett *Mark III* emerged: a man who had found a sort of peace at last with his sexuality, calmer, quieter and, infuriatingly, just when he seemed to be getting somewhere, infected with a bloody virus that had a strong chance of killing him before his 50th birthday.

Finding an identity, maintaining it and adapting it to changing circumstances is an emotional and philosophical chore for the private individual. For the famous – particularly those who aren't meticulously hinged in the first place – it can lead to panic, pills, issues and episodes.

Evolution has given us little intellectual or emotional equipment to deal with fame and none at all to deal with adulation. If you believe yourself worthy of adulation, terrible things happen to your ego. It inflates and inflates until one day it bursts. The resulting feeling of worthlessness can all too easily lead to an acoustic album.

On the other hand, if you don't believe in the adulation, then either you must be an utter fraud who has gulled millions of fans that you are bigger than Jesus and when they find out you've inadvertently pulled the wool over their eyes they're going to be really mad – or, worse still, you begin to disbelieve everything.

If the sacks of fan mail, the crowds, the cheers – all clearly seen, heard, touched and smelled – have no meaning, if they are not 'real' in any usual sense, then why should this piece of cheese be 'real', or this hat, or this table, or the universe? And when thoughts like this invade your head, more likely than not, next thing you know you've signed up for a cult. Or moved in with an Amazonian tribe. Or written a bloody novel. Or started sitting in a Parisian street café, toying with an absinthe spoon and muttering, "forever I shall be a stranger to myself" and "despair is suffering without meaning".

The other difficulty is that the adoring public, wherever you go, reflects your identity back at you. "Say, 'All in the best possible taste', Ken." "Do something wacky." This can grow tiresome in the pub or the supermarket, even more so when the identity they reflect is one you cast off, or tried to cast off, years ago – like asking Glenda Jackson MP to reprise some of her nude scenes from *The Music Lovers,* or David Bowie to sing *The Laughing Gnome.* Strategies have to be developed.

"I was writer on *It's Tommy Cooper,*" says Barry Cryer, "and one day we finished early and Tommy said, 'Come on, let's go to the pub.' It was so early the pub was quite deserted and this man came up to us and sort of punched Tommy on the arm. And I thought, 'Oh boy.'

"The man said, 'Can I tell you a joke?' and Tommy said, 'Don't you know?' Which I thought was quite funny.

"Then the man said, 'I've got to tell you this. Two men go into a pub....'

"And Tommy turns to the barman and says 'Excuse me, I'd better write this down, have you got a bit of paper? Sorry go on.'

"So he starts up again, 'These two men go into a pub....'

"'Have you got a pen? Sorry, go on.'

"And so he says 'These two men ...'

"And by now people are coming into the pub. And they're all spotting Tommy Cooper, but the man ploughs on. 'These two men go into a pub ...'

"'Excuse me – is it any particular pub?' says Tommy. He's pretending to write everything down. 'Has it got a name in this joke or is it just any old pub?'

"The man's now going red, 'Any old pub. These two men ...'

"'They're just 'men' are they? I mean the joke's got nothing to do with their jobs or anything?'

"'No, Tommy...' The man is now dying by inches and people are gathering round. One of the cameramen came in. Tommy calls him over. 'Harry, come here! You've got to hear this joke. Will you start again?'"

Tommy Cooper was a 6'4" ex-soldier, ex-boxer. Kenny was a 5'5" ex-winner of a Saturday morning cinema skipping competition. Humiliating blokes in pubs was never an option.

The public were relentless, forever shouting, "Oi, Everett, let's bomb Russia, too right, ha, ha, ha," from the other side of a crowded street, or wanted him to "do Sid Snot" while he waited for his latest test results at the doctor's surgery. It was, of course, fair enough. They paid his wages. They put him where he was today. If they stopped the harassment, where would that leave him? But all the same it was horrible.

"I think generally he was concerned about being liked," says Andrew Marshall. "I got the impression he used to really hate the idea of anybody not liking him. I think that was quite a worry for him. Which is odd because I can't imagine anybody who wouldn't like him.

"But I've been driving in a car with Ev and we'd stop at the traffic lights. You'd be aware of people in adjacent cars looking at you. And they're saying, 'Who's that bloke with Everett? There – it is Everett, isn't it?' And Kenny would be sitting there going, 'Oh, please, let the lights change.'"

One incident particularly upset him. Kenny was on his way to work one morning when a scaffolder dropped his pants and wiggled his member, shouting, "Come on, you like this, don't you?"

It preyed on his mind. "For years afterwards," says Andrew, "he used to get very worried about the builders outside his flat – about what they were going to say to him when he went out. He'd actually get quite nervous and say, 'Ooh, will you come out with me, Andrew, in case the builders say something?' 'What are they going to say, Kenny?' 'Oh you terrible old queen or something.' 'What could they possibly say that would hurt you?' Of course, they wouldn't anyway, but he used to worry."

Perhaps another aspect of Kenny's eagerness to be liked was the way in which the exact nature of his paranoia was adjusted to accommodate the perceived predilections of a given companion. Just as Andrew Marshall might respond to a terror of homophobia, he assumed – mistakenly as it turned out – that Francis Butler, from a solid middle-class family, would sympathise with snobbery.

"We'd go out together," says Francis, "and wherever he went he would be confronted with fans, which used to upset him terribly. He called them peasants – 'Get me out of here. Take me away from these peasants' and all the rest of it. The word 'pleb' he used a lot. Once I fell out with him over it. Once we were driving somewhere in the car and I said, 'You can't talk about people like that, Kenny' and he stopped the car and threw me out."

Kenny enjoyed making audiences laugh – "It's the next best thing to jumping into the audience and making passionate love to them all" – but he had never possessed the atavistic need that drives real show people back onto the stage night after night because it's the only place they can feel truly alive. He was not, in other words, the kind of person Irving Berlin had in mind when he wrote 'There's No Business Like Showbusiness'. He did not find everything about it appealing.

Years after their meeting for that first ever radio gig on the *Midweek* programme, Kenny had a drink with its producer, Wilfred De'Ath. "I think he'd had a few drinks, or he was stoned, and he said, 'I wish sometimes you'd never taken me out of the pond. I wish you'd thrown me back.' I said, 'Come on it's not that bad, you're doing very well,' but he was adamant. I don't know whether he was just being melodramatic. He said, 'I wish you'd never discovered me,' and I said, 'Well actually I'm very proud of you, Kenny. You've made a fantastic name for yourself.' But he wouldn't be snapped out of it."

⋆　⋆　⋆

The fifth series of *The Kenny Everett Television Show* was the last.

Errol Brown, the bald lead singer with Hot Chocolate, played a boiled egg. Terry Wogan made an appearance in the torture chamber. They tried a new soap opera, *Cobbers,* a parody of *Neighbours* in which

Speedo–clad surfers sat around drinking Fosters. "Where's your cozzie, mate?" they ask Kenny, who, like the pom he is, wears suit, collar and tie. By the end of the series, Cupid was gone. "She'd turned into a monster," Barry said.

It wasn't vintage stuff.

"Kenny Everett used to have the courage to fail and outrage," said Andrew Hislop in *The Times*. "I trust that his anodyne, uncontroversial return in *The Kenny Everett Television Show* (BBC1) merely reflects his own creeping cuddliness, not BBC restraint."

Kenny was bored, tired and distracted. As early as 1984, he had told the *News Of The World*[102], "I don't get a kick out of dressing up you know. It's extremely painful wearing false eyelashes. Lipstick takes an age to get off, and brings half your lips with it. Those latex boobs are extremely big and heavy and give me a painful rash on my nipples. Fishnet tights rub your hair up the wrong way and hobbling around on high heels is not my idea of fun."

"I don't think Kenny even looked at the material on that last series," says Andrew Marshall. "He just turned up at the studio every day."

Except when he didn't.

"I can remember that he didn't turn up to a recording first thing in the morning at the BBC on the day they were actually recording an episode," says Shelia Steafel, the fine comic actress who frequently guest-starred on the show. "They couldn't find him anywhere and were getting frantic and rather cross. Eventually they phoned him at home and said, 'Where are you?' and he said, 'Well, I came to Television Centre and the Commissionaire wouldn't let me park my car in the VIP area in the front – so I went home again."

Sheila was used to this sort of thing. "I can remember inviting him over for a dinner party with people that he knew. I think Cryer was there. Kenny didn't turn up. He didn't phone. He just didn't turn up. And the next morning when we all got down to the studio at the BBC, he handed me a little tape recorder – a little personal tape recorder – as a gift and to thank me and to say, 'I'm sorry I didn't turn up.' But he didn't apologise or anything and he didn't give any reason."

Kenny was, figuratively and literally, in a strange place.

"One day I found myself dangling from the ceiling of Studio Four in the BBC Centre on a wire," he told the *Daily Mail*[103], "dressed as

Quasimodo, with a false glass eye, a broken nose, a hairy wig, wearing sackcloth, itchy and uncomfortable, doing the bells sketch. Then the camera broke down. So I was left dangling there for half an hour, slowly revolving while they fixed the flaming camera. I was frying in the heat and I suddenly thought, 'This is no way to spend the rest of your life, Ken!'"

The day after the transmission of the last show in the series, Kenny, Barry and Paul Ciani, the show's producer, assembled on the sofa for *Open Air,* a daytime TV show presented by Pattie Coldwell. They talked about how the complaints had dwindled. Pattie asked whether they'd gone soft. Barry protested that the show had been put on at an earlier time, almost as kids' television – something they'd had to take into account. They would all have preferred a post-watershed slot. "I'd prefer three in the morning," Kenny says.

Kenny seems particularly subdued, keen to distance himself from the suggestion that he could break out at any time and do something wacky or outrageous. The previous day he'd been on *Pebble Mill At One.* Pamela Armstrong, the presenter, had come on with a riot shield. "And of course, it threw me into respectability. Why don't you put it away, Pam? I'm 43."

Finally, Pattie asks whether they're planning any more series. "Of course, many, many, many series," Kenny replies. "You still have time to leave the country, folks." She turns to Barry and Paul and asks, "And will you both be on board?" Barry and Paul shuffle their feet and say, "Hopefully."

"It was over," says Barry Cryer. "We all said it's over. We had a good time – but in the last series he wasn't as happy as he'd been. I knew, bless him, everyone knew that he wasn't that happy"

"And I admit with regret that I began to make life difficult for the people I worked with," said Kenny.[104] "Because when I was getting fed up clowning around, I was getting stroppy and saying things like, 'If you don't put some silk or winceyette lining on the inside of this thing you want me to wear, I'm not wearing it. So they were furiously stitching extra lining in the frocks and costumes to keep me happy. Then I'd say again, 'I'm not wearing that, it's uncomfortable.' They'd mumble 'Oh he's being difficult again.' I suppose I did become a bit of a prima donna."

Barry Cryer is kinder to Kenny than Kenny was to himself.

"He was fed up with stuff being stuck on his face and costumes and wigs and everything. He coped well but it wasn't his world. He'd rather be in a radio studio. He was very polite – he didn't do any star nonsense with the make-up and wardrobe people but he got fed up with it a bit. Of course, what we didn't know was he wasn't well. He wasn't feeling good and he was just coping. Looking back it's a bit sad because he was exhausted and we didn't know."

CHAPTER FOURTEEN

Staying fit was the thing – whatever it took to stave off further complications for as long as possible. Millions were being ploughed into research. A new drug, AZT, was proving very promising. And anyway, even without drugs, only nine out of 10 people infected with the HIV virus actually succumbed to AIDS and died. Stay positive. Stay healthy. Look to the future.

Plans, or at least pipe dreams, to conquer America were afoot. Kenny had been in contact with Bruce Gowers, a director/producer who'd worked on some of his London Weekend programmes all those years ago and had gone on to make the groundbreaking 'Bohemian Rhapsody' video for Queen. Bruce had been working in Los Angeles on *Solid Gold,* a show with vague similarities to Kenny's – at least insamuch as it featured music, video magic and a dance troupe with a style somewhere between Hot Gossip and Aerobics Barbie (too many twirls, too many teeth and how can lurex *get* so baggy?). He had put together a compilation of Kenny's shows. LA producers were interested. There was talk of a series. Twenty shows. Lorryloads of money.

"Bruce just rang me up out of the blue and said 'America is ready for you now, darling,'" Kenny announced. "I can't see a good reason why the series shouldn't make me a millionaire."[105]

Americans in the eighties had taken to British comedy in the same way as they'd taken to British pop in the sixties. "I love your *Monty Python* and your *Benny Hill*," they'd say, perplexingly, as if the two were similar species. Tracey Ullman, from Slough, after a couple of Fab 40 hits and some British TV shows with Lenny Henry, French and Saunders and Ruby Wax, had been wooed by writer/producer/director/genius James L. Brooks (*Broadcast News, Terms Of Endearment, Lou Grant, Taxi*) to cross the Atlantic. *The Tracey Ullman Show* was one of the first hits for Fox, the then fledgling network started by Rupert Murdoch's News Corporation. It featured a series of cartoon shorts about a dysfunctional family called *The Simpsons*. From small beginnings mighty empires are built.

Kenny thought he could be the Rolling Stones to Tracey's Beatles.

"I see myself as the male Tracey Ullman. I have got to be bigger than Benny Hill – I've never understood the Benny Hill phenomenon and I still don't."

He told the reporter that he'd be taking Cleo Rocos and Barry Cryer with him to the US but had no plans to become a permanent resident. "I'll just go over for two months at a time, lock myself in a basement and work non-stop."

In January 1988, along with Joan Collins and TV chef Keith Floyd, he was the 'company' on Michael Aspel's LWT talk show *Aspel & Company*. Having regaled the audience with details of a five-day trip he'd made with Nikolai to Russia ("Leningrad is the second biggest city in the world's second biggest country, and Leningrad airport has an *outside loo*"; "There will be no World War Three – they can't even get a cup of tea together"), he talked about his plans to take America by storm. "I want to be the next Joan Collins," he said.

As is the way of these things, it never happened.

"People in America called me up," he told Pattie Coldwell on *Open Air,* "and said, 'Have a trip out to America. We'd like you to do a new series out here and stay at this plush hotel for nothing. Then halfway through our chats, the BBC called me up and said, 'Oh, we are putting all your shows out in America. So I didn't have to even go out there and do it. They're all in tins at Television Centre. They are just sending them over. I hope the Americans understand it."

Kenny's shows were shown sporadically in the USA, but nobody erected a statue. And anyway there was never much hope that, at this stage of his career, he could have worked there. In 1987, the US government had imposed a travel ban on anyone with HIV. Kenny did eventually manage to wangle a tourist visa, but even a top Hollywood studio would have had its work cut out trying to fix him up with a work permit. The ban, by the way, wasn't fully lifted until the Obama administration came to power 20 years later.

Stay fit. Stay positive. Stay healthy. He took a holiday with Cleo to Francis Butler's avocado farm in the south of Spain. It was not a success. Kenny was needy, demanding constant attention. Francis' brother-in-law, the actor Ben Cross, paid a visit. Since his massive success playing Harold Abrahams in *Chariots Of Fire,* Ben had established a solid reputation as a screen and stage actor on both sides of the Atlantic. He had just finished making a film. He was healthy, handsome, happily married with two kids, and had every reason to believe that his success would continue long into the future.

"Kenny started asking about the film," says Francis. "He was saying, 'Well, who are you making the film with? Are you the star?' Ben said, 'I suppose I am the co-star.' Kenny wouldn't let it go. 'Are you the star? I mean, for fuck's sake, either you're the star or you're not.' Ben hurled a tray of drinks at him. We jumped in my car and we went to visit my parents. Kenny spent the whole evening wrapped around my mother, crying."

Instead of conquering America he published *Kenny Everett's Ultimate Loo Book*. Like his unreliable autobiography *The Custard Stops At Hatfield,* it was co-written with Simon Booker, who this time got a credit. Sold as "an Astro-Loogical Guide" and "the world's first paperback laxative", the book comes with a loop of red string attached to facilitate its hanging in the facility.

It takes the form of an almanac, with daily notes ("Happy birthday to Margaret Thatcher; whatever your politics, she's a remarkable woman"), 'Bathroom Brain-Teasers' ('Q: Whose turn is it to pay for lunch? A: Nicholas Parsons') and Kenny's forecasts ("It's not often that you get invited to appear naked on prime-time television, and this week is no exception"), and never pretended to be anything except a useful stocking filler for a difficult teenager or a twinkly uncle.

"Kenny was a very unfocussed sort of person," says Andrew Marshall. "I don't think he ever had a plan about what he wanted to do with his life or anything other than just to do stuff."

The next bit of stuff he did was *Brainstorm,* a science-based quiz show designed to occupy the *Tomorrow's World*'s early evening BBC1 slot when Judith Hann and Kieran Prendiville were on their summer break. Kenny co-hosted with Cleo Rocos, but the space age set, with its flashing lights and contestants in pods attached to Kenny's desk by umbilical cords, dominated the proceedings. There were also celebs (look it's Roger Taylor, drummer from Queen), moments of spurious educational intent – without it, for instance, who would have known that during the average lifetime the heart pumps enough blood to fill Wembley Stadium? – and enough smut to draw complaints. It featured often on BBC's televised suggestions box, *Points Of View.*"Dear *Points Of View,* Why, oh, why does Cleo Rocos seem incapable of uttering a simple phrase like "wellie-warmers" without everybody in earshot braying like farm animals."

KENNY: Why don't polar bears eat penguins?
CONTESTANT: Do you want the sensible answer or the silly one?
KENNY: Ooh! Let's have the silly one.
CONTESTANT: Because they can't get the wrappers off.

The scoring was in wattage of Brainpower. If a contestant got a question right, all the other contestants would lose some Brainpower – the score indicator was a throbbing fluorescent tube beside each pod. When they had no more Brainpower left they were 'evaporated' with a whoosh of dry ice and vanished. The prizes, in BBC style, were educational models of classic inventions: Stephenson's *Rocket*, Edison's telephone and so on.

In the last episode, Kenny got down on his knees and begged for a second series. Nobody took any notice.

More stuff included an ad for a board game called *Therapy,* and frequent appearances on all available chat and quiz shows. There he is chatting to Mavis Nicholson again on *Afternoon Plus*, change the channel and there he is again on *Give Us A Clue* failing to convey, using mime only, the song *He's A Hillbilly Gaucho With A Rhumba Beat* to Lionel Blair.

He was less comfortable promoting his *Ultimate Loo Book* on the sofa of Gay Byrne's *Late Late Show*. The interview starts well with Kenny earning his keep by doing his best aeroplane anecdotes. Then fellow guest Sinéad O'Connor interrupts.

"There's one question I'm burning to ask and I hope you won't be offended," says Sinéad, ominously.

"Uh-oh," says Kenny.

"Uh-oh" says Gay Byrne.

Sinéad goes on to ask him, given his support for the Tory party, where he stands on Clause 28 – an addition to the Local Government Act, introduced by the Conservatives, forbidding local authorities from promoting homosexuality in schools or promoting "the teaching in any maintained school of the acceptability of homosexuality as a pretended family relationship".

Kenny, clearly panicking, tries to duck the question and dissociate himself from Tory policy in general.

Sinéad persists, asking whether he'd be prepared possibly to join a demonstration against Clause 28.

"I was never asked. But I would if it was a jolly occasion. This isn't getting any laughs."

Sinéad will not let it lie. "Do you think there's a duty for certain people who are in the public eye to stand up for what they believe in?"

In Kenny's Fab 40 of Embarrassments, having to talk about his homosexuality is somewhere around number three. Having to talk about politics is perhaps number two. Number one by a long chalk is the horror of being serious on television. He squirms.

"There's also a duty," he says, embarking on something that could almost pass as a minor manifesto, "for people in the public eye to amuse and entertain so that people who think, (*disapproving voice*) 'Eh, he's gay, isn't he?' will also think, (*approving voice*) 'Yeah, but he's funny.' They look at you and they see you're not a thing with horns and you're not inhuman and you can be amusing or you can sing good and they think, 'Hey, these people are humans after all.' And I think that's better than marching through the streets and going, 'We're All Right. We're Just As Human As You Are And You'd Better Believe That Or We'll Come Over And Give You A Bunch Of Fives.'"

All of this is spoken with his back to Sinéad, direct to Gay Byrne, with pleading in Kenny's eyes – help me, help me. Gay does the necessary footwork which allows Kenny to move on to an anecdote about an old lady in a supermarket.

There were the regular gigs, too. In 1988, Capital split its FM and AM frequencies and Kenny, for the fourth time in his career, was present at the birth of a new radio station. The main station, renamed Capital FM, continued to provide Top 40 magic to its target 15 to 25 year olds, while the AM frequency was given over to Capitol Gold, bringing nostalgia to the mums and dads. After a few months of weekends-only transmissions, the new station went full time – with the Four Tops' 'Reach Out (I'll Be There)' the first record played – on November 28.

Capitol Gold was one of the first stations to devote itself entirely to 'revived forty-fives'. In what has since become a standard rite of passage for all DJs, Kenny, Tony Blackburn and 'Diddy' David Hamilton were promoted from the juniors to the seniors.

It made little difference to Kenny's show. He'd never paid much attention to the music anyway and his tastes had always veered towards the sweet, the melodic, the cheerful and the Beatles. The nervous energy that had once driven him to spend days preparing fiddly bits had now morphed into something still funny, still entertaining but a lot less worryingly manic and so relaxed he could have phoned the show in, which on one occasion he did. A London Underground strike brought traffic to a standstill. Kenny, stuck on his way from his flat in Earls Court to the Capital studio, had his carphone patched through. David Symonds, who had made it to the studio, played the records. "If you see a dirty grey BMW behind you," Kenny said, "get out of the way, so I can get to the studio."

Another regular gig was a team-captain's seat on the long running quiz show *That's Showbusiness* hosted by Mike Smith.

The questions made Kenny feel his age. "I know everything about Muffin the Mule and Tony Hancock, but when they show me clips about Fun Boy Three, I don't know what they are talking about."

"I'm happy because I haven't got to be funny. I just turn up and they tell me who the guests are. I say, 'Oh, that's nice. She's a jolly person,' or 'I've never met him before.'"

One of the jolly people Kenny had never met before was Rowland Rivron, the drumming half of French and Saunders' in-house band,

Raw Sex, and later feted winner of *Let's Dance* for *Sport Relief*. He found his team captain underpowered.

"He certainly wasn't leading the mayhem. He was on the back foot. He seemed quite stoned. Kind of vague."

It has to be said that Rowland's presence can overawe.

"I blotted my copybook rather by making up some old bollocks about seeing [a well-known pop star] offering his arse to drunk Scottish people coming out of pubs. I probably shouldn't have said something like that on an early evening quiz show. I didn't know Kenny was gay then. I thought Kenny and Miss Big Tits – Cleo Rocos – were an item."

They were, near as damn it. Kenny was 22 years older than Cleo. He was short. She was statuesque. He was gay. But in most other ways they were a perfect couple.

"Kenny and I used to sit and talk," Cleo told the *Independent* in 1998[106], "and because we never talked about age, we used to talk as though we were the same age. And we'd talk about the one thing that really was paramount, and what everyone sadly underrates, and that is humour above all else. Before he was ill he said to me, 'Clee, when we are both 99 and we are sitting in our bathchairs and we are all gnarled up and we haven't got the energy for anything else, we'll still be able to laugh.'"

"He always looked at everything as if it was the first time he'd seen it. He never lost appreciation of, particularly, anything to do with nature. One thing he would always do was carpet the atmosphere with the most perfect fumes. When we were driving to a friend's house in the country he would put on a cassette, and he would time it so that, as we drove up the driveway, the last chord of the last bit of Brahms would resound, and I never knew how he did it. Even that he timed perfectly."

"Do you think he might have driven round and round in circles beforehand?" asks the interviewer, Marcus Berkmann.

"Now you come to mention it…" she laughs. "But we'd always be chortling like loons anyway so I would never have noticed."

One night, slightly pissed, Kenny asked for Cleo's hand in marriage. The engagement lasted four days before the happy couple came to their senses.

"We had a meal once over at Cleo's," says Barry Cryer. "Ev had rung me up and said, 'Oooh you, me and Cleo – we're going to celebrate our engagement.' I thought – oh my God! We had a meal and laughed a lot and the engagement was never mentioned at all. Maybe it was just a sort of a joke thing, but I think it broke her heart – she meant it. Bless her. Would never have worked."

Kenny had split with Nikolai sometime in the middle of 1988. He still saw the Russian from time to time and they remained friends, but they never lived together again.

"Now, he couldn't stand all that in yer face gay business," says Francis Butler. "He couldn't cope with being with people like Freddie Mercury. He wanted to be with sensible, successful middle-class people. It was where he was at his most comfortable."

He and Cleo took healthy walking holidays with his bank manager, Eric Gear and his family. Eric had met Kenny in 1979 when he was working at a bank in Bond Street and Kenny had come in to ask for a loan. Eric was horrified to discover how clueless Kenny was about his finances and gave him a lecture. Kenny took him out to lunch and they remained close friends until Kenny's death.

"He felt Eric was a very, very solid, good friend," says Barry Cryer. "Ev liked to feel safe and he thought, 'I'm with Eric so I'm all right. I feel safe with Eric, he's my good friend.' They shared this passion. People didn't realise that Ev was a rambler. He loved just going off into the countryside and rambling. He liked a nice hotel at the end of the day, though."

"We went out quite a few times with Lulu," says Francis Butler. "We used to go to the Coq d'Or at the bottom of Kensington High Street. With somebody like Lulu or having lunch with my parents – he was in seventh heaven. He was at his most happy and comfortable when there were normal people around. Maybe that's what he craved – so he could chat about washing powder."

Kenny's preoccupation with housework had become borderline obsessive. "I'm turning into a Howard Hughes character. I'm getting very fussy and can't stand untidiness and dirt."

"When I go home, I sit down in my flat and I'm completely relaxed. I vacuum everywhere – even my balcony. I have plastic grass on my balcony, which I vacuum once a week. I don't particularly like vacuuming but it's a euphemism for being normal, so I do a lot of it.

I've changed drastically. I don't stay up until dawn swigging champagne and doing naughty things any more.

"As a comedian you never really grow up. You're not allowed to. You've got to be an eternal child. I want to discover what ordinary people do; to find what's so great about life that makes other people content to sit at home and not make fools of themselves in front of TV cameras. I think I'm beginning to realise what it is. It's called peace and quiet.

"I'm 45. I've got to change my life and start taking things easier. I don't know yet what I'm going to do for the next 45 years, but I'm sure God will give me a gentle push me in the right direction."[107]

"Mark, my partner, and I went round to his flat," says Andrew Marshall. "He gave us a fondue. We had a fondue party. Can you imagine? It was that thing he had about gadgets – he was very fond of gadgets. I remember he had one of the first mobile phones and he had a phone in his car. He came over for a meal with us once in Wood Green and we kept getting these phone calls saying, 'Hello Andrew I'm at a roundabout – what do I do? Now I'm at some traffic lights – now do I go forwards or sideways?' He used to have a little map inside his flat with pins to show him where he'd parked the car. He'd put a pin in it to remember. He had a wonderful studio in his flat that had tape recorders and those leads with the plugs on hanging up in rows – that was kind of like his inner sanctum – that was the holy place – probably what the inside of his brain looked like."

Kaleidoscope, the BBC Radio 4 arts programme, recognised Kenny's importance as a 'sound-sculptor' when it included a trip to his inner sanctum in a piece, presented by David Roper, celebrating the history of BBC's Radiophonic Workshop.

Roper is astonished by the speed at which Kenny works. "I've been doing it so long it's like driving a car," Kenny tells him. "I can sort of do it in my sleep now. Every button is at arm's length and my fingers automatically go to the right one."

The pride and enthusiasm with which he shows off his tape recorders is undiminished from the time when Elsie Fleming, the market researcher, had come to Hereford Road 30 years earlier to talk about his Grundigs. He explains the way you can "just toss sound backwards and forwards from one to the other and do harmonies. I mean, you could sound like a chorus or an orchestra. 'Cos I used to be a choirboy, you know, so I know which notes to hit."

He plays a sample jingle that, with church harmonies, goes: "Dear God in heaven / Please let this show be OK / With no major boobs or goofs / Or is that gooves?"

He adjusts EQ to demonstrate how he can make his voice telephonic or sound as if it's coming from next door.

He introduces his latest pride and joy "this Japanese thing that I bought last year, the Yamaha Rev 5, which costs approximately the earth but it does anything you like with your voice."

He adds echo until his voice disappears into the "depths of the cosmos".

He changes its pitch up to Mickey Mouse then down to a Russian bass.

He presses an automatic stereo pan button that bounces his words from speaker to speaker, faster and faster – "if you're listening in mono this won't mean a thing, but if you're in stereo it'll sound very peculiar indeed. He flanges. He phases. His big finale is to put his own voice and a Vaughan Williams symphony through a Vocoder. His words become an orchestra.

He could lose himself in that studio. He'd disconnect the phone and miss appointments. "When he went off to record his programmes," says Francis Butler, "he would disappear for two weeks, three weeks, however long it was and no one would see him. He had tremendous self-discipline When he worked there'd be zero alcohol, zero social life. He was a consummate professional."

And to the end, the world's most devoted tape recordist.

In October 1989, Kenny and Cleo embarked on a mammoth trip – a couple of months in America, then hop across the Atlantic to spend Christmas with his family in Australia.

He fell ill in New York. In Phoenix, Arizona, he had to be briefly hospitalised. When he arrived in Australia at the beginning of December, he told the *Hobart Mercury* that he was planning to stay. The cold English winters had left him with an 'arthritic knee'. "The gay star, who earns an estimated $320,000 a year, wants to join his parents who live in Western Australia. He said: 'They are up at seven and run along the beach. Here I am in London with creaky knees. It's terrible.'"

He was back in January. There were other vague plans to buy a place in Wiltshire and do his Capital show from there, "... a nice little cottage with some fields around and I'll be happy. I'm going to have several cats – because you know where you are with cats – a herb garden, an Aga cooker and my wonderful new recording studio, with triple glazed windows so I wouldn't annoy the rest of the villagers. Capital have worked out that to attach my house, wherever it is, to the nearest town and then get a line from British Telecom to the station would cost less in a year than they pay for my car park space. When I'm all set up I might even be able to do my shows without getting out of bed."[108]

In the end, though, the lure of the rubber gloves, the fondue set and the plugs hanging up in rows kept him wedded to his Earls Court flat. He decorated in peach and apricot and installed a state-of-the-art shower that was like "standing in a rainforest". The décor was minimalist. Some have described it even as 'corporate', impeccably tidy, with very little indication of the occupant's personality. He liked to change into his pyjamas as soon as he got home and listen to Brahms, Puccini and Mozart on his fancy stereo. He went to the gym three times a week and ate salads "like there is no tomorrow". He cut back on the drink and gave up drugs entirely.

Illness made him more chippy than ever. In 1990, there was a revival of Noël Coward's play *Private Lives* at the Aldwych Theatre, starring Joan Collins, Keith Baxter, Edward Duke and Sarah Crowe. Edward Duke was a friend of Francis Butler's. He invited Kenny to the opening night. Kenny showed up with a friend. Edward had arranged for two tickets to be left at the box office, one for Francis and one for Kenny. There was no ticket for Kenny's friend. He was outraged and "stormed off surrounded by a thousand cameras". It was the last time Francis ever saw Kenny.

Nikolai died in October 1990. "I went to the foot of the stairs in my house and cried for several minutes. Then I thought 'How dare you leave without me. I took you round the world so many times and here you are going off somewhere without me'. Then I had to go on air and be jolly. I thought I was professional that day, because I laughed and joked and I actually was jolly for the time it took to do the programme. It was the last thing I wanted to do but I couldn't ring up and cancel the broadcast."[109]

Look to the future. Stay positive.

Mike Batt, the ginger haired composer whose name, whether he likes it or not, will always be linked with the Wombles, had written a musical show built around Lewis Carroll's epic poem, *The Hunting Of The Snark*.

The score had known many manifestations. In 1984, it had been launched by the London Symphony Orchestra, with Paul Jones among the cast. In 1986 it had been a concept album featuring an astonishing array of stars including Art Garfunkel, Roger Daltrey, John Hurt, Cliff Richard, Stephane Grappelli and Captain Sensible. On April Fool's Day 1987, it had been performed in full costume at the Royal Albert Hall, again with a stellar cast, this time including Billy Connolly and Justin Heyward. A West End opening seemed inevitable.

For some reason he got it into his head that Kenny Everett would make a fabulous star of musical theatre. He made the approach.

"He said, 'I've got this wonderful West End thing I'm going to do – five and a half million pounds, a 32-piece orchestra on stage. Would you like to come and sing and dance and juggle and do funny lines?"[110]

Kenny had never done theatre. He'd barely even seen theatre. He couldn't learn lines. Live audiences put the shits up him. He demurred a few times. But Mike Batt, determined to the last, would not take no for an answer. "You'll only have a few lines, you'll just have to come on, huge applause, wallop, then off."

In the end Kenny agreed.

The gadget fan must have enjoyed the production's lavish use of technology: state-of-the-art lights, state-of-the-art sound, 12,000 animated slides projected from 152 computer-linked projectors. The orchestra, 50-strong, not just the 32 previously promised, was right on the stage, and supplemented by a rock band suspended above in a gantry. Two more gantries, the upper a precarious 30 feet from the stage, together with its access staircase, swung back and forwards as the action demanded. Sets included a moving galleon with flying fishes below, a courtroom with the moving legs and a tropical rainstorm. Batt had sunk an estimated £2.1m of his own money into the show and its forebears.

Rehearsals began.

The poem, and the musical, tells the tale of a voyage made by several people whose jobs begin with the letter B – Banker, Baker, Bellman, Barrister and so on – who set off, as the title suggests, to hunt a creature called the Snark. It has, over the years, been subjected to a great deal of analysis and interpretation. Symbols and hidden meanings have been teased out. Is it, some ask, an allegory on the search for happiness, for civilisation? Or is it a satire on the meaning of meaning? The clue could be in Carroll's own description of the poem. "An agony in eight fits."

Kenny played the Billiard Marker, a character mentioned only twice in the original poem in which his sole action is to chalk the tip of his nose.

In Batt's version, though, the part had grown. Kenny only had one solo, 'The Snooker Song' in Act Two ("I'm going to snooker you tonight – Love is the game, snooker is the same") but he was given more and more lines, and dance routines, too. There could be no mucking about. Unless he performed *these* steps to land *here* on *this* beat, the choreography would be a nonsense, the other dancers would look like lemons, the lighting effects wouldn't work. And with gantries swinging and courtrooms on the move, there was even a faint possibility that people could die.

A week before the opening, Angela Levin of *You* magazine visited the rehearsal room.

"He [Kenny] paced around the room like a caged animal. When he sat down he squeezed his elbows into the sides of his body and squirmed this way and that as if trying to free himself from bodily chains. He occasionally put his head on the table and pretended to fall asleep."

"He's thrilled, he says, at his chance to go on stage. 'People have said that I am being brave and I agree with them. It will be like hanging over the edge of a skyscraper – terrifying and exciting at the same time. To go into a West End spectacular from a standing start is a bit extreme. At first when Mike Batt asked me I thought I couldn't do it. Huge amounts of people terrify me, but after I thought about it, I said yes. Apart from anything else I have such a lot to learn and I'm having to wake up my memory which has been dormant for years.'

"'I am more awake than I have ever been in my life.

255

'The one thing they won't be able to say is that I didn't try. I'm working really, really hard.'"

But Kenny didn't see it as the start of a career in musical theatre.

"I think it will be my swan song. I shall be retiring in about two years. Money is my version of security and I have been very good at being strict with myself and putting some away. I've put huge amounts into a pension fund and I shall tour Europe and especially Italy."

The interest in Italy may have been influenced by Kenny's current relationship with a handsome Italian called Chicco, who had been, on and off, sharing his flat for some time. They were to remain close to the end.

Barry Cryer wasn't sure that Kenny would make it to the opening night: "He'd turned down various stage things Ray and I had thought up before for him. It wasn't his world – turning up every night and two matinees a week and all that. And he wasn't well either. It was a personal thing – he liked Mike Batt. They liked each other and he trusted him."

Starring in a stage musical would also, Kenny knew, make his mum an dad proud. He spent practically his entire fee for the show on bringing them over from Western Australia, first class.

"I really enjoyed the opening night. And that's the only thing I did it for. So I could say I'd done a West End musical spectacular."

The reviews were mixed but you have to look in odd corners to find the good ones.

The Australian *Courier Mail* for instance, declared, "Womble Whips Up A Winner".

The (now defunct) *Masquerade* magazine reported, "Kenny is fine. An adequate singer, he carries off his part perfectly well."

But the *Independent* quoted the "old lady from Wigan's remark on seeing St Peter's in Rome, 'Well, you can see there's a lot of work gone into it.'"

The Daily Telegraph said: "You can almost see the panic in Kenny Everett's eyes, as he tries to make a zany character out of the Billiard Marker, with only a snooker cue and a desperately unfunny song to work with."

Revered theatre critic Michael Coveney, then working for the *Observer,* now remembers the show with a rueful smile, "I was rather rude about it, I'm afraid. I wasn't alone."

"The lowlight," he wrote, "is provided by Kenny Everett's unctuous Billiard Marker, waving his cue at Victoria Hart's lissom Beaver and singing, 'I'm snookering you tonight.' Suddenly, chorus girls materialise in Sally-bowlers and 'Pot Black' leotards. The song bounces off various cushions and ends in baulk. We should have been prepared for the worst after a first-act closer prophetically titled, 'Dancing Towards Disaster.'"

"I hope he had a good laugh about it later on," says Michael.

The show closed seven weeks later.

Halfway through the short run, Freddie Mercury announced that despite his having told the press that his test for HIV had come up negative, in fact he had known for four years that he was infected and the infection had developed into AIDS. He died the following day.

Kenny didn't go to the funeral. He said he didn't like funerals and anyway what was the point? "Freddie won't be there."

More stuff came and went. In March 1992, Kenny presented *Gibberish*, a daytime celebrity panel game for BBC1. It was vaguely related to the long running radio show *I'm Sorry I Haven't A Clue* inasmuch as the panellists were given 'silly things to do' – word games and so on. Comedy at 10.30 in the morning is an odd scheduling decision, nevertheless, thanks to quality contestants (Barry Cryer, Steve Punt, Danny Baker et al) it did vaguely work. Being asked to finish a sentence which included the words "… playing with men's…" reduced Derrick Griffiths to helpless laughter for nearly a minute.

The series of 40 shows took it out of Kenny. By the start of 1993, he was beginning to look unwell. Reporters followed him when he kept hospital appointments. The *People* ran the headline "Friends Concerned Over Health of Kenny Everett". Frequent illness meant that stand-ins often had to sit in for him on his Capital Gold show. There was speculation.

'Diddy' David Hamilton tried to scotch the rumours: "Kenny does seem to be off a lot more than a lot of us. But I don't think there's anything you can read into that other than he seems to get a lot of colds and flu. He's just a lot more fragile than the rest of us."

A more formal statement from Capital said that Kenny was suffering with his teeth and put Kenny's problems down to a couple of 'bad fillings' – without a hint of grim double entendre.

Kenny took a holiday in Italy and returned to find a gaggle of hacks on his doorstep.

Finally he gave in. A *Sun* journalist asked him outright, "Are you HIV positive." Kenny said yes.

He could have taken the same route that Freddie Mercury chose and not told the press that he was ill until he was practically on his death bed, but Kenny had had enough.

A few days later at an impromptu press conference on his doorstep, he admitted, "I would have kept it quiet if it hadn't been forced out of me."

Jokey and chatty, he handled the whole situation with remarkable grace and courage: "I've been wondering what to put on my tombstone and I think it will be 'No punchline – ring Barry Cryer.'"

Perhaps still feeling Lee's influence, he talked about reincarnation. "I can't imagine I was nowhere before this. I'd like to come back living in Spain or Italy or somewhere. As long as I don't come back as bald or in Bosnia, I don't mind."

When one of the journalists asked him whether he'd infected Nikolai, he puffed himself up with mock anger. "No, he probably infected me, the bastard. I'll get him back for this."

Stephen James, an AIDS counsellor with an organization called the Body Positive, commented in *Today*[111]: "No matter how rich and famous you are, openly admitting to having AIDS or being HIV positive creates problems. While Kenny lives and works in a showbiz world that is very tolerant and has a high proportion of openly gay people, he will not be immune from those who are less sympathetic. He must have gone through a lot of heart-searching before reaching his decision. Even someone as well-known as Kenny will have trouble getting life insurance or a mortgage – and he could still be around for many years yet.

"I would ask anyone to think very carefully before announcing to the world that they are HIV positive or have AIDS. If Kenny feels it is the right thing for him to do, that's fine – but it's a private decision. Nobody should be condemned for choosing to stay silent."

In fact Kenny did experience problems with his private health cover. He'd been with PPP for over 20 years – since before the existence of AIDS was known – yet still it refused to pay for his treatment.

Gibberish was his last TV show. He wouldn't give up radio, though, even though he often had to drag himself to the studio. "How healthy do you have to be to play 'Da Doo Ron Ron'?"

There'd usually be a knot of reporters and fans waiting for him to arrive. He tried disguise, wearing an oversized trench coat and a pulled down baseball cap. But there weren't that many five-foot-five skinny blokes going in and out of the building. He got caught nearly every time. He smiled, pretending to bask in the attention. "I should do this more often."

Inside he got on with his show announcing to his listeners: "What a palaver! Sorry about filling up your front pages with my ugly mush but you know how the papers are."

On July 15, he told the *Independent*[112] he'd refuse medication. "I have decided not to take anything when it starts getting hideous because that way I'll go faster. I'd hate to cling on because I'll be more beautiful and fabulous in my next life. I hope they don't find a cure just after I've spent the last of my pension."

He told them he was in a relationship with a man – without naming Chicco – but they didn't have sex. He'd been celibate for four years. "It's like the priests used to advise us at training college, to rush off and play rugger as soon as we had any naughty thoughts. Sex can become an obsession and you lose track of everything else. The person I'm having a personal relationship with is not in showbusiness, so he does not want anything in print about him. I have lots of really nice friends and one rather special one, but we don't do rude things, unfortunately."

Kenny claimed to be fit apart from the HIV virus and hoped to be one of the 10 per cent of carriers who didn't get full-blown AIDS. He even claimed that HIV had taught him a lot, and given him a new, more relaxed, philosophical outlook on life and death. "I don't really care how I go," he said. "I'd hate to live forever and be alive when all my friends have died of old age."

The following February he was in Sydney, Australia, taking part in the Gay And Lesbian Mardi Gras, waving a banner and dancing the night away with underdressed lifeguards, cross-dressed nuns, bikers and hula girls to Kool and the Gang's 'Celebration'.

In the spring of 1994, he was awarded a Gold Sony Radio Academy

Award for Lifetime Achievement. His old friend Michael Aspel introduced him. "Independent, irrepressible – one of broadcasting's major stars. He has constantly bewitched audiences across BBC and independent TV and radio with his comic talent, outrageous antics and wacky style. He's been with Capital Gold since its launch in 1986."

George Martin, the Beatles' producer, made the award. Kenny, looking frail, and dressed, incongruously among the dickey-bows and starched collars, in his dog-tooth sports jacket and scrap of a tie, kept his acceptance speech short.

"Wow... Thank you to Sony for making so many lovely toys for grown-ups and thank you for this delicious award, which is richly deserved... I mean after playing 'Da Doo Ron Ron' and 'Doo Wah Diddy Diddy' for 30 years I deserve something. Thank you very much."

Towards the end of May, he contracted pneumonia. While undergoing treatment at Chelsea and Westminster Hospital the doctor broke the news that he had developed full-blown AIDS. He sobbed.

Later he told the press, "I'm not angry, but resigned. We all have death hanging over us. It's just that I'll probably get there before most people do. But I'm still here. And I'm still on the radio. But we're all getting older. I'd like to think that if I got as ill as Nikolai, I'd have one last party with lots of champagne and afterwards throw a lot of pills down. But I suppose I'll be hanging on with my fingernails to the end."

A few weeks later, he had lunch with Ivan Waterman of *Today* newspaper. Kenny was laying the black humour on good and thick, but underneath his pain is obvious.

"Looks like I'm going to be making my next long journey in a box in the back of a Land Rover. Yes, I'm afraid the grim reaper is on his way. Everything is out of my hands, out of my control. I have been a very silly boy. Scared? You bet I'm scared. Don't believe anybody who tells you otherwise."

He didn't have the energy to put much preparation into his shows any more. They were off the cuff. Some have said that his last programmes were most like his first, out at sea, on the *MV Galaxy*.

His eyesight was failing. He wore large owly glasses now. Then his hearing started going in one ear. "Can you imagine," he said, "a DJ with a hearing aid? Too much."

It would have been fitting if he'd stayed true to tradition by getting himself fired from Capital for some outrage. It wasn't to be. He left in July 1994, "for six months' leave".

"We will welcome him back with open arms whenever he wants to return," Capital announced. He never did return. The 30 year career that had started with *The Maurice Cole Fifteen Minute Radio Show* was over.

In the summer, Kenny took his usual walking holiday with his friends, Eric and Jane Gear and Eric's brother George. They went to Tissington Park in the Peak District, famed for its rolling limestone countryside and banks of wild flowers. They had brilliant walking weather. "You could see that he was there to have fun," said Eric. "You could see the way he looked at the scenery. He could go very serious. As he stood there and looked out over a dale, or a vale, or a hill, I had the feeling that he realised that there wouldn't be too many more walks. And there weren't."[113]

In November, he went again to Australia, returning to London for Christmas and his 50th birthday. He was a very sick man.

In January, his sister, Kate, travelled to London to look after her brother. She moved into his flat and devoted herself to his care during the last months.

Kenny began the excruciatingly painful business of saying goodbye to his friends.

While he was still well enough, he left the house for lunch with Dave Cash.

"It was a sad occasion. And we sort of both knew that this would be it. I said, 'Listen, I'll come round and see you.' And he said, 'No, no, please don't. I'm still OK now, but I don't think I'm going to be OK for much longer. Let's keep in touch on the phone or something like that. I don't want you to see me in the later stages of this.' I respected that – I would have liked to have seen him some more. But that's the way he wanted it."

John Birt, his producer on *Nice Time* over a quarter of a century earlier, was also treated to a farewell lunch. "He confessed – with a look that combined both a gleam of mischief and a tear – to having the fondest feelings for me."

He was suffering from tinnitus, dizziness and had lesions on his arms when he met Cleo. She described the occasion in her memoir, *Bananas Forever*:

"He smiled at me and squeezed my hand.

"'Clee' he said 'we've been so perfect with each other, haven't we?'

"'Yes Kenny.'"

He pointed out that in all the time they'd known each other, he had never once seen her without he make-up on. Even when she was sick. Even when he inadvertently set fire to her hair in a restaurant.

And now he told her that, as his illness took hold, he didn't want her to see him 'without his make-up' on, either. They were both fabulous people, he told her. Her memories should only be of him being utterly fabulous.

Barry Cryer went to the flat. "Whenever I went there in the past he'd be hoovering around and he'd say, 'Ooh where's Mrs Ashtray,' and he'd produce an ashtray and I'd have a cigarette. This last time, his sister was there and she came to the door and I said, 'Hello' and went in. He was lying on the settee and I thought – I don't like this. He still talked and laughed same as ever but I didn't like it. I mean, I didn't really know the full extent of the HIV. He was lying down – lively as ever. Then things got worse."

Kenny and his big sister talked and listened to music together. Kenny hated hospitals so his bedside was fitted with a saline drip and a morphine pump. They hired a specialist nurse to help Kate when help was needed.

The week before Kenny died, Kate asked him whether he wanted to see a priest.

Father William Hofton, a young priest from the local Catholic Church, Our Lady of Victories, came often during those last days. Kenny took Holy Communion.

On April 3, Kenny made his will. He left everything he had to Kate.

At 10 o'clock on the morning of April 4, Eric Gear came round to see him. Kate was there, of course, and Jo Gurnett, Kenny's friend and agent. Kenny died at 10.43.

Kenny had told Sue Lawley in 1993: "I think I'd like to die serene. I haven't been very serene in this life. It's been a sort of turmoil-ish sort of life going on in front of the cameras and being silly and potty. I think I'd like to try a bit of serenity."

Wilfred De'Ath, the man who first put Kenny on the wireless, quite by chance one day met Father William, who told him about the last moments.

"He said, 'I heard Kenny's confession and gave him absolution and the last rites and I told him, 'Right. You've said it all. You've told me everything and now you can go. And he died immediately after that.' The priest said, 'Now you can let go,' so off he went."

The body was immediately taken to the funeral parlour in Westbourne Grove. They all knew that as soon as the news got out, the street would be filled with press. Jo Gurnett prepared a formal statement.

In January, Kenny had been to the funeral of his friend, the actor Edward Duke, who had also died of AIDS. It was held at the Church of the Immaculate Conception in Farm Street, Mayfair and had been a beautiful and moving experience. This was the church that Kenny and Kate chose for his funeral.

Kate's daughter, Joanna, read the bidding prayers. Jo Gurnett read the lesson. Father William spoke movingly and in a mercifully non-judgemental way about Kenny. He told the congregation: "I rely on the fact God has the most wonderful sense of humour. Anyone who gets given the gift of laughter and humour will be a very welcome guest in heaven."

He also described how he imagined Everett whispering his life story into God's ear and bringing "a wonderful smile" to his face.

It was a full requiem mass. The music included Fauré's 'Requiem' and Puccini's 'Symphonic Prelude' – the piece that Kenny had chosen to have on his Desert Island if all his other gramophone records were washed away.

"It is the most beautiful record that I've ever heard. If I ever do die, I think as I'm hoiked aloft in a ray of God's lovely sunbeam I'd like this to be on the gramophone. It's God. God with knobs on."

Everybody who was anybody in radio queued up to pay tribute.

"He was the only one of us," said Paul Gambaccini, "who used the studio instead of tolerating it."

"At the funeral I did a reading from the Bible," says Barry Cryer. "It was strange. I had the same feeling that Ernie Wise had at Eric's funeral. I half expected the coffin lid to suddenly burst open and Ev to leap out shouting 'Hello'. Before the service I was stood outside the church with

Ev's agent. A helicopter swooped low over us and in unison we said, 'He's late again.'"[114]

Alan 'Fluff' Freeman said, "It was one of the most beautiful services I have ever been to. I am sure that Kenny, from afar, appreciated it greatly. And I am sure that had he been alive he would have said something very funny about it all, as beautiful as it was."

Chris Tarrant said, "This is the number one man. None of us could compare to him. He opened the door for us."

Lee was there too with her husband, John Alkin, although they'd had little contact with Kenny during his last years.

Kenny's elderly parents, Thomas and Elizabeth, didn't come over from Australia. They had been besieged by reporters who camped outside their sheltered housing complex in a western suburb of Perth. Few of their neighbours knew who their son was and they retreated from the publicity.

Another notable absentee was Cleo Rocos. Because Kenny told her that he would love to have a bright red sleek Porsche, Cleo went to Harrods and bought a child's pedal Porsche and to echo their childish preoccupations with bananas (her autobiography was called *Bananas Forever*) filled the thing to the brim with bananas. Cleo then took the whole thing tied up with yellow ribbon to the undertakers so that it could accompany the coffin to the church.

It was deemed "inappropriate". Cleo, devastated, felt unable to attend the funeral.

The coffin, covered with yellow flowers, was taken from the church to Mortlake Crematorium. The last music played was the Beatles' 'Strawberry Fields Forever'.

Half of the ashes were scattered in the Cotswolds: the other half in Dovedale, in the Peak District where he had spent his last walking holiday with the Gears.

In St Paul's Cathedral there is a memorial to its architect, Christopher Wren. It says (in Latin), "If you seek his monument, look around you." If you seek Kenny's monument look, and listen, to every TV comedy, every radio show and You Tube video. Look at the way people talk and walk. Listen to the lilt of catchphrases. Feel the speed.

And now... *this*.

SOURCE MATERIAL

1   *In The Best Possible Taste – The Crazy Life Of Kenny Everett* – David
    Lister, Bloomsbury, 1996.
2   *Daily Mirror*, September 17, 1979
3   *The Custard Stops At Hatfield* – Kenny Everett and Simon Booker,
    Willow 1982
4   *You* magazine – October 20, 1991
5   *ibid*
6   *Bananas Forever – Kenny Everett And Me* – Cleo Rocos, Virgin
    Publishing 1998
7   *Sunday Telegraph* – July 15, 1990
8   *Mail On Sunday*, November 1, 1987
9   *The Custard Stops At Hatfield* – Kenny Everett and Simon Booker,
    Willow 1982
10 *Daily Mirror*, September 17, 1979
11 *Sunday Express*, October 10, 1982
12 *Evening Standard*, June 9, 1978
13 *News Of The World*, August 20, 1978
14 *Mail On Sunday*, November 1, 1987
15 *Spike & Co* – Graham McCann, Hodder & Stoughton 2006
16 *Daily Mirror*, September 17, 1979
17 BBC interview – 1981.

18   *ibid*
19   *ibid*
20   *Here's Kenny* – BBC Radio 4, 2008
21   *The Custard Stops At Hatfield* – Kenny Everett, Willow, 1982
22   Quoted *http://www.youtube.com/watch?v=M5wZXkFppeg*
23   *The Guardian* – March 8 2008
24   BBC Interview – 1981
25   *ibid*
26   *He Sounds Much Taller* – *Memoirs Of A Radio Pirate* – Dave Cash, Amazon Digital Services, 2012
27   *Here's Kenny* – BBC Radio 4, 2008
28   *ibid*
29   BBC Interview 1981
30   Richard Porter http://www.beatlesinlondon.com
31   BBC interview 1981
32   *In The Best Possible Taste* – David Lister, Bloomsbury, 1996
33   Reproduced with permission – Richard Porter http://www. radiolondon.co.uk/jocks/kenny/kenbeatlesint.html and http:// www.beatlesinlondon.com
34   *The Custard Stops At Hatfield* – Kenny Everett, Willow 1982
35   *The Guardian* – March 8, 2008
36   *The Dee Jay Book* – Bill Williamson, Purnell, 1969
37   *Poptastic* –Tony Blackburn, Octopus, 2007
38   In conversation with the authors in 2003.
39   From an interview in *The Londoner* – March 23, 1968
40   *ibid*
41   *Treatments of homosexuality in Britain since the 1950s* – *British Medical Journal*, February 19, 2004.
42   *The Homosexual Role* – Mary McIntosh, Social Problems, Vol 16, No. 2 (Autumn 1968)
43   *The Custard Stops At Hatfield* – Kenny Everett, Willow, 1982
44   *Kinds Of Loving* – Lee Everett Alkin, Columbus Books Ltd., 1987
45   *ibid*
46   *The Harder Path* – John Birt, Time-Warner, 2002.
47   *The Dee Jay Book* – Bill Williamson, Purnell, 1969
48   *Daily Mirror*, April 19, 1969
49   *The Harder Path* – John Birt, Time-Warner, 2002

50 Don't try this at home, kids. LSD can no more make homosexuals into heterosexuals or heterosexuals into homosexuals than it can make the blind see. It can, however, make the sighted go blind and frequently leads to a condition know as "Silly Art".

51 *Daily Mirror*, September 17, 1979

52 *As Time Goes By* – Derek Taylor, Davis-Poynter, 1973

53 *The Sun* – December 16, 1969

54 *The Times* – July 22, 1970

55 *Daily Mail* – July 25, 1970

56 *Daily Mail* – July 25, 1970

57 We are indebted for much of this information to http://www.vivarchive.org.uk/articles/articlekettering.htm

58 *The Times* – July 15, 1972

59 *The Times* – August 5, 1972

60 *Kinds Of Loving* – Lee Everett Alkin, Columbus Book, 1987

61 *Daily Mail* – April 8,1974

62 *The Times* – October 16, 1973

63 http://mikesmithinlondon.blogspot.co.uk/2012/10/all-in-best-possible-taste.html

64 *Sunday Mirror* – September 22, 1974

65 *Daily Mirror* – March 21, 1986

66 *The Custard Stops At Hatfield* – Kenny Everett, Arrow Books, 1982

67 *Celebrity Regressions* – Lee Everett, Foulsham, 1997

68 *Capital Radio 194 Fun Book* – ed. Annie Wallace, Capital Radio 1976

69 *The Custard Stops At Hatfield*

70 *Freddie Mercury: The Definitive Biography* – Lesley-Ann Jones, Hodder and Stoughton 2011

71 *Daily Express* – November 1, 1976

72 *Halfway To Paradise* – Spencer Leigh and John Firminger, Finbarr International, 1996

73 *London Evening Standard* – June 9, 1978

74 *Daily Express* – July 26, 1978

75 *News Of The World* – August 20, 1978

76 *Cosmopolitan* – September 1979

77 *Sunday Mirror* – September 16, 1979

78 *The Times* – February 18, 1980

79   Mike Smith's blog – http://mikesmithinlondon.blogspot.co.uk/2012/10/all-in-best-possible-taste.html
80   *Daily Mirror* – April 12, 1980
81   *Sunday Telegraph* – July 15, 1990
82   *Bananas Forever* – Cleo Rocos and Richard Topping, Virgin Publishing 1998
83   *News Of The World* – December 19, 1982
84   *The Custard Stops At Hatfield* – Kenny Everett, Willow 1982
85   *The News Of The World* – September 19, 1984
86   *The Times* – July 23, 1983
87   *Daily Mirror* – April 11, 1981
88   *Life And Laughing: My Story* – Michael McIntyre, Michael Joseph 2010
89   *The Guardian* – August 22, 2008
90   *Daily Express* – May 23, 1984
91   *Sunday Mirror* – October 6, 1985
92   *Daily Mirror* – October 31, 1985
93   *Daily Mirror* – March 21, 1986
94   *Woman's Own* – September 1986
95   *Daily Mail* – August 14, 1986
96   *Daily Mirror* – May 13, 1985
97   *Woman's Own* – September 1986
98   *Sunday Mirror* – October 6, 1985
99   *Stick It Up Your Punter – The Uncut Story Of The Sun Newspaper* Peter Chippindale and Chris Horrie, Mandarin, 1999
100   *News Of The World* – November 30, 1986
101   *Mail On Sunday* – November 1, 1987
102   *News Of The World* – September 16, 1984
103   *Daily Mail* – June 2, 1990
104   *ibid*
105   *Today* – November 30, 1987
106   *Independent* – September 1998
107   *Daily Mail* – June 2, 1990
108   *ibid*
109   *Daily Express* – April 1991
110   *Desert Island Discs* – BBC Radio 4, 1993
111   *Today* – April 6, 1993

Cupid Stunts

112 *Independent* – July 15, 1993
113 Interviewed in *The Unforgettable Kenny Everett*, Carlton TV, 2000.
114 *Butterfly Brain* – Barry Cryer, Orion, 2010

269

INDEX

273